Literary Translation and the Making of Originals

Literatures, Cultures, Translation

Literatures, Cultures, Translation presents a new line of books that engage
central issues in translation studies such as history, politics, and gender
in and of literary translation, as well as opening new avenues for study.
Volumes in the series follow two main strands of inquiry: one strand
brings a wider context to translation through an interdisciplinary inter-
rogation, while the other hones in on the history and politics of the
translation of seminal works in literary and intellectual history.

Series Editors
Brian James Baer, Kent State University, USA
Michelle Woods, The State University of New York, New Paltz, USA

Literary Translation and the Making of Originals

Karen Emmerich

Bloomsbury Academic
An imprint of Bloomsbury Publishing Inc

B L O O M S B U R Y

NEW YORK · LONDON · OXFORD · NEW DELHI · SYDNEY

Bloomsbury Academic

An imprint of Bloomsbury Publishing Inc

1385 Broadway	50 Bedford Square
New York	London
NY 10018	WC1B 3DP
USA	UK

www.bloomsbury.com

BLOOMSBURY and the Diana logo are trademarks of Bloomsbury Publishing Plc

First published 2017

Library of Congress Cataloging-in-Publication Data
Names: Emmerich, Karen author.
Title: Literary translation and the making of originals / Karen Emmerich.
Description: New York : Bloomsbury Academic, 2017. | Series: Literatures, cultures, translation | Includes bibliographical references and index.
Identifiers: LCCN 2017007921 (print) | LCCN 2017026208 (ebook) | ISBN 9781501329920 (ePub) | ISBN 9781501329937 (ePDF) | ISBN 9781501329906 (pbk. : alk. paper) | ISBN 9781501329913 (hardcover : alk. paper)
Subjects: LCSH: Translating and interpreting.
Classification: LCC P306 (ebook) | LCC P306 .E46 2017 (print) | DDC 418/.04–dc23
LC record available at https://lccn.loc.gov/2017007921

ISBN:	HB:	978-1-5013-2991-3
	PB:	978-1-5013-2990-6
	ePub:	978-1-5013-2992-0
	ePDF:	978-1-5013-2993-7

Series: Literatures, Cultures, Translation

Cover design: Daniel Benneworth-Gray
Cover image © Creative Commons

Typeset by Fakenham Prepress Solutions, Fakenham, Norfolk NR21 8NN
Printed and bound in the United States of America

To find out more about our authors and books visit www.bloomsbury.com. Here you will find extracts, author interviews, details of forthcoming events, and the option to sign up for our newsletters.

Contents

Acknowledgments

This book is as unoriginal as the "originals" it discusses. It is the product of countless hours spent in the company of the ideas of others—with their writings, their translations, their conversation. It is also the product of the generous support of various individuals and institutional bodies who gave me the time and space to channel that "outside" more effectively, as Jack Spicer might say. *Words Without Borders* solicited an essay in 2013 that provided a first opportunity to articulate some of these thoughts in writing. Lawrence Venuti read that piece, and encouraged me to turn it into a book. Michael Cronin was an early supporter of the project; Michelle Woods and Brian Baer enthusiastically accepted it for their series at Bloomsbury, where Haaris Naqvi, Katherine de Chant, Kim Storry, and James Tupper have eased its entry into the world. Amanda Doxtater, Leah Middlebrook, Lanie Millar, Marc Schachter, and Casey Shoop were my intellectual community throughout the writing of this book; they read every word, and made them all better—as have Helen and David Emmerich, Hilary Plum, and Douglas Robinson. Jen Bervin, George Economou, Michael Emmerich, Peter Gizzi, Nikolaos Kakkoufa, Emmanuela Kantzia, Noah Kaye, Kevin Killian, Renata Lavagnini, Peter Shillingsburg, Satoko Shimazaki, Matvei Yankelevich, and Konstantina Zanou also read parts of the book and gave invaluable feedback, as did anonymous reviewers for *Comparative Literature* and *Translation Studies*, where parts of two chapters appeared. To have had so many engaged and demanding readers is already more than I could have hoped for.

That list of readers is, of course, only the tip of the iceberg. Of my many mentors, Dimitri Gondicas stands out for the unfailing generosity of his support over the past twenty years; Karen Van Dyck has also been a steadfast supporter. Peter Constantine and Edmund Keeley were early champions of my translation habit; Lawrence Ventui has continually challenged and sharpened my thinking on translation; while conversations with countless translators and publishers of translated literature over the years not only broadened the range of my ideas about translation, but made me endlessly grateful to have fallen into a community characterized by such generosity of spirit. Michelle Woods and John Davis both allowed me to cite unpublished material in this book. Jen Bervin, who kindly gave permission for me to reproduce an image from *The Dickinson Composites* in Chapter 3, has been a model to me for many years in her dedication to creative forms of scholarship. My professors, colleagues, and students at Columbia University, the University of Cyprus, the University of Oregon, and Princeton University have also been important interlocutors, while the institutional support I have received from each of those universities has been crucial, if not for the actual drafting of this book, then for the cumulative intellectual experiences that have made it possible. A timely semester off from the Department of Comparative Literature at Princeton, before I even arrived on campus, allowed me to focus my energies on research and writing when it was most needed. Recent invitations to speak at Indiana University, the University of New South Wales, San Francisco State University, Simon Fraser University, and twice for the Program in Translation and Intercultural Communication at Princeton gave me opportunities to formulate some of the thoughts articulated in this book, as did work-in-progress talks in the Comparative Literature departments at both UO and Princeton. Martin Worthington was kind enough to answer naïve questions from a stranger; Dimitris Kousouris, Andreas Galanos, and Panayiotis Pantzarelas answered equally naïve questions, though all are far from strangers. Bill Johnston, Chet Lisiecki, Cate Reilly, David Greetham, Michelle Woods, and Alex Zucker are thanked in footnotes for their help, but I'll do so here as well. Evi Haggipavlu and Konstantina Zanou are constant interlocutors, even from a distance; Eliza Strickland always shows up when needed. My parents, Helen and David, make the word "support" seem pale and feeble; my brother, Michael, is a role model in all things. The privilege and joy of talking translation, literature, and ideas with family, friends, students, colleagues, and mentors is a gift for which I am thankful every day.

*

the author. Originally published in *Unfinished and Uncollected*, published in 2015 by Shearsman Books.

Unpublished material from the Jack Spicer Archive at the Bancroft Library, University of California, Berkeley reproduced with permission of the Bancroft Library, Peter Gizzi, and Kevin Killian.

"The Item in the Paper" and "The Photograph" from C. P. CAVAFY: THE UNFINISHED POEMS by C.P. Cavafy, introduction, notes, commentary, and translation copyright © 2009 by Daniel Mendelsohn. Used by permission of Alfred A. Knopf, an imprint of the Knopf Doubleday Publishing Group, a division of Penguin Random House LLC. All rights reserved.

Excerpts from "Poetry as Magic Workshop Questionnaire," "After Lorca," and "The Heads of the Town Up To the Aether" from *my vocabulary did this to me: The Collected Poetry of Jack Spicer*. © 2008 by the Estate of Jack Spicer. Published by Wesleyan University Press. Used by permission.

"Η φωτογραφία" and excerpts from "Το έγκλημα" from *Ατελή ποιήματα (1918-1932)* by C.P. Cavafy, philological edition and commentary copyright © 1994 by Renata Lavagnini. Published by Ikaros Publications. Used by permission of Renata Lavagnini and the Cavafy Archive.

Introduction: Difference at the "Origin," Instability at the "Source": Translation as Translingual Editing

And I returned, you might say, like a stranger to a world stranger than I.
Everything was inconceivably familiar yet at the same time inconceivably
distant—it's hard to explain. I don't mean the people. I expected to find
them changed. But the books? How had even the books managed to
change as they had?

> —Vassilis Vassilikos (tr. Emmerich)[1]

This book has the perhaps immodest goal of challenging the time-honored tradition—long upheld by readers, reviewers, publishers, literary scholars, even many translators and scholars of translation—of referring to the objects of literary translation as if each were a known quantity, a singular entity whose lexical content is stable or fixed: "the original," "the Arabic original," "the original French text," "the source text," "Kafka's German," and so on. It is a truth now widely acknowledged (though at times still bemoaned) that a translation is in part the product of a particular individual's (or group of individuals') interpretation of a work she herself encountered in a different language (or languages).[2] Give seventy translators an identical swatch of text and, unless divinely inspired, they will produce seventy different translations that accord with their diverse understandings of what the text means, and of the relative importance of its various features. It is a truth less widely

---

[1]   In keeping with the textual instability I discuss throughout this book, I have revised my translation here from the published version of 2002.

[2]   To be honest, to call the interpretive nature of translation widely acknowledged may be wishful thinking on my part. While translators and scholars of translation are certainly aware of the interpretive work involved in the creation of any text in translation, many general readers, students, and even scholars of literature continue to see translation as a communicative endeavor, a (failed) transfer of an invariant meaning via the construction of textual equivalents. The tenacity of this flawed understanding of translation can be seen in the countless reviews, casual conversations, and classroom encounters that continually describe translation as loss—even, as I argue elsewhere in this book, in the recent popularity among literary scholars of the discourse of untranslatability, which likewise rests on the assumption that translation attempts a transfer of some semantic invariant. One of my goals in this book is to challenge this rhetoric of transfer, and to replace it with an understanding of translation, or at least literary translation, as interpretive iteration.

acknowledged that most literary works exist in more (sometimes many more) than one textual form, even in the language(s) in which they were initially composed. German texts we complacently treat as Kafka's have been multiply mediated by numerous editors over the years, beginning with his friend Max Brod. The Arabic "original" of what many refer to in English as *The Thousand and One Nights* has a history of cross-lingual composition and circulation as complex as the stories it tells, including the translation into Arabic, and then back out again, of tales first published in eighteenth-century French. Virginia Woolf's novels, typeset and printed in both the U.K. and the U.S. from two separate sets of proofs, exhibit slight but (some would say) significant differences across these editions, complicating the task of a translator who seeks to settle on a "source text" for one of Woolf's works.

And yet when it comes to translation, we often revert to rhetoric that suggests that the changes supposedly wrought by translation are inflicted upon an otherwise stable source. Even in a post-poststructuralist intellectual environment that accepts textual instability and semantic indeterminacy as inherent to literary works, most readers, including literary scholars, continue to treat "originals" as categorically richer texts than translations, and to discuss the process of translation as if it began with a "source text" already in hand, and labored solely to create a text in another language to stand in that first text's stead. But the "source," the presumed object of trans-lation, is not a stable ideal, not an inert gas but a volatile compound that experiences continual textual reconfigurations. The works we translate often exist in multiple manuscript, print, or digital forms. Excerpts of novels are published in magazines; authors revise for new printings or editions; poems or short stories appear online before a collection has even been planned; plays differ, lexically and otherwise, every time a new production is staged, and playscripts can differ along with them. The textual condition is one of variance, not stability. The process of translation both grapples with and extends that variance, defining the content and form of an "original" in the very act of creating yet another textual manifestation of a literary work in a new language. Translation may be conceived as a form of translingual editing, by which a translator both negotiates existing versions and creates a new one of her own, in a language other than that (or those) in which the work was first (or previously) articulated.

In order to give concrete shape to these fairly abstract claims, I begin with an origin story of my own for the preoccupations that gave rise to this book—a story that demonstrates the conceptual confusion that persists in our discussions of translation, by probing the difference at the origin I encountered during my first major project as a professional translator. The first book-length translation I was commissioned to complete was published by Seven Stories in 2002 as *The Few Things I Know About Glafkos Thrassakis*. My contract with the press, which I had signed two years previously, required that I provide a "faithful rendition into idiomatic English" of "the work now entitled *Glafkos Thrassakis*" by Vassilis Vassilikos; my translation would "neither omit anything from the original text nor add anything to it, other than such modest verbal changes as are necessary in the translation into English." Following this phrase was an asterisk referring to a hand-typed addendum in the lower margin of that page, which stated that "the version of the text Karen Emmerich is to translate will be approximately 500 pages in length." The task of editing the "original text" down to that length would be shared by myself and another individual, also a translator from Greek.

From my current vantage point, even these few seemingly forthright sentences are rife with confusion and contradictions. The rhetoric of faithfulness, with its attendant prohibition against adding or subtracting and its grudging acceptance of only "modest verbal changes," is standard in the contracts U.S. and U.K. publishers ask translators to sign. References to this vague notion of faithfulness or accuracy crop up time and again in reviews and popular discussions of translated literature, and even in many translators' descriptions of the work they do. Yet this stance betrays a misconception as deep as it is widespread. Translation has no truck with modest changes. The entire translation is a text that didn't exist before: *all* the words are added; *all* the words are different. A translation adds a new iteration, in a different language, to the sum total of texts for a work. As the case of *Glafkos Thrassakis* will demonstrate, it can sometimes even be the catalyst for new textual iterations in the language in which it was first composed. Yet this is not the change most people are talking about when they say translations "change" originals. That "change," like the contractual prohibition against subtraction and addition, belies a mistaken understanding of translation that rests on a series of problematic assumptions: that translators are in the business of textual replication rather than textual proliferation; that this replication is a process by which meaning is transferred, to the extent possible, between texts; that readers who can understand both the "original" and the translation will be able to ascertain whether this invariant material has in fact made it through unscathed; and, most basically, that we can safely judge whether words or phrases in different languages are to be treated as "equivalent" to one another in a particular context, and perhaps independent of context.[3]

---

[3] Equivalence remains one of the most powerful and most contested paradigms for thinking about translation; a critique of the concept runs through this book. On the particular question of adding and subtracting, consider the following passage by Theo Hermans: "Timothy Buck tells us [in his critique of Helen Lowe-Porter's translations of Thomas Mann] unambiguously what he associates with 'faithful translation': the

Contrary to these assumptions, translation doesn't move an invariant semantic content across linguistic divides, like a freight train carrying a cargo of meaning to be unloaded on the far side of some clearly demarcated border. Rather, as Naoki Sakai (or Sakai Naoki) writes, translation seeks to "create continuity at the elusive point of discontinuity" (71) between languages whose boundaries are themselves unstable. Translation continues the iterative growth of a work in another language whose otherness *and* self-sameness are always provisional. Translation requires a complex set of interpretive decisions that are conditioned by the particular context in which a translator (or translators) is working. At least as regards the words and punctuation that comprise them, translations are radically different from the prior texts on which they are based. But the creation of difference is not synonymous with change. Translations are textual supplements; for most readers, they serve as substitutes for something written in a language they cannot access.[4] Translators use one or more texts for a work as the basis from which to formulate another text in another language. They decide what a work means (to them), how it means (to them), and which of its features (diction, syntax, linguistic register, rhythm, sound patterning, visual or material aspects, typographic form, and so on) are most important for the particular embodied interpretation they hope to share with others. They also decide how to account for those features in the new text they are writing. Even more basically, translators often decide—if sometimes unwittingly—what the "original" or the "source text" *is*, or at least what *their* original or source text will be. If one is to translate Flaubert's *Madame Bovary* (first published in installments in the *Review de Paris* in 1856, then in a two-volume bound edition in 1857, and in many additional editions since then, even just in French), one must decide which (singular or plural) of these many French texts one will use as one's "source." In some cases, the available versions will differ only a little; in other cases, they will differ quite a lot.

In our current moment, we might assume that translators of contemporary literature would be contractually obliged to translate the particular

---

translator should neither add nor subtract from the content of the original, respect the author's intentions and refrain from offering 'wild interpretations.' Could it be that his criticism of Helen Lowe-Porter's practice reveals little more than the clash between diverging conceptions of what translation is or should be? Is translation possible without adding or subtracting or interpreting, wildly or not, and who is to judge? What if we set this case against translations from other times and places in which the original content was added to or subtracted from, authorial intentions were violated and wild interpretations were rife—and the texts in question were still called 'translations'?" (Hermans 1999: 5).

[4] See David Bellos's excellent take-down of the cliché that "translation is no substitute for the original" in *Is That a Fish in Your Ear?* (37–9).

version of a work put into circulation by the publisher from whom the translation rights have been obtained. The example of my translation for Seven
Stories calls even this into question. Contemporary contractual language
in the Anglophone publishing world conflates "work" and "text" in such a
way as to elide the existence of *multiple* textual or editorial manifestations
of a given work.[5] As a consequence, contracts rarely specify that a particular
edition should be followed—an oversight few but textual scholars are likely
to notice, and which most translators are unlikely to consider significant to
their task. With works that have entered the public domain, a choice between
versions may make the process of settling on an "original" far more complicated—if, that is, a translator sees it as her decision to make. By the same
token, even when specific texts have been assigned to a translator working
on commission, some degree of what we generally call editing is often part
of the translation process. My contract with Seven Stories makes the editorial
aspect of the task of translation unusually explicit: though the two most
recent Greek editions of the novel were over 750 pages long, I had agreed to
translate an "original text" of no more than 500 pages. My contract called, in
other words, for a "faithful rendition" that added and omitted nothing—yet
it also required me to abridge the work's most current form by roughly one
third.

   Glafkos Thrassakis is an autobiographical novel (or, in my translation
of Vassilikos's neologistic description, a "biogranovel, an autonovegraphy,
a novistory")[6] that describes the experiences of leftist Greek intellectuals
during the 1960s and 1970s. The novel's eponymous character, a writer
who flees Greece during the dictatorship of 1967 to 1974 and returns after
the junta's fall, is a kind of alter ego for Vassilikos. The work has seen many
incarnations in Greek, evolving along with the author's life. The first seed for
the character of Thrassakis appeared in a two-page vignette in a collection
of short stories published in 1971. Then came an entire story in 1973, next
a full-fledged volume in 1974. "I thought at the time it would end there,"
Vassilikos has written (in my translation of the Spanish version of what I
assume to be an originally Greek text, included as an author's note to Ángel
Peréz González's 2014 Spanish translation of the novel), "but that summer
saw the fall of the colonels' junta and I decided to fictionalize my return to
Greece after six and a half years of living in exile" (2014: 9). This fictionali-
zation, in other words, unfolded in tandem with the return itself: Vassilikos
both lived and wrote his sequel, which was followed a year later by yet

[5]   The distinction between "work" and "text" is central to this book; see page 16 for defini-
     tions and further discussion of these terms.
[6]   As quoted in my translator's note to the novel (Vassilikos 2002: vii). The Greek neolo-
     gisms appear on the back cover of the Gnosi edition (Vassilikos 1988).

another. Not long afterward, a 620-page volume brought all three books of this makeshift trilogy under a single cover.[7] "To complete this historical tour," Vassilikos continues in his author's note to the Spanish translation, "I should add that Thrassakis visited me once more in 1978, when another book saw the light of day: the *Hidden Texts,* which later became *Roman Notebooks.*" Both titles suggest that this latest book will give the reader access to the fictional Thrassakis's previously unpublished works, yet what it actually offers are only further rewritings: an unnamed narrator's descriptions and interpretations of stories whose texts the reader never sees. From that point on, no new books featuring Thrassakis were written—yet "various revisions" of the existing publications followed, "in which I personally reworked the material, the last time in 2008 in a *definitive* edition—if one can speak in such terms about a *work in progress* of this sort" (Vassilikos 2014: 10; italics in the Spanish).

My translation fell during the period of these "various revisions," which are far more extensive than Vassilikos's passing mention would suggest. In fact, my translation, though in a different language and not produced by the author, could be considered one such revision. Seven Stories had obtained translation rights from Livanis, whose 1996 edition included the *Roman Notebooks* and some other bits and pieces. Like the subsequent 2008 edition, the Livanis edition had been billed as "definitive" when it appeared, as had the previous (and substantially different) edition released by Gnosi in 1988. Before I even started working on the translation, Vassilikos told me he now preferred the 1988 version, which was by then long out of print. I tracked down a copy to bring to our first meeting in Athens, where we sat in a hotel bar and wondered how we would manage to turn a 763-page book into a 500-page one. In the end, Vassilikos decided that one large section of the book wasn't of a piece with the rest, and carefully tore that chunk of roughly 150 pages out of the copy I had been at such pains to procure. When I finally sat down at my desk to begin translating, the "original" before me was a physically altered copy of an out-of-print edition of a novel that had already appeared in numerous other versions in Greek. The book from which I was translating was therefore original in a different sense: one of a kind, an utterly unique object.

It was also still at least a hundred pages too long to please the American publisher. So, with occasional help from the individual mentioned in my contract, I continued to edit as I translated, making cuts that ranged from sentences to paragraphs to entire chapters. In creating my translation, I

---

[7] The precise dating and details of these publications remain obscure. Vassilikos refers in his author's note to a 580-page edition of the trilogy-in-the-making, but I was unable to verify the existence of such a volume.

was thus envisioning and inventing new textual manifestations in English *and* Greek for this shape-shifting work. Yes, not only in English but in Greek, too: I edited this unique "original" as I went, crossing out passages and pages in order to make my copy of the Gnosi edition correspond with the translation I was producing, rather than the other way around. When the translation was ready, I sent it to Vassilikos, along with a list several pages long that catalogued all of these cuts; he read and approved the translation, and seemed to pay little attention to my meticulous documentation. Yet while the specific changes I'd made were less important to Vassilikos than the overall feel of the end product, the very existence of this edited English version did affect the subsequent editorial life of this work in Greek: when I saw him a few years later in Greece, Vassilikos told me that the publication of the U.S. edition had spurred him to rethink the book's structure once more. This reevaluation resulted in the third "definitive" edition of the novel, the one published in 2008.

Another six years later, Peréz González's *Lo poco que sé de Glafcos Zrasakis* was released. Judging from its title, which echoes that of the English translation (chosen not by me but by the American publisher), one might assume that the Spanish translator had followed my editorial decisions. But while he incorporated many of my cuts, his text reflects additional editorial work that makes his version unlike all other versions to date. Any attempt to compare Peréz González's Spanish text to my English text, or either of them to any of the several Greek texts a reader might find at a university library or bookstore in Greece, would quickly become an exercise in frustration. In the author's note published in the Spanish edition, Vassilikos makes the following (now, perhaps, to be expected) parting shot: "I consider the present edition the most representative of the work and it will remain as presented here in its reissue—this time final—in Greece in 2015" (2014: 10). If the most representative version to date is a translation that incorporates certain elements of a prior translation, whatever "final" version eventually appears in Greek (2015 came and went with no sign of it) will thus have been mediated by the editorial efforts of two translators, working in two separate languages and literary traditions, in collaboration with numerous named and unnamed individuals, at the behest of publishers who, though unable to read any of the Greek versions, had ideas of their own about the preferred textual makeup of this novel. So much for adding or omitting nothing; so much, indeed, for the notion of adhering to an "original."

Some of you may be surprised to learn of the extensive editorial interventions that went into the production of my translation. You may even be unsettled by the way a work from a supposedly minor language was reshaped to suit the demands of a trade publisher in the United States. In some ways, this seems an apt example of what Lawrence Venuti has described as the "insidious domestication" in which translation can engage, the "reconstitution of a text in accordance with values, beliefs and representations that preexist it in the target language, always configured in hierarchies of dominance and marginality, always determining the production, circulation, and reception of texts."[8] The fact that Vassilikos was receptive to these edits doesn't necessarily make Venuti's concern any less valid.[9] Neither, I suspect, will it lessen the discomfort some readers may feel at the power vested in me as a translator of this work—a discomfort that may reflect, too, a belief that this is an exception to the rule of what translation is, or should be. But while extreme, the case of Glafkos Thrassakis and his many guises is not at all exceptional. On the contrary, it merely crystallizes issues that commonly arise from the textual instability of literary works, while highlighting the significant (if rarely acknowledged) role that translators, among others, play in shaping these works for new audiences. It is not an exaggeration to say that there is no translation without editing: each new textual manifestation of a work, including those in translation, embodies assumptions about what a work is and where its boundaries lie; each new iteration of a work, in the same language or in a different one, shifts those boundaries at least a little, and sometimes quite a lot. Each new published text in translation is both a translation *and* an edition. Editing and translating are mutually implicated interpretive practices that further the iterative growth of a work in the world.

In placing this argument at the center of *Literary Translation and the Making of Originals*, I hope to bring attention to aspects of translation that have long been elided in both scholarly and popular discussions. I also hope to encourage more translators and scholars of translation to consider the relevance to their task of aspects of literary production that those in other fields already take for granted. It is probably not news to a scholar of early Persian literature, for example, or a scholar working with born-digital primary sources, that translators may need to negotiate multiple versions of a given "original," or that a work of literature may comprise textual

---

[8]   1995: 16, 18. See also many of the essays in Sandra Bermann and Michael Wood's 2005 edited volume *Nation, Language, and the Ethics of Translation*, including Spivak's "Translating into English" (93–110). The politics of translating from languages with fewer users into the major languages of international commerce and culture are also central to Apter's 2013 *Against World Literature: On the Politics of Untranslatability*, though I take issue with Apter's reliance on the term "untranslatability," in that book and elsewhere. See footnote 2, as well as the last section of Chapter 5 for a critique of this term.

[9]   Vassilikos, I should note, is not indiscriminately receptive to all translingual editing of his work: in the author's note from which I have been quoting, he takes the 1978 French translation, *Un poète est morte*, to task for having "butchered" his novel.

manifestations in several languages. Valerie Henitiuk has written that, while translations "are routinely judged in terms of faithfulness to the original," "in the case of premodern literature, what is 'original' is far from self-evident"; the notion "of a sacralized, authoritative source text is obviously problematic when the only extant manuscripts date from centuries after composition and reveal variant textual traditions" (2007, 6). Ferial Ghazoul describes *Majnun Layla*, a work that circulated in many languages across Western and Central Asia over the course of several centuries, as a work with "no original text or authentic source," which "lies on the borderline between orature and literature," and whose fluidity "cancels out the categories of fidelity or infidelity that are so often used when discussing translation" (375). Ghazoul suggests that this work, whose identity is continually "preserved but modified, in a process one might call *textual becoming*—a textual identity in progress—rather than a *textual being*," therefore "poses a special problem in translation studies" (377). Rita Kothari's discussion of "everyday practices of translation" in contemporary India focuses on romances, detective novels, and so on, which are often not marked as translations and which routinely disregard the textual makeup of their presumed "sources." The "uninstitutionalized and popular practices" that Kothari groups together in this category of "unofficial and 'low-brow' translation activity" (both because of the genres in question and because of the modes of translating employed) "continue to escape the awareness of a fixed text" (262–5).

This last phrase may indicate just how entrenched the notion of translation as transfer is: even in a piece that opens our discussion of translation to include forms of cultural production for which stability is not the norm, Kothari refers to a "fixed text" as something of which one could have an "awareness"—in other words, as something that is indubitably there, whether or not we are aware of it. My argument is precisely the opposite: textual instability is there, whether or not we are aware of it. Instability is not limited to nonliterary texts, or quasiliterary texts, or works from ages past. It is not in fact the "special problem" Ghazoul suggests, but part and parcel of what translation *is*. High-brow and low-brow translations of high-brow and low-brow literature from various places and periods may differ in the norms of acceptability to which they adhere—but all engage in translingual editing, because all present new, translingual editions of extant and ever-growing works, to whose proliferative growth they also contribute.

A spate of recent scholarly engagements with news translation have described it as a form of "transediting" (Stetting, quoted in Valedon: 442) in which multiple sources may be "reshaped, edited, synthesized and transformed" (Bielsa and Bassnett 2009: 2) to produce a news item in another language, making it nearly impossible to trace a discrete source for any given translation. This description is certainly true to the reality of translingual news production. Yet as Christina Schäffner points out, if the term "transediting" is used "as a substitute for and/or in opposition to the term translation, there is the danger that translation continues to be understood in a narrower sense of a purely word-for-word transfer process" (883). While the discussion of news translation falls outside the purview of my book, which focuses exclusively on the translation of literary texts, I join Schäffner in claiming that editorial work is involved in nearly all translation, in all genres. On the surface, this may not sound like an entirely new argument: translation scholars working in the tradition of the so-called manipulation school already view translation as one of many processes by which texts are shaped by political, social, and aesthetic agendas in the "receiving" culture. What my book contributes is a demonstration that translation doesn't just edit or manipulate some preexisting, stable "source," but rather continues a process of textual iteration already at work in the language of initial composition. André Lefevere's 1992, *Translation, Rewriting, and the Manipulation of Literary Fame*, gave translation pride of place among other forms of interpretive mediation that included editing, anthologization, literary criticism, reviewing, adaptation, and dramatic performance, yet Lefevere treated editing and translating largely as separate activities, one preceding the other.[10] Theo Hermans subsequently drew on Lefevere's work to further combat the contemporary understanding of equivalence as ahistorical and unhelpfully proscriptive. "What do we do, for example, with a translator like Antoine Houdar de la Motte," Hermans writes, borrowing an example from Lefevere's book, "who renders the *Iliad* into French at the beginning of the eighteenth century and blithely informs us in his preface that he, the 'mere translator', reduced Homer's twenty-four books to twelve," cutting out what Lefevere describes as "superfluous repetitions, trivial descriptions, anatomical detail and long speeches"? (Hermans 1999: 48).

Hermans argues against the notion of translation as transfer by referring to practices that allow for texts to be "reduced" or edited in translation. Yet the rhetoric of his passage does nothing to challenge the stability of "Homer's twenty-four books," elsewhere referred to as "Homer's original"— an "original" that was in fact composed over the course of centuries and arose in part from an oral tradition, whose authorship is the subject of much debate, and whose twenty-four books were editorial constructions of subsequent centuries rather than a mythical "Homer's" own. I certainly do not

---

[10] See also *The Manipulation of Literature* (1985), a collection of essays edited by Hermans, which introduced many of the theoretical concerns that would drive scholarship in the field in the years that followed.

mean to suggest that Hermans believes the myth of Homer, or is ignorant of the textual history of the *Iliad*. On the contrary, I choose this example precisely because of Herman's astute description of translation as a form of translingual editing, to show how, even here, in the best of circumstances, the rhetoric employed to talk about supposed "originals" reinforces a distinction we already know is flawed, between the iterative work of translation and the supposedly textually consolidating work of canon formation. The textual complexities of "originals" have historically not been considered relevant to the translator's task, and are often glossed over even by those aiming to bring issues of textual instability in translation to our attention. If pushed on the issue, most scholars who write about "originals" and "source texts," about "Homer's original" or "Kafka's German," would likely acknowledge that such phrases are placeholders, and misleading ones at that. It is one goal of this book to push translators and translation scholars on the issue with more lasting, less localized results.

In arguing that translations further the iterative growth of a work in new languages, I also seek to intervene not only in the field of translation studies, but in that of textual scholarship. If translation studies has yet to grapple in a concentrated fashion with the consequences of the textual instability of nearly all objects of translation, the field of textual scholarship has likewise rarely recognized translation as a process that shakes the foundations of the editorial project as widely understood. Textual scholars have long been concerned primarily with the history of a work's production and trans-mission within a single language (usually its language of composition), or with constructing editorial forms that best represent a particular version or versions of that work. That might mean comparing all extant texts of a work to see which is a more likely representative of some lost "original," or determining whether rhetorical or grammatical punctuation should be used in a new edition of a nineteenth-century novel whose author likely would have expected a publisher to impose house style. Translation seems to stand in opposition to such projects, which focus on particular lexical, syntactic, or even typographic details in the language of a work's initial composition. Translation could in fact be considered the ultimate case in which a work of literature "survives" despite the wholesale replacement of one text with another that differs from it in constitutive ways, including the basic fact of its being written in a different language.

Yet just as translation is increasingly recognized as an interpretive activity that creates something "new and different" in another language (Venuti 2013: 10), so too is editing now seen to be an interpretive endeavor that doesn't restore a lost "original" but presents a new textual as well as bibliographic configuration of the work in question. In the words of Peter Shillingsburg, "every attempt to edit a work, even when the aim of the edition was to restore earlier or more authorial or otherwise authentic readings, is not, in the end, an act of restoration but is instead a new creative act that merely adds to the accumulating stock of available editions" (2006: 7). Swap "edit" and "edition" for "translate" and "translation" and the sentence rings equally true. This argument is, moreover, not just a theoretical one: Shillingsburg offers specific policy recommendations, as it were, for how editors can make readers aware of the status of the text they are reading and the processes that shaped it. "The new text emerging as a result of editorial work," he writes, "should declare itself for what it is: a new iteration of some previous iteration as found in one previously existing physical object, or more" (19). Editors should, in other words, name and describe their sources, announce their methodology, and be forthright—in introductions and afterwords, or in supplementary articles and essays—about how their edition reflects their interpretation of the work in question and shapes others' interpretations in turn. While publishers rarely give translators space to discuss their approach, Shillingsburg's recommendations are very much in line with what many translators and scholars of translation would like to see happening in that domain as well.

Despite their lack of communication, the fields of translation studies and textual scholarship have recently been undergoing parallel shifts that involve similar reconfigurations of the metaphorical terrain onto which the activities of translating and editing are often mapped. In the wake of Venuti's enormously influential *The Translator's Invisibility* (1995), translation studies has exhibited an increasing concern with the marginalization of translators in the publishing industry and the academy. Many scholars have encouraged translation practices that seek to resist what Venuti calls the "hegemony of transparent discourse" (304) and to bring translators back into view, not just in book reviews and jacket copy, but within the texts of translations themselves. Likewise, a growing number of textual scholars seek to counteract what David Greetham calls the "disappearing act" by which editors have long been complicit in minimizing the visibility of their interventions into the texts they treat, and to focus readers' attention on the "phenomenologically fraught and powerful role" (1996: xiii) editors play in the formation of literary texts. Ever greater numbers of scholarly editors are eschewing the so-called eclectic method, with its customary emphasis on the author's supposed final intentions, in favor of methods that recognize the collaborative or social aspect of textual production and the validity of varying versions of works, while underscoring rather than obscuring the interpretive effort that goes into the preparation of both scholarly and popular editions.

This book seeks to consolidate, further, and enhance the rigor of the conceptual shifts taking place in these two fields by bringing them into sustained and explicit contact—or rather, by demonstrating that, like translating and editing, they are already standing on much the same ground, however unstable that ground may be.[11] Textual scholars and translators have always been called upon to negotiate a tension between the one and the many, between the metaphysical and the material, between an understanding of the work as an abstract entity that exists independent of any one manifestation and a close-range focus on the materiality of textual production and circulation. This book presents translating and editing as mutually implicated processes whose points of divergence are also points of contact. I focus primarily on the ways in which those involved in extending the reach of literary works through the production and dissemination of translations—authors, translators, rights holders, agents, editors, publishers, scholars, and so on—both negotiate and further the textual instability that has always characterized literary works, even those from a time before the concept of "literature" existed. Not only do translators (often in collaboration, or contestation, with other individuals) choose between, consolidate, or otherwise negotiate the available versions of the works they translate, they also create others versions of those works, expanding a shelf (to paraphrase Shillingsburg's claim for scholarly editions) on which there will always be more room.[12]

Literary Translation and the Making of Originals questions the often unexamined assumption that the object of translation is a single, stable lexical entity whose existence predates the process of translation. I argue that each translator creates her own original, fixes a particular text as the "prior" text to be translated—fixes it sometimes before translating, and sometimes during and even by way of the process we tend to think of as "translation proper." So-called originals are not given but made, and translators are often party to that making. In saying this, I do not mean to claim that translations are original creative products "in their own right" (to borrow that common phrase of backhanded praise). This may be true, but it is incidental to what this book is about. And if it is true, it is so only insofar as *any* text can be called an "original" creative product: "originals," too, are shaped by generic conventions and a nearly infinite list of ghostly "sources." My point, on the contrary, is that a particular text becomes an "original" only when

---

[11] Esther Allen, too, points to the fact that translation "can and does" involve the activities Greetham includes in his definition of textual scholarship ("the discovery, description, transcription, editing, glossing, annotating and commenting upon texts," quoted in Allen: 210). Gary Taylor, meanwhile, views editing and translating as parallel modes of "regulated transformation" (citing Derrida), and even suggests that we reconceptualize editorial theory "as a special subset of translation theory" (99).

[12] Shillingsburg (1996: 114): "each new scholarly edition, unless carelessly produced, extends the shelf on which there is still space."

another, derivative text comes along to *make* it so. Thus while I invoke the language of originals and sources throughout this book, I do so largely to contest the understanding of translation that these terms represent. One of my central goals in challenging the assumption that a stable original preexists the process of translation is precisely to make us more aware of the assumptions embedded in the language we use to talk about the objects and products of translation.[13] An "original" is distinct from a "copy." The adjective "original" stands in counterpoint to "derivative," "imitative," "banal." In common parlance, translations are derivative, while the texts we translate are originals, no matter how derivative, imitative, or banal those prior texts may be. The very idea of a textual "origin" or "source" not only ignores the many sources upon which an "original" may itself rest, but rhetorically strips translations of *their* potential for what we conventionally (if problematically) call "originality."

Translations *are* derivative, of course—but so are so-called originals. If we begin to recognize the extent to which translations are not only shaped by but also shape those "originals," we may finally be able to let go of the rhetoric and ideology of faithfulness, and to replace an outdated under-standing of translation as a transfer or transmission of some semantic invariant with a more reasonable understanding of translation as a further textual extension of an already unstable literary work. As a consequence, we may also become more open to experimental forms of translation we have tended to dismiss as not really translation, or other forms we have yet to encounter or conceive—forms that may currently be hidden in plain sight.

Unexceptional editing

Works of literature almost always exist in multiple forms even in the language in which they are first composed. These forms are shaped, directly or indirectly, not only by those named as their authors, but by patrons, amanuenses, scribes, editors, publishers, typesetters, designers, and so on, not to mention the histories of literary production that precede the particular works in question. The longer a work survives and the more widely it is distributed, the greater the number of forms it is likely to take. My university library currently has seventy-nine different holdings for *Robinson Crusoe* in

---

[13] For excellent reflections on the metaphorical language we use to talk about translation, see Gambier and van Doorslaer's *The Metalanguage of Translation* (2009), and James St. André's edited volume *Thinking through Translation with Metaphors* (2010), particularly Maria Tymoczko's contribution, as well as Chamberlain (1988) and Michael Emmerich (2013).

English, including the first printing of 1719 (whose title was in fact *The life and strange surprising adventures of Robinson Crusoe, of York, mariner, Who lived eight and twenty years, all alone in an un-inhabited island on the coast of America, near the mouth of the great river of Oroonoque; Having been cast on shore by shipwreck, wherein all the men perished but himself. With an account how he was at last as strangely deliver'd by pyrates. Written by himself*); four additional printings of that edition that appeared within the year; and numerous subsequent editions, some illustrated, some abridged, some (particularly those intended for young readers) illustrated *and* abridged, some facsimiles of earlier editions, some digitally available, published under widely varying titles and often supplemented by editorial paratext of various sorts. Then there are the translations (into twenty-two languages, including Esperanto) and the continuations (two by Defoe and many more by others); the translations of the continuations; the adaptations, literary and filmic; a comic opera, the libretto for which has also been translated numerous times; scores for pantomimes and children's songs; and so on. *Robinson Crusoe* is a tree whose branches beget branches that themselves beget others.

If you think I've chosen an isolated example—admittedly a bit extreme—to prove my case, I invite you to walk over to your bookshelf. Try to find a work of literature for which you are entirely sure that the text in the book on your shelf is the only text there is: no hardcover or paperback or digital edition that might differ from it, either lexically or bibliographically, no excerpts in anthologies or internet prepublications, no audiobooks, no abridgements, no scholarly editions bristling with annotations, no revised versions or as-yet-undiscovered manuscripts. You may find such a work, but I very much doubt it. When we introduce the specter of translation into the mix, the number of potential texts becomes, for all intents and purposes, infinite. Each of the many textual manifestations of a work in its language of composition could potentially become an object of translation. Likewise, each version of the work in another language will not only be the product of a translator's (or translators') interpretive efforts, but will take shape in an edition of its own—or many editions over time, particularly if the translation achieves a canonical status. The widespread practice of so-called relay translation (a term that houses an embedded spatial metaphor of translation as transfer), in which a translation serves as an intermediary text for another translation of the same work in a third language, demonstrates that translations can in fact be objects of further translation, notwithstanding Walter Benjamin's thoughts on the matter.[14] Each of these cases demonstrates the

---

[14] The relevant passage from Benjamin's "Die Aufgabe des Übersetzers" reads, in Stephen Rendall's translation ("The Translator's Task"): "The more distinctive the work, the more

fundamental theoretical tension between the one and the many that we encounter when talking about works of literature: we often operate as if works were singular, unified entities, though they in fact assume multiple textual forms that are often quite different from one another.

In distinguishing between *work* and *text*, I am drawing on the usage of those terms in contemporary Anglophone textual scholarship. A work, Shillingsburg writes, is a "product of the imagination" that can take shape in many versions corresponding to different moments in the work's development; a text is "the actual order of words and punctuation contained in any one physical form, such as a manuscript, proof, or book," or in digital or oral forms.[15] When encountering, interpreting, and discussing particular textual instantiations of literary works, many readers, including the professional readers of the academy, tend to overlook both the contingency of those texts and the ways in which they have been editorially shaped by any number of hands. In a 1958 lecture, textual scholar Fredson Bowers complained that "many a literary critic has investigated the past ownership and mechanical condition of his second-hand automobile, or the pedigree and training of his dog, more thoroughly than he has looked into the qualifications of the text on which his critical theories rest" (5). Bowers was speaking at a time

it remains translatable, in the very fleeting nature of its contact with sense. This is of course true only of original works. Translations, on the contrary, prove to be untranslatable not because the sense weighs on them heavily, but rather because it attaches to them all too fleetingly" (2012: 83).

[15] See Shillingsburg (1996: 42, 46) for these quotations. Shillingsburg is trying in this passage to encourage greater uniformity among scholars' usages of terms that have historically been quite slippery. While my own use of *work* and *text* corresponds fairly closely to what he proposes, there are some crucial differences, arising first and foremost from my attempt to open up the "work" to accommodate *translingual* versions, i.e., translations in other languages. The definitions Shillingsburg offers focus explicitly on authorial intent: a "version" of the work is not only "one specific form of the work," but "the [form] the author intended at some particular moment in time" (44), while each text "represents more or less well or completely a version of the work" (46), i.e., an authorially-intended form. While Shillingsburg recognizes the sociological nature of textual production and the plurality of individuals whose work contributes to the existence and circulation of texts for a work, his schema may need to be tweaked in order to accommodate the confluence of authorial and translatorial intention that translation seems to involve. I note, too, that the desire among textual scholars for a clear distinction between "work" and "text" is complicated by the nearly opposite definitions of *oeuvre* and *texte* given by Roland Barthes in *De l'oeuvre au texte* (translated by Richard Howard as "From Work to Text," Barthes 1986), which greatly influenced the use of these terms by subsequent literary scholars. For further discussions of twentieth-century developments in textual scholarship and the ontology of the work and the text, see McGann (1983); Tanselle (1989); and Groden (1991). See also Cohen (1991) for a number of excellent essays on the role of theory in textual editing, and the paradigm shift in the field of textual scholarship. These books, while now a few decades old, remain key contributions to a field of whose advances many literary critics and translation scholars remain only marginally aware.

when New Criticism, infused with ideas from the Russian formalists that encouraged a focus on the mechanics of a text in isolation from its history of production and circulation, held sway in Anglo-American literary studies, and when the rift between textual scholars and literary critics was growing ever deeper. Textual scholars largely focused their efforts on attempts to reconstruct lost or never-fully-realized texts corresponding to an author's "final intentions" for a work. Meanwhile, literary scholars—unschooled in the specialized labor of scholarly editing and trained by the era's dominant methodologies of reading to treat a text as an autonomous entity ready for the hermeneutic touch—often took for granted the reliability of the texts on which they based their interpretations. In other words, scholarly editors downplayed the interpretive nature of their work, while literary critics treated textual scholarship as a "preliminary operation" by which a text was fixed that they could proceed to interpret.[16]

On the whole, Bowers' caustic description of literary critics' disinterest in the editorial history of the texts and works they treat may still hold true. Just as academics in any number of fields routinely decline to cite translators when quoting works in translation ("According to Jacques Derrida," "As Karl Marx writes," or, "In the words of Walter Benjamin," followed by words for which Derrida or Marx or Benjamin can be held only partly responsible), literary scholars, while certainly aware that editing happens, often proceed with the work of interpretation as if it didn't. This may be particularly frustrating to those in the field of textual scholarship, which in the past several decades has undergone what George Bornstein calls a "sea change" in its conception of its own goals and purpose; in the methodology by which editions are constructed; and in the tools editors use to make editorial activity visible within editions themselves. The notion of textual finality has been undone by the recognition that works often exist "in several versions no one of which can be said to constitute the 'final' one" (McGann 1983: 32). An author's "intention to *mean*" has been judged ultimately unrecoverable. And while her "intention to *do*," i.e., to put certain words to paper, "may be at least partially recoverable from the signs written," that intention is often qualified by the author's explicit or implicit expectations about what others would do with her text, including publishers, editors, copyeditors, and designers, all involved in the process of bringing a piece of writing into print or digital form (Shillingsburg 1996: 34). Scholars such as Shillingsburg, Bornstein, Jerome McGann, and D. F. McKenzie have thus dismissed the notion that a quest for authorial intentions should necessarily drive editorial

---

[16] The phrase "preliminary operation" dates at least to Austin Warren and René Wellek's *Theory of Literature*, first published in 1949.

activity, promoting instead an understanding of literary creation as a social rather than a solitary endeavor. While an author's intentions still figure as one factor among many to be taken into consideration during the process of constructing an edition, these scholars also recognize the legitimacy of various versions, the importance of actors other than the author, and even the significance of what McGann calls the "bibliographical code" (1998: 123), a set of nontextual elements including page design, the incorporation of illustrations or images, binding, page size, paper weight, and so on, all of which affect a reader's experience of a work. Web platforms and digital devices offer still other nontextual elements that likewise affect the reading experience.

This fundamental reexamination of the nature of the literary work and its relationship to its various texts has, meanwhile, encouraged editors to reconsider the structure and purpose of the editions they produce. As Philip Cohen and David Jackson note, "an editor's assumptions regarding literary ontology ... determine the stages of the editorial process as well as the form of the edition itself" (104); a change in our understanding of what a work is and how (not what) it means necessitates a new set of editorial methodologies that better account for these new conceptual frameworks and interpretive priorities. Recent decades have thus seen a flood of new editions, print and electronic, that seek to represent more adequately both the textual mutability of literary works and the potential significance of elements that had previously been overlooked, including the visual and material aspects of texts.[17] This proliferation of new editorial forms, including an increasing array of digital archives and editions, invites literary critics, in turn, to explore a diverse set of intellectual arguments that treat instability as a central aspect of the textual condition, and of the particular works they choose to discuss. Moreover, since the creation of an edition is itself an act of criticism, textual scholars continue to urge students of literature at all levels, from undergraduates to senior scholars, to equip themselves with basic information about the composition and publication history of the texts they interpret, and to cultivate a sufficient understanding of editorial methodology so as to "read" not just the text at hand but also the edition that gives it shape.

---

[17] Chapter 3 of this book will discuss a number of editions of Emily Dickinson's work that seek to do just this. I cannot hope to give a representative list of examples here, but a few might include the Rossetti Archive, McGann's hypermedia archive of the writings and images of Dante Gabriel Rossetti; Morris Eaves's digital archive of the work of William Blake; the Homer Multitext Project, an open source project to offer digital editions of extant manuscripts; and Jack Stillinger's 1995 *Coleridge and Textual Instability: The Multiple Versions of the Major Poems*, which includes an edition of Coleridge's best known poems, an account of his process of self-revision, and a critical text about how such texts should be presented.

In many realms, scholarly editing has historically been a cross-lingual endeavor: think of the centuries of classical Chinese texts given scholarly apparatuses in other languages in Asia, or the long-lived European habit of writing textual apparatus in Latin, or the use of Hebrew as an interlanguage by scholars of ancient Semitic languages. Yet even as the modern field of textual scholarship moves outward from its nineteenth- and early-twentieth-century fixation on authorial origins and intent, contemporary discussions of textual theory and editorial methodology continue to be deeply rooted in single-language literary traditions, exhibiting what Conor Fahy calls a form of intellectual "national isolationism" (401). Moreover, we rarely think of books in translation as translingual editions of works (a fact that, in my view, shows rather surprisingly just how much their own thing we think translations are). A translation is widely understood to be a derivative text that both embodies a particular interpretation and also contributes to what Walter Benjamin famously called the "*Fortleben*" of an "original," its "afterlife," or "continuing life," or "surviving life" (depending on which English version of Benjamin you read).[18] Yet a translation is also widely understood as contributing to that ongoing life not by *living* it but by *pointing* to it; translations continue to be considered "no substitute for the original," even if, as David Bellos points out, that is precisely how translations often function.[19] All the *Crime and Punishment*s and *Crimen y castigo*s and *Verbrechen und Strafe*s in the world, while giving us wonderful ways to spend long, lazy afternoons, seem inevitably, inexorably also to disclose their own crimes of murdering

---

[18] Or, of course, any number of translations of this word in the many languages that host interpretive iterations of Benjamin's piece. (The three English terms come from the translations by Rendall [2012], Zohn [2004], and Hynd and Volk [1968].) For a field putatively concerned with cross-linguistic networks of meaning, translation studies as practiced in the United States and Europe has done a very poor job of considering the fact that many of its key terms may not resonate in languages spoken outside these locations. In fact, even within the Western European context the presumption of equivalence between key terms in various languages is highly problematic. As Robert Young has pointed out, much translation theory "assumes that there is a unitary global concept for practices called (in English) translation": the field proceeds as if "there is in fact an equivalence among the terms 'translation,' 'traduction,' 'Übersetzung,' and so on" (2014: 51)—not to mention the many other words in languages primarily spoken outside Europe. Maria Tymoczko has described translation as a cross-cultural "cluster concept" comprised of a "wide range and variation of conceptualizations, ideas, norms, practices, and histories," attention to which, she hopes, will "[begin] to open up the domain of translation far beyond the ideas of transfer, fidelity, and so-called equivalence that have been valorized in Eurocentric cultures" (2014: 168; see also Tymoczko 2010). See also Ricci on Java conceptions of activities akin to translation, and how recentering the discipline elsewhere might lead to *different* descriptions and conceptions of what these activities are.

[19] Bellos (2011: 37). See also footnote 4.

this or that aspect of a Russian text or texts we ourselves cannot read—the dreaded "violence" of translation, which many scholars treat as if it were something more than metaphor.[20] The commonplace insistence on an ideal of translational "fidelity" means that promiscuity is for originals alone; the last thing we want is for a translation to go messing around with an unstable text, much less with several at once.

Translation's deictic gesture seems, in a way, to roll readers right back to 1958: when it comes to texts in translation, our understanding of textual instability as a basic characteristic of literary works flies out the window, and we revert to speaking of an "original" or "source text" as if it were a stable entity whose self-sameness could be taken for granted. While we recognize that a given work of literature can give rise to multiple translations, we are less willing to admit that a translator might, in the course of her work, need to negotiate the existence of multiple texts for that work, or even engage in the editorial finessing of a new so-called original. In other words, with regard to translation, the understanding of textual scholarship as a preliminary operation seems alive and well: we may recognize semantic multiplicity as an unavoidable feature of language, and thus the "source text" as open to any number of interpretations, but the actual words of that source are often assumed to be more or less fixed, even by scholars of translation. Yet this assumption simply ignores the reality of the textual condition. If we can't count on a work being lexically stable even as a theoretical ideal, and if any new edition of a work in its language of composition presents not a definitive text but an interpretation of the materials at hand—if, that is, the "afterlife" begins not with the translation but with those "originals" themselves—translators are suddenly faced with the problem of how to arrive at a "source text" to begin with, and how to adjudicate between potentially conflicting versions or editorial presentations of a work in the language from which they are translating.

Textual instability is the rule rather than the exception. The more a translator digs into the composition and publication history of a work, the more likely she is to find entirely new sets of choices to be made concerning the constitution of her "original" and how to present it to a new set of readers. Like editors, translators shape the forms in which readers encounter literary works. The editions they help to create are based on existing shapes, but also give new and different shapes to those works, ones that help define for a new readership what and how those works mean, and even what they are, where their margins lie. The more aware of

---

[20] See Douglas Robinson's chapter on Philip Lewis in *What is Translation?* (1997) for a remarkable contestation of the rhetoric of violence in translation studies.

this we are, the more concertedly and creatively we may try to make our readers cognizant of some of the many decisions that comprise the process of translation, and the construction of the edition that presents our "final" product—whose shape, of course, may change as our translations, too, enter new printings, new media, new contexts of reception, and are perhaps even taken up and revised or responded to by subsequent generations of translators, editors, or both.[21] Inviting readers to recognize how translation both negotiates and contributes to the textual instability of literary works can also help us combat more effectively the mistaken idea that translation involves a transfer of some invariant "meaning." After all, the fact that translations rarely have only one possible source not only makes such a transfer impossible, it also makes word-level comparisons between a translation and an assumed original both practically and conceptually problematic.[22]

The convoluted translingual publication history of Vassilikos's novel is certainly a case in point. And while it may be an extreme case, extreme is not the same as exceptional. Among the several books I have translated, of poetry and prose, I am hard pressed to find a single one for which a stable text could be said to exist in Greek. Conversations with others

[21] Consider, for instance, D. J. Enright's editing of Terrence Kilmartin's reworking of C. K. Scott Montcrieff's translations of Proust. Likewise, the first time I read the poetry of C. P. Cavafy was in Edmund Keeley and Philip Sherrard's translations, as published by Princeton University Press in 1992. However, the instructor of the course I was taking preferred the slightly different translations in the 1972 edition, and asked us to laboriously "correct" some of the translations in our copies of the 1992 edition, which was subsequently followed by another edition in 2009. When readers refer to the "Keeley and Sherrard translation" of a particular poem by Cavafy, they may not know just how many such translations are currently in circulation, both in printed books and in online citations, as on the English-language website of the Cavafy Archive (www.cavafy.com). In other words, translations need be no more stable than "originals" in their published forms.

[22] In his landmark *Descriptive Translation Studies–and beyond* (2012; 1st edn 1995), Gideon Toury noted that, any time we hope to investigate a translator's choices by comparing a source text with a translation, we first have to determine what source was used, since "a multitude of candidates for a source text may exist" (74). Toury's methodology for determining a source rested, paradoxically, on comparing the translation with potential sources. There are several problems with this approach. First of all, the source may not be publicly available—it may, for instance, exist in a unique copy on the translator's shelf, as with my altered Gnosi edition of Vassilikos's novel. Second, the translator might have drawn on multiple sources, in one or more than one language. More importantly, the kind of comparison Toury suggests would likely enable one to determine only between sources that differ quite radically, rather than sources with subtle differences in wording. Likewise, this comparative method seems to rest on an assumption of a lexical transfer of content, in which every word of a source could be accounted for. See Chapter 5 for a contestation of this notion.

in the translation community have shown that my experiences are not uncommon.[23] Translators frequently work with living authors who see a translation as an opportunity to revisit a work, tailoring content for an audience abroad or revising a book according to their own changed aesthetic sensibilities. A translator is likely to read the text or texts she is working with as closely as anyone ever will, and her response to textual details (including, at times, factual errors) can elicit changes from an author, even to a book that is already in print. Particularly in an age of digital communication, many translators are in close contact with authors, who often alter texts or rewrite passages as a result of queries, though these revised "originals" may never see the light of day outside of an email thread.[24] Collections of poems or books of short stories in translation often include pieces from several extant volumes, and may even present newly written pieces that have yet to be published in the language from which they are being translated. It is in fact not uncommon for works of literature to circulate first in translation, sometimes because publication in an author's country of birth or residence is made impossible by social or political circumstances. If these works subsequently appear in their language of initial composition, the forms may differ from those that were translated. Works may appear in censored forms

---

[23] To give just one example, a recent panel entitled "Translation as Collaboration" at the 2016 conference of the Association of Writers and Writing Programs featured four translators: Kareem James Abu-Zaid, Edward Gauvin, Shabnam Nadiya, and myself. All of us discussed instances in which our translation work intersected with what might more commonly be understood as editorial work, usually but not always in collaboration with the author.

[24] One consequence is that readers of translated texts who can compare a translation to its presumed original can't ever be sure that the text they have before them is in fact the text on which the translation was based. See, for instance, Madeline Levine's review of Bill Johnston's translation of Magdalena Tulli's *In Red*, in which she wonders why "the entire third paragraph of the Polish original, almost a page long, does not appear in the translation. There is no indication on the copyright page or elsewhere in the Archipelago edition that *In Red* was not translated directly from the 1968 edition, yet here and there one finds in the English version minor changes in descriptions and even entire sentences that do not appear in the Polish. Since it is inconceivable that Johnston would have decided to exercise his creative talents by adding to the original, one can only conclude that Tulli saw the English translation as her opportunity to revise her novel a decade after its publication. It would have been interesting to be told when and why she made the changes" (82). Levine is generous enough with Johnston to assume—correctly, as I learned from a personal conversation with Johnston himself—that he was working from an edited text by Tulli. One can, however, imagine a situation in which a reviewer might not be so generous, and might blame the translator for any perceived divergences in the texts. Levin's "generosity" also rests both on the assumption that translation performs a recognizable transfer of content, and that the exercise of a translator's "creative talents" will properly adhere to certain limitations upon which we agree: it is "inconceivable" that this respected translator would "add" to the text. See also footnote 3 on adding and subtracting.

in one place and in noncensored (or differently censored) forms elsewhere, even in a single language; translations, too, often pass under a censor's pen. In these and many other circumstances, line-by-line comparisons—or, at least, comparisons that seek to evaluate the success of a particular translation by tracing its supposed similarity to the textual configuration of a "source"—are rendered futile. (They are often misguided to begin with, since such comparisons are usually based on an understanding of translation as semantic transfer that does not hold up under scrutiny.)

Consider Alex Zucker's *City Sister Silver*, released by Catbird Press in 2000, a masterful and inventive translation of Jáchym Topol's *Sestra*, which was published in the Czech Republic first in 1994 and again, in revised form, in 1996. Zucker began translating the novel before the revised text was published, and therefore worked from the first edition. Topol reportedly gave him free rein to edit the book as he saw fit, on the assumption that an English-language audience would be less tolerant of culturally specific material than those able to read the book in Czech. Zucker cut a total of about twenty pages, in passages ranging from less than a paragraph to several pages in length. Yet for readers who might want to read a translation of the entire first edition, Zucker and his publisher made most of those deleted passages available on the Catbird Press website as a downloadable file.[25] The 1994 and 1996 Czech versions and the 2000 English print version are thus all quite differently configured, while the textual instability manifested by Zucker's print-plus-digital translation mimics or extends the instability of the Czech. Given that his translator's note to the book makes his interventions clear, Zucker's approach to his task as translator-editor seems in keeping with Shillingsburg's desire that editors disclose their sources and editorial methodology, and also "prepare an apparatus that will make the edition useful to persons wishing that another orientation had been employed" (1996: 26). Zucker's solution to this editorial conundrum points toward the ever more significant role that supplementary texts may play in providing readers with information about the translations before them. While translators are rarely given adequate space to discuss their work within the covers of a printed book, the increasing popularity of digital platforms may enable translators to make hitherto "invisible" aspects of their task more accessible to readers in other forms and contexts.[26]

---

[25] For excised passages of at least a paragraph in length, see http://www.catbirdpress.com/firstchaps/cuts.htm (last accessed 7 May 2017). I am grateful to Alex Zucker for talking to me about this project, and to Michelle Woods for sharing with me an unpublished lecture, "Translating Topol: Kafka, the Holocaust, and Humor."

[26] Karin Littau likewise suggests that hypertext might be used as a tool to present "variant translations," thus "confront[ing] its readers with the very impossibility of a definitive

Decisions regarding the makeup of an "original" can seem even more weighty when one is translating a work by a deceased author who cannot be consulted for assistance or approval. With such works, it may be tempting for translators to hew as closely as possible to the editorial choices of others. After all, works often find their way into print via the painstaking efforts of trained scholars whose expertise differs greatly from that of most translators. Bernhard Echte and Werner Morlang spent years deciphering Robert Walser's Mikrogramme, or "microscripts"—whose penciled letters are barely a millimeter high, such that an entire story can be squeezed into the blank space on a calling card—for their six-volume German-language edition of Walser's later works.[27] If potential translators had to decipher these scripts anew, or if every translator of Kafka's unfinished novel *Der Verschollene* (which Max Brod titled *Amerika* for its first posthumous German-language publication in 1927, and which has since been published in several editions that differ significantly from Brod's) had to decide how to order the chapters, or if translators of *Gilgamesh* had to visit the cuneiform collections of countless museums all over the world in order to piece together an "original," those works might never be translated at all. Many of the examples I discuss in this book are works scholars have spent decades studying, editing, and writing about; these scholars can, even in absentia, serve as collaborators of sorts.

By the same token, the existence of multiple editions for works such as *Gilgamesh* or Kafka's novels means that translators may have to choose between them. Even for works that are not fragmentary or unfinished, works whose textual makeup hasn't been subject to much-publicized contestation, the decision to use a particular edition or editions as the basis for a translation can entail significant intellectual and interpretive positioning. In translating the book-length early poems of Greek poet Eleni Vakalo, I had to negotiate the extensive differences between the first editions, whose visual aspects were designed by the poet herself, and the more commercially available collected edition of her work—also produced during her lifetime, but edited and designed by others—whose pages and spreads looked radically different. My decision to follow the bibliographic organization of the first editions was based on extensive research in the poet's archive, and on an interpretive claim that the collected edition failed to

translation, and therefore also with the impossibility of the closure of the original" (91). Littau argues against the notion of the "faithful translation" and the "blind acceptance of the 'supremacy of the original'" by reconceptualizing translation "as the re-writing of an already pluralized 'original'" (81).

27 See Walser (2011) for an edited selection of texts based on these transcriptions, with images of selected manuscripts. See also Walser (2010) for Susan Bernofsky's translation of a smaller selection of these texts; this edition also includes images of the manuscripts.

account for aspects of these works that I considered crucial to their mode of meaning; my translations thus present embodied interpretations of what *and how* these poems mean.[28] This kind of research is not generally considered part of the translator's task, though it may feel like a natural step for some translators who are also literary scholars, and who see their translation work as part and parcel of a broader intellectual engagement with a field of study that often involves archival research. However, given the dearth of visible public engagement with the role of textual and bibliographic instability in translation, many translators may be less attuned to the fact that determinations regarding the textual makeup of "originals" are an inevitable part of the process of translation—that, in other words, they themselves are often already making these decisions by their de facto endorsement of the prior editorial choices of others. Translators may have little sense that a choice between editions, for instance, may be theirs to make.

And of course that choice is *not* always theirs, and certainly not solely theirs. For premodern and early modern works circulating in the public domain, long-standing editorial convention has often given a remarkably stable lexical form to a particular text or set of texts, which is then replicated across editions, albeit in different bibliographic forms. Translators of Aeschylus, Homer, Dante, or Murasaki Shikibu may not feel they are in a position to question the texts before them, or at least not beyond certain words or passages that scholars already consider contested variants. And yet those texts don't simply appear out of the blue; they are, rather, consolidated by literary or textual traditions, by historical circumstances and processes of canon formation that involve the actions of countless individuals, ourselves included (as translators, editors, readers, writers, teachers). For modern and contemporary works, on the other hand, such decisions may not fall within a translator's legal purview. Many editorial decisions are made or preempted by those who hold the translation rights to particular works, and are inscribed in the contracts translators sign before they even start working; other decisions are manifested in the interventions, sometimes unwelcome, of in-house editors who often have the final say.[29] Publishers,

---

[28] The translations, which embody my argument about the importance of the visual aspect of these texts, were published by Ugly Duckling Presse as *Before Lyricism* (2017). For a scholarly version of this argument, see Karen Emmerich (2013).

[29] See Marilyn Booth's "Translator v. author" (2015), which treats her experience of having an author and editor overrule her own wishes regarding a translation she produced. See also Eva Hemmungs Wirtén's discussion (2011: 38–56) of Tiina Nunnally's decision to withdraw her name from the U.K. edition of Peter Hoeg's *Smilla's Sense of Snow* over objections to the author's and editor's interventions into her translation; the translation was published under the pseudonym "F. David." For one almost comical example of what it might look like for a translator to incorporate a sense of the textual history

especially trade publishers, rarely give (or perhaps even think to give) translators the purview to make basic decisions about "sources," or about the forms of the translations they produce; they also rarely give translators space to discuss their methodology or approach in notes or introductions, thus depriving readers of one opportunity to gain at least a rudimentary sense of the complex processes that have produced the text before them. Translations, we are often told, don't sell, and the more a publisher can do to help a reader overlook the fact that the text they are reading is a translation, the better. Yet in a cultural moment in which forms of citational composition such as the remix, the mashup, the retweet, and the annotated share have become deeply embedded in everyday popular practice, publishers may find that their attempts to protect the supposed authorial purity of the work of literature by downplaying the visibility of translation is no longer quite so necessary, desirable, or even relevant to the way many readers want to read.

Translation is, indeed, an exemplary case of divided authority. And if more and more of us are now willing to treat textual production as a collective enterprise for works in the languages in which they were first composed, the time has surely come for us to recognize the translator's role not just in interpreting a "source text," but in determining what that text is, and in shaping the edition that will present her translation to the world. This recognition may, in turn, help us to understand that translations are not mere derivative works beholden to (yet always failing to adequately represent) a single, stable "original." They are, instead, textual iterations of a work in another language—translingual editions that both represent a work and add to it, extending the growth of that work in new interpretive forms.

---

of a work into the resulting translation, see Manuel Portela's two-volume Portuguese-language translation of Laurence Sterne's *Life and Opinions of Tristram Shandy*, which attempts to imitate the minutest of visual and material details of the first bound edition of the novel. In an essay discussing the challenges of this self-assigned task of "fidelity" to a particular physical manifestation of Sterne's book, Portela notes that the typographical aspect and historical context of this work "face the translator with a number of editorial dilemmas," since "it is often impossible to distinguish between the typographical and the semantic element" (290). There is, too, Sterne's own injunction that future editors "do not presume to alter or transpose one Word, nor rectify one false Spelling, nor so much as add or diminish one Comma or Title, in or to my Romance" (295). Of course, the translation replaces *all* the words of Sterne's text. Yet Portela also attempts to replicate, to the extent possible, the visual and material aspects of the first edition, much to his publisher's exasperation: "my suggestion of actually marbling the paper so that we would have different patterns in each of the 2,000 copies raised serious doubts about my sanity as a translator" (304).

Editing, translation, and the ongoing configuration of the literary work

The task of textual scholarship presupposes the fundamental textual instability of literary works. It also implicitly challenges conventional understandings of the task of translation, and invites us to expand our conception of that task: one cannot think of translation as a transfer of invariant content if one recognizes variation and variability as constituent elements of "originals" themselves. By the same token, translation is a process that challenges textual scholars' traditional focus on the material history of works in a single language, and calls into question some of the most basic premises of scholarly editing as currently understood. That may, in fact, be one reason why textual scholars have been so hesitant to address translation in their work—or at least this was Peter Shillingsburg's supposition over twenty years ago, in a challenge to the field that has yet to be taken up:

> What then IS the work itself and how do texts contain or convey or represent the work itself? [...] When does a work, through change, cease to be a work? What happens to the work if not only the physical document is changed but the linguistic text is substituted? Let us consider a transferal of works of literary art in which no attempt is made to transmit images either visual or aural, transmuting them into something like a total reincarnation—translations. I have often wondered why textual theorists have not explored the relation of translated texts to their originals with the same dedication that they have explored the relation of a transmitted text to its originals. For a while I thought it must have to do with an exaggeration of editorial disdain for the interference of publisher's editors. If a text can be corrupted by a compositor simply by repunctuating a text or by an editor merely regularizing the grammar or level of diction, then surely a translation, in which every word is different, is beneath our contemplation.
>
> I begin to think, however, that the real reason lies in a fear of the results of such an investigation. If we find that the work of art lives in the translation, how can we defend the idea that a novel with changed punctuation or a few altered words, where ninety-nine percent of the text is the same, is a ruined, corrupted wreck? An idea develops from this question: perhaps the work is not made up of any particular words but, finding its expression in words of a variety of texts, the work is a spiritual presence that lives through earthen vessels and transcends the limitations of any particular embodiment of it. This does not mean there cannot be bad translations or bad editions through which it might be

difficult to encounter the "real presence" of the work, but such an idea is consonant with the popular perception that a book like *Moby-Dick* is so great in size and spirit that, as a friend elegantly suggested, "whole hunks of it could be hacked out and it would still be *Moby-Dick*" (1993: 43).

In this passage—whose "earthen vessel" and metaphysical understanding of the work as a "spiritual presence" subject to "total reincarnation" are strikingly reminiscent of Walter Benjamin's "Die Aufgabe des Übersetzers" (translated by Stephen Rendall as "The Translator's Task")—Shillingsburg identifies the distinction between work and text as a fact crucial for editing and translating alike. It is this very distinction between the abstract entity of the work and the physical embodiment of a particular text that allows a work of literature to survive (as we often say) in a translation, in which all the words and punctuation are different from those of the text that has been translated. A work, once it enters the world, is subject to the textual condition, one of variance, difference, proliferation, and iterative growth, including growth in new linguistic contexts. Negotiating the tension between work and text, in and between languages (another embedded spatial metaphor), thus involves the underlying question of the relationship of the one to the many: how different can two texts be before we cease to see them as iterations of the same work? How much of *Moby-Dick* can we sacrifice to the abridger's scalpel, saw, or scimitar? Is *Moby-Dick* still *Moby-Dick* in Urdu?

In drawing a parallel between "transmitted" and "translated" texts, Shillingsburg admits the possibility that a work can be "transfer[red]" in other languages (a choice of terms informed by an assumption of equivalence that I would contest). Yes, *Moby-Dick* in Urdu is still *Moby-Dick*. But Shillingsburg also makes clear that many of his colleagues may not share this view. Their apparent discomfort with translations stems, he suggests, from a sense that the very fact of translation might call into question the conceptual foundations and methodology of scholarly editing as currently practiced. The common use of the term "survival" I noted above reflects an anxiety that a work might, in fact, escape an author's (or editor's) control—that it might *not* survive, and that we as readers may never know the difference. In other words, despite the widespread, if recent, acknowledgment in the field that the role of the editor is not to fix a definitive text that reflects an author's "final intentions" but to facilitate the continual creation of new, interpretive texts for existing works, many textual scholars may not be willing to conceive of a translation as a translingual edition of a given work. And if we face this kind of resistance within a scholarly community that largely accepts the sociological nature of textual production, it may take a concerted and coordinated effort to get general readers to reconceive of translation as an activity that, like editing, shapes the ideas readers form about a particular work by shaping the form of an inherently unstable "original." We will have to counter the lingering belief among readers of all stripes in the primacy of so-called creative literature—an internalization of the image of the poetic genius whose original, self-expressive works can arise only from the ultimate source of a solitary writer.

The widespread, unqualified use of the term "original" implies a hierarchy between writing and translating that has real consequences in the realms of publishing and academia alike. This distinction between a stable "original" and a contingent, "derivative" translation also underlies many of the other metaphors that inform discussions of translation: figures of transfer, transmission, reproduction, preservation, damage, destruction, distortion, and of course the dreaded "loss" all suggest that the object of translation has a fixed identity that precedes the moment of translation. As I have been arguing, however, the fluid textual identity of the work is by no means a special problem that we face when dealing with translations; it is a fundamental aspect of the textual condition. "Developments in textual bibliography," as David Schalkwyk has written, "indicate that it is no longer feasible to posit a single, authoritative text that is a representation of its author's intention" (230). Echoing Benjamin's observation that the process of linguistic change transforms literary works even in the language of their composition, Schalkwyk notes that even were we to have a stable text in our hands, "its iterations across time bring *inevitable* alterations or transformations"; time is always a work's "primary translator" (232). Schalkwyk is writing here about the plays of Shakespeare, a figure so central to the Western literary canon that claims regarding his works' untranslatability approach the status of cliché. Yet Shakespeare's plays are also the best known examples in the English-language literary tradition of works whose contested texts and lack of authorial signature make the project of settling on a single authorial "original" an impossibility. Schalkwyk thus contests the very notion of Shakespeare's untranslatability by pointing out that, since we cannot determine precisely what the "Shakespeare text" *is*, the assumption that there is some invariant to be transferred via a paradigm of equivalence—an assumption on which the notion of untranslatability rests—simply makes no sense.

Textual instability is not an exception to the rule but an underlying condition that translators can choose either to engage or to ignore. So, too, is translation a simple fact of the world that textual scholars can choose either to engage or to ignore. Shillingsburg's insights into the elasticity and resilience of the work—its ability to survive "whole chunks" being removed or one entire text being replaced by another in a different language—find expansion in Schalkwyk's description of what he would like for us to make of Shakespeare's oeuvre: instead of "jealously limiting the Shakespearean text (or 'Shakespeare') to those structures of signs that are either confined to a single language or reduced to the spirit of a particular person […] we could, following recent translation theory, encompass within the name 'Shakespeare' *all* the translations of the texts collected under that name" (232). Schalkwyk is drawing here on Patrick O'Neill's fascinating work on translations of James Joyce, in which O'Neill promotes the idea of a translingual, polyglot *"Joyce"* (author-function rather than author) whose works are to be located not in a single, stable text but in an ever-growing corpus of versions—including those in other languages, over which authority is manifestly shared. Like Shillingsburg, O'Neill acknowledges that individual translations can be, in part or in whole, "seriously inadequate or even unambiguously wrong." Yet even bad translations, he argues, can teach us things about the work in question, and can "contribute in a decidedly interesting fashion" to the "extension" of a literary work that is "still under multilingual construction."[30] Translation, for O'Neill as for Schalkwyk—and certainly for me—is best described not in terms of loss but in terms of perpetual, if uneven, growth and gain.[31]

---

[30] Stefan Helgesson, too, urges us to consider literature in translation as a "serial collective endeavor" (320) that involves not only authors and translators but publishers, editors, critics, and so on, all of whom "contribute to the collective labour of publicly constituting the literary work" (322). See also Isabel Hofmeyr's *The Portable Bunyan: A Transnational History of* The Pilgrim's Progress (2004), which considers this work both in its many rewritings in English and in innumerable translations largely in Africa in the nineteenth and twentieth centuries. Another important recent contribution to this conversation comes in Rebecca Walkowitz's *Born Translated: The Contemporary Novel in an Age of World Literature* (2015). Recognizing the distinction between work and text—or, in her discussion, work and book—she asks, "How many books constitute the work? Does the work consist of an edition in one language? Or does it consist of all editions, including those that may be produced in the future?" (46). Yet while Walkowitz is ostensibly writing about the transformation of literary works into world literature via translation, she, too, treats "originals" as stable objects of translation. Moreover, for a work of scholarship nominally interested in translation, *Born Translated* engages very little with the process or products of translation, or with the practitioners who engage in it. Although she presents translation as a site of "global collaborations" (98), and refers repeatedly to the collaboration between author and translator, her book in fact effaces translation itself—or, rather, folds the work of translation into the figure of the author, by looking primarily at best-selling books originally written in English *as if* they involved translation. The only time a translator is mentioned in her book is in a quote from a text by Ishiguro. For a strong critique of Walkowitz's project, see Venuti (2016).

[31] More recently, in a book on translations of Kafka, O'Neill argues for a concept he calls "macrotextuality": "any literary work potentially or actually involves both an original text and a macrotext that is made up of that text *and* all its translations." The related concept of "transtextuality" recognizes that "the original text is in principle always *extended* by its individual and cumulative translations" (2014: 9). O'Neill's attempt to compile a comprehensive description of this "worldwide Kafka *system*" (3) becomes a kind of genetic criticism in reverse, which examines the transformations wrought by a

This book furthers the discussion of translation as a continual recon-figuration of a work by recognizing, not eliding, the instability of so-called originals. The stress I place on the overlap between translation and textual scholarship will, I hope, allow readers to develop greater nuance in the ways they talk about both the objects and the products of translation. *Literary Translation and the Making of Originals* owes a great debt to the many other scholars of translation who have challenged paradigms of transfer and equivalence alike, and who have championed the notion that translation is an essentially interpretative endeavor. But it comes at the central issue from a different angle: by questioning the fixity of the "original" itself. Like any new edition of a work in its language of composition, each published translation is also a translingual edition, a further iteration of the work. A translator certainly can, and often does, choose to focus her interpretation on a single text—yet that text is rarely the only one the translator *could* have chosen. Whether or not these decisions are consciously made, and whether or not the translator is the one to make them, the process of bringing trans-lated texts the world almost always entails negotiating between multiple versions of a work to be translated; determining what elements of a text or texts (lexical, visual, material, paratextual, and so on) will be considered; and shaping a new version and print or digital edition of the work in its new linguistic context. In representing more adequately what translation does, and in raising awareness even among translators of the implications of textual instability for their task, this book may encourage us to translate differently—to expand our notion of what translation can do, and to imagine modes of translating that break the mold in which the reigning (if often disguised) discourse of originality and derivation seems to have trapped us.

It is in this spirit that I offer a series of case studies in the chapters that follow. Chapter 1, "'A message from the antediluvian age': The Modern Construction of the Ancient *Epic of Gilgamesh*," considers the ways in which the material instability of the Gilgamesh tale affects and is affected by the task of translation. For many ancient works, standard texts were established long ago, and are now largely taken for granted even by specialists. This may, in fact, be a good working definition of a "standard text:" one that is taken for granted even by specialists. However, the work we now know as *The Epic of*

---

body of translingual renderings of an "original text." While I find O'Neill's work exciting, I also am wary of his continued reliance on the term "original text," compounded by phrases such as "Kafka's original text" or "Kafka's German"—a particularly fraught statement with regard to this writer, most of whose works were famously unfinished at the time of his death. O'Neill's methodology of comparing lines from Kafka's novels to multiple translations across languages yields interesting results, but also elides the editorial construction of those works in German.

Gilgamesh is not one of those works. After a history of textual transmission that spanned several languages and at least a millennium and a half, in which stories of an ancient king named Gilgamesh (or, in the earliest versions, Bilgamesh) were told and retold, toward the end of the first millennium B.C.E. the languages and scripts in which they circulated passed into disuse, and the stories, too, faded from cultural consciousness. Only in the mid-nineteenth century, 2,000 years later, did stories of this king resurface, thanks to a number of pioneering Assyriologists whose project of recovery and decipherment was wrapped up in Orientalist thinking and politics of the time. Modern editions tend to present texts based on a twelve-tablet redaction dating to sometime between 1300 and 1000 B.C.E. In addition to the vast historical range of material witnesses to this "standard" Akkadian version, numerous fragments have been discovered elsewhere in the Middle East, composed in other languages or other historical and geographical versions of the "same" language. Likewise, even the "standard" text can't be traced to any *particular* twelve tables, but can only be guessed at on the basis of countless fragments. This chapter explores how modern editions negotiate the question of how to represent a work comprised by such a wide range of linguistic and textual manifestations. Even more crucially, however, I question the mechanisms by which we have come to "know" not only what the text of this epic is, but what the symbols that comprise its language mean. I propose that the very process of deciphering a lost, ancient language in an unknown script involves assigning phonetic and semantic equivalents on the level of the symbol and the word; I explore the role bilingual dictionaries play in structuring the terms of equivalence between ancient and modern languages and their surrounding cultures.

Chapter 2, "'Monuments of the Word': Translation and the Textualization of Modern Greek Folk Songs," addresses the challenges that works of orature, characterized by variation and ephemerality, pose to editors and translators alike. The chapter focuses on the editorial construction through translation of a corpus of modern Greek folk songs. It begins with Claude Fauriel's 1824 bilingual *Chants populaires de la Grèce modern* (*Folk songs of modern Greece*), produced by a French scholar who never traveled to the lands that would later become Greece, and who compiled his material largely through conversation and correspondence with literate Greeks living in Europe, themselves at a distance from the populations whose cultural production the collection supposedly represented. The very year after Fauriel's collection appeared, it was translated into English by Charles Sheridan, a vociferous supporter of the cause of Greek independence. Both of these volumes proved instrumental in garnering European support for the Greek revolution against the Ottoman Empire; they also laid the ideological and practical foundation for a canon of modern Greek literature by linking a supposedly oral "past" with a literate present and providing a set of texts for literate Greeks to reproduce, comment upon, and use as inspiration for written works of their own. In examining how later Greek editions—which framed the songs in terms of political and cultural debates then taking place among Greek intellectuals—made use of the texts and even paratexts of these foreign editions, this chapter explores the role translation has played in shaping some of the foundational texts of a supposedly national literature.

If these first two chapters treat the editorial consolidation of texts for works with no recognizable author, whose numerous versions straddle languages and cover vast swathes of both geography and time, Chapter 3, "On Manuscripts, Type-Translation, and Translation (Im?)proper: Emily Dickinson and the Translation of Scriptural Form," turns to a poet whose work is often seen as bound up with her biography—or at least with the myth of the poet as a New England recluse, for whom poetry was not a public but a private affair. This chapter traces the posthumous editorial history of Dickinson's poetry and considers the consequences for translation of the ongoing scholarly debate over how to best represent Dickinson's idiosyncratic textual and scriptural forms in print, a debate prompted in large part by the 1981 publication of a two-volume facsimile edition of her "manuscript books." Discourse around these issues is steeped in the trope of translation: many scholars contend that to read Dickinson in a standard print edition (or, now, digital transcription) is to read her in translation—and, moreover, in a translation that fails to account for the potential significance of such elements as her handwriting, her unorthodox lineation and punctuation, and the pervasive presence of variants. This rhetorical use of the term "translation," I argue, reifies Dickinson's manuscripts in such a way as to disallow, on a conceptual level, translations of the poems in other languages. While I contest this implicit rejection of the possibility of interlingual translation, I also draw on the interest in the visual and material details of Dickinson's manuscripts to encourage a more capacious approach to translating those important aspects of literary works. The last section of the chapter turns to the work of poet and artist Jen Bervin, whose *Dickinson Composites* offers a model, or at least an inspiration, for a visually oriented translation we have yet to see.

Like Dickinson, Alexandrian Greek poet C. P. Cavafy chose not to circulate his work in conventionally printed editions during his lifetime; unlike Dickinson, however, he shared his writings with a remarkable number of readers, in unique collections of individually printed poems which he compiled by hand and distributed through a network of friends and acquaintances. My fourth chapter, "The Unfinished Afterlives of C. P. Cavafy," explores the effect Cavafy's mode of selective self-publication had on the posthumous circulation of his work in Greek and in translation. I focus on a group of poems Cavafy never had printed, thirty-four poems found in varying states of completion in the poet's archive after his death. While my chapter on Dickinson touches only briefly on the complications that arise when attempting to translate textual variants, Chapter 4 takes the translation of variants as its central concern. Does an edition of an unfinished poem in its language of composition need to account for all textual variants present in the manuscripts? If so, should a translation be held to the same standard? How can one possibly represent variants in translation without reinforcing a mistaken understanding of translation as the production of word-level equivalence? This chapter approaches these questions by looking closely at three existing translations of a single "unfinished" poem, and how their translators approach the question of textual instability; it models a methodology of translation comparison that respects the interpretations of individual translators and questions the divide between "finished" and "unfinished" works, particularly in the case of writers who choose not to make their work commercially available.

The final chapter, "'The Bone-Yard, Babel Recombined': Jack Spicer and the Poetics of Citational Correspondence," takes a slight turn. Other chapters probe the ways translators negotiate, intervene in, and contribute to the unstable histories of literary works. Chapter 5 considers the boundary between writing and translation from a different angle, by treating both as ultimately citational practices. Rather than claiming originality for translations, I present "original writings" as themselves tissues of citation, explicit and implicit alike. At the same time, I make a case for more experimental modes of translation that move beyond notions of equivalence and transfer. This chapter focuses primarily on Jack Spicer's 1957 *After Lorca*, a book that combines translations of Federico García Lorca's poetry, pseudotranslations of nonexistent "originals" attributed to Lorca, and letters to the deceased Spanish poet that many scholars take to be Spicer's most cogent statements on poetics. Taking seriously Spicer's assertion that his "own" poems were written by "dictation"—a statement that abandons all claims to originality or authenticity not just for his translations but for his supposedly original writing as well—this chapter promotes translation as a form of creative work that, like other modes of writing, exists in dialogue (or in what Spicer calls "correspondence") not just with a single source but with an infinite number of sources, some traceable and others not. Spicer's work thus poses a challenge less to the assumed existence of a stable original than to the notion of stable authorial originality—a notion that underwrites many of the assumptions that *Literary Translation and the Making of Originals* seeks to disrupt.

I end the book with a brief coda, "Toward a Pedagogy of Iterability," which argues for the importance of incorporating discussions of textual instability and translation into as many pedagogical contexts as possible. In his "Call to Action" at the end of *The Translator's Invisibility*, Venuti insists that "no translation should ever be taught as a transparent representation" of a "source-language text" (1995: 312). Yet as my book demonstrates, no "source-language text" is ever a transparent representation of a literary work, either. I thus follow André Lefevere in calling for pedagogical approaches that account for translation's status not only as an interpretive act, but as one form of rewriting among others.[32] The level of engagement with these issues can range from gestures as small as a recognition of editors and translators on syllabi and in audiovisual materials in the classroom, to entire courses devoted to modes of textual iteration. Such a focus—which I invite not only in literature classes but across the humanities and social sciences—can attune students to the mediated nature of the many texts they encounter, on a daily basis, both inside and outside the academic sphere. In raising the visibility of these forms of textual mediation, we may also begin to chip away at the unfortunate, arbitrary, and ultimately reversible disciplinary divides and divisions of labor that keep translators, scholars of translation, textual scholars, and literary critics apart.[33]

I end with this coda on pedagogy not only because of my commitment to promoting translation as a legitimate scholarly activity, but also because I believe that in order to gain acknowledgment for the practice of translation within the academic sphere we must raise both awareness of and respect for the products of translation at all levels, in disciplines across the university. Translators who are also academics are often expected to check their translator's hat each morning at the university gates—or, in the best case scenario, to wait until we have tenure to spend time on such a risky intellectual endeavor. We are advised to downplay our translation work in job materials and tenure files, since our temporal investment in translation is seen as taking away from our "real" work as scholars. Even most scholars of translation rarely draw explicitly on their translation work in writing about translation, though the knowledge they gain through their practice is, understandably, often at the core of their thinking on

---

[32] See the introduction to Lefevere (1992).

[33] This is, of course, a false distinction: by virtue of the extensive knowledge of the language, culture, and history of a place or places that translation entails, nonacademic translators can also be true independent scholars both of the sphere they translate from or within, and of translation itself.

this subject. To my mind, the academy's resistance to acknowledging the hard-earned knowledge, intellectual rigor, and compositional flexibility required to translate almost any text, from an internet meme to a scholarly article to a best-selling novel, does a vast disservice not only to translator-academics, but also to our fields. In promoting only a few acceptable forms of scholarly writing at the expense of others, including translations, we are depriving generations of scholars of all ranks—including our students, those most junior scholars among us—of the many philosophical, historical, art historical, literary, anthropological, and other texts that those of us with the necessary linguistic training and disciplinary knowledge could have been translating all along.

This introductory chapter and my closing coda argue explicitly for the importance of scholarship that draws on a committed practice of translation; the book as a whole seeks to embody and present some of the forms of knowledge that my practice as a translator has made possible. To my mind, this book could only have been written by someone for whom translation is an intellectual habit, a daily mode of thought. It is a risky book, for many reasons—including my choice to delve into time periods, works, and literary traditions with which I was, until undertaking this project, only glancingly familiar. I am sure that, despite my obsessive research, a multitude of errors of various sorts remain. But if translating has taught me anything, it is that generous, engaged, critical readers will often be found to correct, complicate, or build on whatever argument or interpretation one ventures to share. I hope this book will be so lucky.

1

"A message from the antediluvian age": The Modern Construction of the Ancient *Epic of Gilgamesh*[1]

Ever do we build our households,
ever do we make our nests,
ever do brothers divide their inheritance,
ever do feuds arise in the land.

Ever the river has risen and brought us the flood,
the mayfly floating on the water.
On the face of the sun its countenance gazes,
then all of a sudden nothing is there!
—*The Epic of Gilgamesh* (tr. Andrew George)

At some time we build a household,
at some time we start a family,
at some time the brothers divide,
at some time feuds arise in the land.

At some time the river rose (and) brought the flood,
the mayfly floating on the river.
Its countenance was gazing on the face of the sun,
then all of a sudden nothing was there!
—*Babylonian Gilgamesh Epic* (tr. Andrew George)

For over 2,000 years, beginning in the late third millennium B.C.E., oral and written stories of a legendary king of Uruk circulated in several languages in the region between the Tigris and Euphrates rivers. The wide distribution of these tales was facilitated by the spread of a series of empires throughout the region that brought canons of scribal texts to the far ends of their dominions.

---

[1]   An earlier version of this chapter appeared in *Comparative Literature* in Fall 2016.

Toward the end of the first millennium B.C.E., as these empires gave way to others with different languages of administration, the writing system in which these stories had been consolidated and copied out by generations of scribes was replaced by new, more efficient scripts. Cuneiform was forgotten, and the stories with it. Only after another two millennia of dormancy were tales of this king brought to light by explorers and early archaeologists who unearthed countless fragments of inscribed clay tablets, and by pioneers of the field of Assyriology who set out to decipher these unfamiliar scripts and languages.

What we now know as the epic of Gilgamesh has been the object of a century and a half of decipherment, scholarly reconstruction, and translation, involving fragments found all over the Near East that date to many historical eras. These bits of text were inscribed in several historical and geographical varieties of the Akkadian language, including Assyrian and Babylonian, as well as in Hittite and in the Sumerian of the oldest surviving tales, whose hero was named Bilgamesh. Most current-day readers encounter *Gilgamesh* in editions based on the so-called Standard Babylonian version, which circulated throughout the Middle and Neo-Assyrian Empires, traveling widely over space and time. This version included a prologue inviting readers to open "the tablet-box of cedar," lift out the tablets, and read out "all the misfortunes, all that Gilgamesh went through" (quoted here from the more scholarly of Andrew George's two published translations of the reconstructed epic, 2003b: 2). Gilgamesh, a formerly unruly and unjust leader, has been broken by the loss of his friend Enkidu and tamed by his own subsequent soul-searching wanderings in distant lands. He has returned to Uruk with a "message from the antediluvian age" (539), a lesson learned both from Uta-napishti, survivor of a great flood, but also from his own encounters with the deep: his confrontation of the sheer fact of human mortality and his consequent attainment of "the totality of knowledge of *all*" (in Maureen Gallery Kovacs's translation: 3). Gilgamesh returns, rebuilds the "ramparted walls of Uruk," and "Engrave[s] all his hardships on a monument of stone" (in Benjamin Foster's translation: 3), a story that then finds its way onto the tablets in the box of cedar (or copper, depending on the translation), where it waits to tell its cautionary tale for the benefit of future generations.

The epic's message, as it has come down to us, is thus in part about the importance of societal or cultural continuity in the face of human mortality, a continuity to which the tale seeks to contribute. Yet the history of the epic's loss and rediscovery has additional messages to impart: about the *dis*continuity of traditions, and about the transience not just of people but of ancient texts and their meanings, which can only be "revived" by shaping an original in the image of a translation, rather than the other way around. Just as Gilgamesh must travel far afield and experience deep loss in order to return a better ruler, the tale of the epic's rediscovery also involves a series of journeys, conquests, departures, and domesticating "returns," as European Orientalists traveled to the Near East and traced a reverse journey carrying extracted archaeological materials "back" (a word they used, and which I repeat in full irony) to private collections, museums, and other institutions in the West. And just as the initial dissemination of texts about Gilgamesh was made possible by the spread of a series of empires through the ancient Near East, so too was its rediscovery wrapped up in expansionist European politics. Even the deciphering of Akkadian was discussed by scholars of the day in profoundly nationalist terms. Yet this new rhetorical realm could ultimately picture its discoveries only in the light of inherited discursive regimes, resulting in what David Damrosch calls the "profoundly assimilative" (2003: 57) ways of reading the epic that abounded in the nineteenth century, as *Gilgamesh* reemerged into a society obsessed with origins and progress, travel, science, and encounters with the unknown, and whose far-flung intellectual adventures were so often undertaken in the hope of discovering that society's *own* true past. These assimilative readings are, of course, the basis for our own twentieth- and twenty-first-century understandings of what *Gilgamesh* is and means.

This chapter explores these tropes of origins and reproductions, travel and domestication, in order to probe the pervasive paradigms of equivalence that have structured modern readers' encounters with this ancient work and with the languages in which it was written. In it, I challenge the notion that a stable original exists upon which translations might be based. Setting aside the many other ancient versions of the tale, our texts for even the twelve-tablet Standard Babylonian version are derived not from any *particular* set of tablets; they are, on the contrary, composite texts formed by piecing together multiple textual witnesses.[2] And unlike the Homeric epics, for which texts that began to assume relatively fixed form in the tenth century C.E. are now often taken for granted as objects of study even by specialists,[3] the textual makeup of even this one version of *Gilgamesh* continues to shift,

---

[2] For an excellent account of this process, intended for a popular audience, see George's "Appendix: From Tablet to Translation" in his Penguin Classics edition of the epic (2003a: 209–21).

[3] Recent scholarship has begun to question the single-text approach to reading the Homeric epics. The Homer Multitext Project, for instance, declares "the aim of determining an original [...] self-defeating," since attempts to do so "end up sacrificing accuracy in reporting the status of variations." This electronic, web-based edition "offers the tools for reconstructing a variety of texts as they existed in a variety of times and places" (www.homermultitext.org/about.html (last accessed 7 May 2017)).

as excavations turn up new fragments and as we revise our understanding of its language and surrounding culture. Yet I do not mean to set *Gilgamesh* aside as an exception to the rule of how we encounter ancient works, or any works for that matter. On the contrary, I use it as a limit case that invites us to question our conventional reliance on other supposedly fixed texts as well. It may be easier for us to get on with the business of interpreting works attributed to Sappho or Homer if we can all agree on what the texts (however fragmentary) for their works are—but this is a matter of convenience, not truth. Claims to textual stability are either disingenuous or naïve, for ancient and modern works alike.

But a more crucial contribution of this chapter lies elsewhere: in its unpacking of the ways in which the task of re-membering the epic, of assembling its fragments, has gone hand-in-hand with an assimilative "remembering" of these forgotten languages. I show the process of deciphering cuneiform and codifying the meaning of Akkadian words to be steeped in the rhetoric and practice of a certain *kind* of translation, by which phonetic and semantic equivalents are assigned to cuneiform symbols such that presumed equivalence on other levels can follow. This, too, is a system for establishing conventions rather than of establishing truths. I am particularly interested in the role bilingual dictionaries play in structuring a paradigm of seeming equivalence between this ancient language and modern ones. I am also interested in the tension between a post-poststructuralist suspicion of the very idea of stable textual meaning and the fact that this ancient literature—if it is literature, and even if it isn't—can be experienced only in translations for which these dictionaries are crucially enabling. For these cuneiform texts, and for ancient Mesopotamian languages more generally, lexical equivalence is, I suggest, less discovered than assigned. And while the results continue to be contested and debated—is the tablet box copper or cedar?—the process of decipherment nonetheless entails building at least a partial, functional consensus that ventriloquizes ancient texts in terms of likeness to (and difference from) an ever-changing contemporary context.

This argument has consequences far broader than the case study I have chosen; it bears, too, on certain disciplinary modes of language pedagogy, and on the policing of translations via word-level comparison with dictionary definitions, which obscure the fact that such definitions arise from a process of building consensus rather than of discovering truth. I turn to *Gilgamesh* because, as a language lost in antiquity and rediscovered in the modern era, Akkadian offers a prime site for an investigation of this kind. In the following pages, I trace the fraught processes of the decipherment of this language and the textual "reconstruction" and reception of this work in four sections. I begin with an overview of early Assyriologists' modes of assimilating ancient Near Eastern texts to the current concerns of their day, which I follow and substantiate with a close look at a single instance of translation comparison that, while intended to demonstrate the success of decipherment, actually reveals some of the fault lines in this project. I then move to the great Akkadian dictionary projects of the twentieth century, which, I argue, exhibit a tension between a practical need to assign concrete, usable definitions to words and a desire to elaborate forms of encyclopedic knowledge that resist attempts to assign word-level equivalents. Lastly, I touch briefly on some contemporary editors' and translators' ways of dealing with the textual uncertainty of the *Gilgamesh* materials. What binds these sections together is the fluctuating pull and push of what we might call domesticating and foreignizing impulses, both in translation and in the broader discursive approach to a culture so distant in place and time.[4] Throughout, I argue that the constitution both of "original" texts and of the translingual schema that enable translation are highly contested processes whose results can only be taken for granted insofar as the contestation itself is willfully or otherwise forgotten.

Foreignizing domestications: The assimilative mode of Orientalist thought

The nineteenth century was, as Edward Said has shown, the grand century of Orientalism, a set of discursive practices that rationalized the political domination of the inhabitants of the Near East by portraying them as exoticized, infantilized others. In Said's formulation, the colonial enterprise cannot properly be understood as a mere show of imperial force; rather, this violent annexation was bolstered and even facilitated by forms of knowledge about the Orient created by and for individuals and institutions in the West.

---

[4] This use of "domesticating" and "foreignizing" draws, of course, on Lawrence Venuti's elaboration of those terms, particularly in chapter 1 of *The Translator's Invisibility*; see his definition of "domesticating practice" as "an ethnocentric reduction of the foreign text to receiving cultural values, bringing the author back home," and of "foreignizing practice" as "an ethnodeviant pressure on those values to register the linguistic and cultural differences of the foreign text, sending the reader abroad" (1995: 20). I use these terms to refer not only to the textual practices of translation, but to a confluence of broader social, cultural, and political practices that include, for instance, the physical removal of archaeological materials from the sites where they were found, and the incorporation of those materials into frameworks that are both domesticating and foreignizing at once, bringing the objects back home while also coding those objects as profoundly other.

Materials from the Near East were acquired wholesale by Western travelers and disseminated back at home "as a form of specialized knowledge [...] reconverted, restructured from the bundle of fragments brought back piecemeal by explorers, expeditions, commissions, armies, and merchants into lexico-graphical, bibliographical, departmentalized, and *textualized* Orientalist sense." This textualization, Said writes, involved the creation of "dictionaries, grammars, commentaries, editions, translations, all of which together formed a simulacrum of the Orient and reproduced it materially in the West, for the West" (Said 1994: 165–6).

It is difficult to imagine a more apt description of the process of deciphering the languages of ancient Mesopotamia: fragments of inscribed tablets and paper pressings of monumental inscriptions were sent to institutions and private collections in Britain and Europe, where they were pieced together, copied, printed, made legible, discussed in lectures and essays, unpacked in grammars and dictionaries. Alongside this textualization of the Orient came its literal objectification. For instance, the wild success of Austen Henry Layard's *Nineveh and its Remains* (1849)—a memoir of the excavations that turned up, among other things, the first known textual fragments of the Gilgamesh story—fueled the construction of the Assyrian wing of the British Museum, which was built in part to house the massive statues of winged bulls and lions that Layard shipped to England from the field.[5] This fetishization of unique oriental "originals" was, meanwhile, accompanied by their rampant reproduction for popular consumption, ranging from the drawings in Layard's memoir, to jewelry and knick-knacks modeled on Assyrian motifs, to Frederick Charles Cooper's *Diorama of Nineveh*, an archaeological simulation that appeared in London's Gothic Hall in 1851.[6] The intellectual conquest of the Near East, enabled by and complicit in its political conquest, thus also gave rise to a series of reproductions that both domesticated and exoticized these textual and material finds.

Not coincidentally, this period of "Assyromania" was also one of intense debate over the age of the world and the origins of human history, a debate that involved the 1859 publication of Charles Darwin's *On the Origin of Species*. "Had the Victorians internalized ideas about deep time (the 4.55

---

[5] Layard himself is a prime example of how the discursive construction of the Middle East as a place containing secrets about the history of Western civilization was imbricated in the project of colonial conquest: not just an adventurer in search of the ruins of Biblical cities, Layard was also a spy during a time of expanding British political ambitions in the region. For an account of Layard's political activities in the region, see Malley (2012). See Damrosch (2003: 39–77; and 2007) for more on Smith's role in the discovery of the epic, and the prejudice both he and Hormuzd Rassam faced.

[6] See Malley (2012) and Bohrer (2003) for discussions of these popular reproductions of Assyrian materials.

billion years of history in which we now believe)," literary scholar Vybarr Cregan-Reid has suggested, "then the rediscovery of the *Epic of Gilgamesh* would have been of interest principally to antiquarian specialists rather than the newspaper- and periodical-reading masses" (4). As it stood, George Smith's discovery in 1872 of a tablet describing a flood, a boat, and a series of birds set loose in search of dry land fueled a fascination with the idea that Biblical stories, including the account of the creation of mankind, might be verified by earlier written sources. Smith was an engraver who often walked to the British Museum during his lunch hour to study the mass of cuneiform tablets that had been shipped to the museum two decades earlier from Layard and Hormuzd Rassam's excavations of Nineveh. Smith wasn't just casually sifting through these materials, he was actively seeking fragments that might include names or episodes known from the Old Testament. When he found a fragment from what we now know as the eleventh tablet of *Gilgamesh*, he quickly assimilated this story of a flood to the story of *the* Flood. A few months later, he presented his translation before the Society of Biblical Archaeology in London in ceremoniously Biblical terms as "The Chaldean Account of the Deluge." Soon afterward, the *Daily Telegraph* agreed to sponsor a trip into the field in search of further materials, hoping to be given first crack at a potentially sensational story. From across an ocean, the *New York Times* joined in the chorus of voices supporting the conjecture that further investigations might confirm other Biblical stories: "[Smith] can almost put his hand on the place where Noah's story is told in full, with that of the Creation, the building of Babel, and the rise of diverse tongues—nay, all the great legends of the Bible may find here their fountain-text; and he may even hit upon the real *editio prima*, the actual clay or stone from which all of these were copied."[7]

This desire for an Ur-text behind these Babylonian texts—and, by extension, behind the stories in Genesis—would prove chimerical. In fact, the very idea that an *editio prima* could exist for these materials reveals a misunderstanding of the modes of textual production and reproduction in ancient Mesopotamia. Smith's journey did, however, turn up further fragments of numerous Babylonian texts, including significant portions of the Gilgamesh story, which he continued to read through a Biblical lens.[8] While Smith's truly pioneering work should not be underestimated, his persistent equation of Gilgamesh with Nimrod offers a clear instance of confirmation bias: "I have always felt," Smith wrote in his 1876 *The Chaldean Account of Genesis*,

---

[7]   Quoted in Cregan-Reid: 53.
[8]   See Damrosch (2003: 57), as well as Smith (1876), whom I quote in the following sentences.

"that Nimrod, whose name figures so prominently in Eastern tradition, and whose reign is clearly stated in Genesis, ought to be found somewhere in the cuneiform text" (180). And so Smith found him, confidently asserting that "the translations and notes given in this book will lead to the general admission of the identity of the hero I call Izdubar"—Smith's provisional transliteration for the name we now read as Gilgamesh—"with the traditional Nimrod," with whom he "agreed *exactly* in character." "When this result is established," Smith continued, "I shall myself abandon the provisional name Izdubar, which cannot possibly be correct" (182–3).

The theory that these materials told the story of Nimrod survived at least as late as Paul Haupt's 1889 *Das Babylonische Nimrodepos*, the first book to present cuneiform texts for as much of the Gilgamesh epic as was known at that time. And the Biblical was not the only mode of assimilative reading to which these materials were subjected: ancient Greece frequently made an appearance, arguably even in the characterization of this brief text as an epic.[9] While contemporary inhabitants of the region were foreignized as cultural others, its ancient cultural products were thus assimilated as evidence of a continuity of culture that led not to the modern Near East, but to modern Europe, rhetorically positioned as the rightful inheritor of that tradition. Yet if the reception of Smith's work demonstrates how nineteenth-century theological, philological, and scientific debates shaped the terms according to which his findings could be made legible even to Smith himself, his trouble transliterating the name of the hero gives some indication of how difficult it was to assign phonetic values, much less meanings, to cuneiform signs. It was not until 1889, over two decades after Smith's early death of dysentery in the field, that Thomas Pinches triumphantly announced in a short notice titled "Exit Gistubar!" in the *Babylonian & Oriental Record* that he had finally hit upon "the long-wished for reading of the name of the well-known hero, and it is neither Gistubar, nor Gisdubar, nor Gisdubarra, nor Izdubar, nor finally, Namrasit, but *GILGAMEŞ*" (264).

Today, this "long-wished for reading" is one we take for granted, while the history of how scholars arrived at it is largely forgotten. The first sustained attempts to make sense of cuneiform had begun only in the 1840s, when Sir Henry Creswick Rawlinson, an officer in the British East India Company, became fascinated with the ancient ruins that dotted the landscape of the Near East, including a massive trilingual inscription carved on a sheer rock face on Mount Behistun, in current-day Iran. Rawlinson risked life and limb

---

[9] In the discussion following Smith's 1872 lecture, for instance, Prime Minister William Gladstone "praised the new discoveries in Mesopotamia for giving 'a solidity to much of the old Greek traditions which they never before possessed,'" referring explicitly to Homer (Damrosch 2003: 53).

(first his own and then those of local boys) to climb the rock, transcribe most of the signs, and produce paper pressings of the rest.[10] Rawlinson was not the first to concern himself with this inscription: earlier in the century, German epigrapher Georg Friedrich Grotefend guessed that the Behistun inscription might refer to the genealogy of Hystaspes, Darius, and Xerxes. Grotefend located places in the text where he thought those names might appear and proposed sound values for a number of symbols in the Old Persian inscription on the basis of those hypotheses. This was not an uncommon method for making an initial attempt at decipherment: since proper nouns are usually transliterated rather than translated, scholars often began by looking for patterns in unknown scripts that might correlate with the repetition of names known from texts in other languages. In the case of the Rosetta Stone, for instance, the ancient Greek text on the stone was treated as lexically equivalent to the hieroglyphic text it accompanied, and proper nouns served as initial anchors of assumed equivalence.[11] In a lecture before the Royal Asiatic Society in London in 1850, Rawlinson declared the Behistun monument "as important for the decipherment of cuneiform as the Rosetta Stone has been for the hieroglyphs."[12] Like the three inscriptions on the Rosetta Stone, the texts on the Behistun monument were presumed to be word-for-word translations that said the same thing thrice. And while all three of the languages on the Behistun inscription—now identified as Old Persian, Elamite, and Babylonian—were unknown, a similar method was employed. Even in the absence of a parallel Greek text, scholars' encounters with the Behistun inscription were framed by a knowledge of the ancient history of the region supplied by *other* ancient texts, many in Greek. The initial stages of deciphering cuneiform thus involved structuring a system of phonetic equivalence between an unknown script and one that, while known, was entirely absent from those inscriptions. Greek was, in a way, a ghostly, inferred presence that gave scholars a foothold in the topography of these unfamiliar scripts.

Transliterations, meanwhile, were usually offered in Hebrew or Roman characters. Hebrew was ideologically useful, given the goal of assimilating these texts to Biblical stories. It was also a practical choice, since Akkadian

[10] For discussions of Rawlinson's role in the early deciphering of cuneiform, see Adkins (2003), Larsen (1994), and Budge (1925), though Budge's economic accounts must be taken with a fairly large grain of salt.

[11] For an excellent discussion of the ways in which the process of deciphering the Rosetta Stone involved the structuring of equivalence between the three, "level[ing] out the phenomenological distinctions of languages, bracketing the critical differences between them," see chapter 2 of Michael Allan's *In the Shadow of World Literature: Sites of Reading in Colonial Egypt* (2016: 41).

[12] Quoted in Larsen: 218.

was found to be an early Semitic language, and cuneiform words could thus be not only transliterated but also translated by way of analogy to other Semitic languages, including Hebrew and Arabic. Pronunciation and meaning were at first tackled independently, under the assumption that an understanding of the former must precede the latter. In 1848 Rawlinson wrote to a friend, "I can *read* pretty well to my satisfaction all the Inscriptions Median as well as Babylonian given by Westergard—but this does not enable me by any means to *understand* a Babylonian Inscription, of which I have not a translation. The language as I have often told you has to be reconstructed 'ab origine.'"[13] Rawlinson's distinction between reading and understanding— which we might gloss as one between transliteration and translation—is remarkable, given what scholars now take to be the case for the family of dialects collectively known as Akkadian: they use a syllabary rather than an alphabet, and also include ideographic holdovers from Sumerian, an older, non-Semitic language that continued to be used in the scribal tradition long after it ceased to be commonly spoken. Particular signs can represent either ideographs or syllables, and can have multiple pronunciations and meanings. A scholar might hypothesize one transliteration for a set of symbols, find that the ensuing translation did not suit the particular context, and modify the transliteration to accommodate a better semantic match. Grammar and syntax, too, had to be unraveled—or, as Rawlinson wrote, reconstructed "ab origine," not *from the origin* but *anew*, since it is impossible to know whether the system put forward corresponded to a preexisting system of language or was simply a convincing simulacrum for which the measure of success was what worked. Indeed, significant uncertainty regarding both transliterations and translations is unavoidable: in comparing Grotefend's initial trans- literation of the Behistun inscription to the "correct" one, contemporary scholar Cyrus Gordon qualifies the latter as "correct in the sense that it is now accepted" (51). We could in fact see the decipherment of cuneiform as a movement toward increasing agreement regarding the plausibility of certain proposals. The resulting consensus subsequently swallowed up the history of its formation—a history as fraught with disagreement as it was marked by the successes of those theories that became generally accepted.

In his 1877 *Lectures Upon the Assyrian Language*, A. H. Sayce noted the potentially democratizing nature of all readers' ignorance before these signs: "The teacher is but a little in advance of the pupil [...] and even in the act of teaching, is making fresh discoveries, and rectifying old conclusions. There is no authoritative standard to be referred to, no tradition to be appealed to, no dictionary to be consulted" (2). Of course we quickly run up against the

---

[13] Quoted in Larsen: 119.

limits of this democratization, since even the pupil must come from a place of quite impressive prior training: "all must be worked out by the laborious comparison of texts, by extensive knowledge of cognate languages, by ready combination and hypothesis, and by the trained judgment of scientific research" (2–3). Sayce also codes the democratic potential of this enterprise in distinctly nationalist terms. He sees his lectures as inaugurating a new "era in national education" that opens "a fresh realm of conquest [...] before the mind" (3), in much the same way as the lands where these tablets were unearthed had been forcibly taken by British military conquest. This likening of intellectual to political conquest makes clear how the competitive yet ultimately collaborative assigning of phonetic and lexical equivalents to cuneiform signs comprises precisely the sort of cumulative textualizing enterprise Said identified as a hallmark of Orientalism. Particularly fitting is Said's description of the growth of knowledge as "a process of selective accumulation, displacement, deletion, rearrangement, or insistence within what has been called a research consensus" (176)—in this case, a consensus that would, with astonishing rapidity, open up the contents of cuneiform and its languages, like the tablet-box in the prologue to *Gilgamesh*, to reveal long-lost messages from a nearly antediluvian age.

And yet the messages contained in that box may be less revealed than inscribed by the very process of decipherment itself, which fashioned simulacra for this ancient text, script, language, and culture partly out of materials already at hand: from the selection of excavation sites on the basis of Biblical geography, to the assumption that multilingual inscriptions repeat stories already known from other ancient works, to the translation of words and phrases on the basis of presumed likeness to words in other languages both ancient and modern, this project was guided by a search for confirmation of presumed knowledge and dearly held beliefs. We might, I suggest, see decipherment as a multifaceted project of domestication that explained an unfamiliar script and language in unavoidably assimilative terms, making sense of the unknown through the lens of the already known.

"The grand desideratum of language"

During the 1840s and 1850s, philologists and epigraphers began to compile pronunciation keys and vocabularies, slowly establishing many of the things we now believe to be the case about cuneiform. The process was by no means a smooth one, and a teleological account that focuses only on the steps that bring us to our current understanding risks obscuring moments of discontinuity and discord that challenge the consensus-building enterprise of decipherment. Writing in 1847 to George Renouard of the Royal Asiatic Society, Rawlinson expressed his disbelief about Edward Hincks's claim to have made headway on the translation (as opposed to the transliteration) of cuneiform texts. The day was still far distant, Rawlinson wrote, "in which we shall be able to read and understand independent Babylonian and Assyrian inscriptions, for we want the grand desideratum of language."[14] A year later, he wrote again of his "great distrust" of "announcements of a sudden and complete solution," noting with obvious annoyance that "[Eugène] Burnouf has declared he can read and *understand* the Khorsabad Inscriptions, and [...] is now preparing a paper on the subject. I really however cannot believe this, for where the deuce did he get his language from."[15]

It is therefore worth examining in some detail an event many have taken as initial proof of the accuracy of the system of decipherment developed thus far. A mere decade after Rawlinson scoffed at the idea of a "sudden and complete solution," pioneering photographer and dabbler in cuneiform William Henry Fox Talbot tried his hand at translating an inscription describing the conquests of Tiglath-Pileser I, an Assyrian king of the eleventh century B.C.E. (who, like many figures who caught the attention of early Assyriologists, earns several mentions in the Old Testament). At Talbot's urging, the Royal Asiatic Society invited three leading figures in the field, Rawlinson, Hincks, and the Frenchman Jules Oppert, to produce translations of their own, all working independently. A committee would then compare the four translations, and if the texts were determined to be sufficiently similar, "[a]ll candid inquirers," as Talbot states in a prefatory letter to the 1857 volume that presents these translations, would have to acknowledge that the results "have the Truth for their basis" (4).

In an elaborate staging that evokes another moment of preeminent "truth" in translation, in which the Holy Spirit was believed to have inspired seventy identical translations of the Hebrew Bible into Greek, the Royal Asiatic Society collected the translations in sealed envelopes and opened them before a gathering of its most esteemed members. Comparison determined that the texts demonstrated "a very remarkable concurrence," even a "curious identity of expression as to particular words" (5). The judges declared that "the result of this experiment—than which a fairer test could scarcely be devised—may be considered as establishing, almost definitively, the correctness of the valuation of the *characters* of

---

[14] Quoted in Larsen: 181.
[15] Quoted in Larsen: 184.

these inscriptions" (9). Rather than calling the system of decipherment into question, "occasional differences in the mode of interpreting some words and sentences" were merely proof of the "fairness of the translators" (8). The last lines of an introduction to the volume written by the society's president go so far as to suggest that "several of the *seeming* differences" between the translations could perhaps have been "explained satisfactorily" had the scholars been able to confer, "and that an opportunity for re-consideration might have modified the translation of particular passages" (16, emphasis added).

In other words, breaking the code meant a production of sameness in which any differences would either be ignored as insignificant or resolved via the collaborative determination of what was in fact the *correct* translation of a given word. In setting sameness as proof of correctness, the judges projected the idea that an identicality of translations was not only possible but in fact the ideal outcome—a notion that seems to shape the very format of the volume. Many early editions of cuneiform texts are presented with a transliteration and Latin or English translation below each line of printed or hand-drawn cuneiform, an interlinear format that implies the feasibility of word-for-word translation. Demonstrating a similar investment in the close comparison of texts, the Royal Asiatic Society chose to present the four English translations of the Tiglath-Pileser inscription in parallel columns reminiscent of the multilingual, multicolumn inscriptions that were the primary objects of these early Assyriologists' investigations. And just as the texts on these inscriptions were thought to offer translingual copies of the same content, the process of decipherment was to produce an unchanging semantic value that could be transferred both into and between modern languages. After all, the committee's only serious regret was that Dr Oppert, not a native speaker of English, "did not translate into French, in which language his version would have been more clear and precise, and might have been compared [to the English versions] with equal facility" (6). Modern European translations of the Tiglath-Pileser inscription could thus be considered unproblematically equivalent both to the ancient text and to one another—an equivalence doubly established (i.e., both accomplished and "proven") through word-for-word textual comparison across linguistic divides.

Ironically, the volume's format actually lets us see how substantially the translations diverge. While accounts of the decipherment of cuneiform often declare this event a turning point, we can just as easily read the translations as arguing *against* the grand claims made in the volume that contains them. Consider the following lines (70–1), presented in Rawlinson, Talbot, Hincks, and Oppert's versions, reformatted here to fit the pages of this volume:

Rawlinson.

Whoever shall abrade or injure my tablets and cylinders, or shall moisten them with water, or scorch them with fire, or expose them to the air, or in the holy place of God shall assign them a position where they cannot be seen or understood, or who shall erase the writing and inscribe his own name, or who shall divide the sculptures (?), and break them off from my tablets,

Talbot.

But He who my stone tablets and my memorial records shall injure, or shall destroy them: with water shall efface them: or with fire shall consume them: or shall deface the writings; or shall write his name (*instead of mine*): or shall cut away the emblems: or who shall break in pieces the face of my tablets:

Hincks.

He who shall hide or obliterate my tablets and my floors shall wander on the waters, shall be suspended in the fires, shall be besmeared with earth, shall be assigned by adjudication an unpleasant place in the excellent house on high. He shall survive Jew years, and shall write his name *where, some enemy shall speedily deface it,* and shall *have it* (*i.e. the tablet containing it*) *broken* against my tablets!

Oppert.

He who hides or defaces my tablets, and my angular stones, who throw's them into the water, who burns them with fire, who spreads them to the winds, who transports them to the house of death, to a place without life, who steals the cylinders (?). who engraves on them his name, and ...... who injures my tablets:

Even in this brief passage we see how substantially the four translations diverge. The general sentiment may remain constant, but nary a word is the same across all versions, while Hincks offers entirely different interpretations than the others regarding the grammatical subjects of most clauses. This particular passage seems presciently to foretell the very situation in which these scholars find themselves: they, too, are facing an inscription that has been "abraded," "injured," "hidden," "defaced," or "obliterated" by the effects of time, placed "where [it] cannot be seen or understood." And while they are attempting to repair that damage and restore it to legibility, in some sense they themselves may also be objects of the curse, since their translations quite literally take the place of Tiglath-Pileser's inscription, and the volume puts their names, "instead of [his]," at the top of each column—a hubris the text itself condemns.

And the promised punishments for such acts of defacement are harsh:

Rawlinson.

Anu and Vul, the great Gods my lords, let them consign his name to perdition; let them curse him with an irrevocable curse; let them cause his sovereignty to perish; let them pluck out the stability of the throne of his empire; let not offspring survive him in the kingdom [doubtful and faulty in text]; let his servants be broken; let his troops be defeated; let him fly vanquished before his enemies. May Vul in his fury tear up the produce of his land. May a scarcity of food and of the necessaries of life afflict his country. For one day may he not be called happy (?) May his name and his race perish in the land.

Talbot.

May Anu and Yem, the great gods, my lords, utterly confound him; may their curses fall upon him; may they sweep away his kingly power; may his enemies carry off his royal throne; and may the memory of his reign perish; may they break in pieces his weapons; may they take his army prisoners; and may he dwell an exile for ever in the land of his enemies. May they establish a race of strangers in his place, and may his name and his race perish for ever from the land!

Hincks.

May Anu and Iv, the great gods, my lords, *energetically punish* him! and may they curse him with a *destroying curse*! May they *depress* his kingdom! may they remove . . . . the throne of his dominion! may they *scatter the attendants* on his majesty! may they break his arrows! may they affect the destruction of his army! may they make him sit *submissively* before his enemies! may *Iv depopulate* his land with *pillars of devastation*! may he lay upon his land *heavy weights of calamities* and *large measures* of blood! may he not *promise him life* for even a single day! may he *disgrace* his name and his family in the land!

Oppert.

May Anu and Ao, the great gods, my lords, load his name with infamy; may they curse him with the worst imprecations! May they subdue his sister; may they deport the districts of his kingdom! May they confound the language of his authority! May they destroy his servants! May they defeat his army! Into the hands of his antagonists may they give him for ever! May Anu, in bad intention, dismember his land! . . . . . . May he spread calamities over the country! May he excite sickness without remedy! May he entirely annihilate his name and his race!

Here, too, the differences among the four versions are striking. We have, for instance, four different transliterations of one god's name. And since cuneiform texts are not punctuated, each translator breaks phrases and sentences where he deems appropriate. The four also utilize a range of punctuation marks, from Rawlinson's and Talbot's subdued semi-colons to the energetic exclamation points of their colleagues. Meanwhile, Rawlinson's bracketed aside and Talbot's and Oppert's ellipses acknowledge that the text itself may be "doubtful" or "faulty." All four translations indicate displeasure at the thought of someone defacing the inscription, yet the proposed consequences vary widely: from a loss of power and authority, to the subduing of the wrongdoer's sister, to the perishing of his own name and the establishing of "a race of strangers in his place" (a note that also speaks to the replacement of the inscription by these translations). And while a general gesture may suffice for this sort of curse, in other passages semantic precision could be important, depending on who wants to use the translation, and for what purpose. The orchestrators of this event might not much care whether Tiglath-Pileser hunted elephants or wild buffalo, as we read elsewhere, or whether he killed them or took them alive, but for natural historians that information might make all the difference.

Only at one point in this fascinating volume is any uncertainty expressed regarding the degree of independent confirmation these translations provide. One judge, though concurring that the test offers "almost definitive" proof, notes that the nearly exact agreement in thirty-nine place names across the four versions of a particular paragraph "is no doubt, in part at least, owing to [the translators'] adoption of the values proposed previously by Sir H. Rawlinson and Dr. Hincks" (9). Indeed, Rawlinson, Hincks, and others had been proceeding by way of an odd kind of competitive collaboration, continually refuting, adopting, revising, and elaborating on one another's work, while slowly building up shared lists of phonetic values and meanings. It is hardly surprising, then, that these scholars would arrive at similar results when drawing on the same interpretive codes and tools. We could thus see the *Inscription of Tiglath-Pileser I, King of Assyria B.C. 1150* less as a proof of decipherment than as a snapshot in a long process of contestation and provisional agreement between scholars that continues to the present day.

Not even a decade after this experiment, we find serious divergence of opinion even between two of its participants: Hincks explicitly framed his 1866 *Specimen Chapters of an Assyrian Grammar* as a corrective to Oppert's Assyrian grammar of a few years earlier, "of which I have already stated," Hincks wrote, "that, besides minor errors, it was pervaded by three erroneous general principles, 'so as scarcely to leave a page free from what I consider pernicious error'" (2). Rather than simply offering a "dogmatic" statement of "what I believe to be the grammatical rules of the Assyrian language," Hincks proposed instead to "deduce them from those leading positions on which all are agreed, by inductive proofs" (3). This complex gesture of combative consensus-building draws on the language of science to frame the project of grammatical analysis as competitive and collaborative at once. The tension between these two impulses remained central to the field of Assyriology as grammars, syllabaries, and word lists grew in certainty, specificity, and length, leading to the great dictionary projects of the twentieth century and beyond.

The conceptual autonomy of the Babylonian wor(l)d?

In a 1960 article in *Current Anthropology*, leading Assyriologist Leo Oppenheim stressed "the difficulty of synthesizing data coming from a deeply alien civilization, a civilization that is reflected solely in the dull and distorting mirror of documents written in a dead language. It is necessary, but extremely difficult," he continued, "to free oneself consciously and consistently from one's own ingrained conceptual conditioning in order to organize adequately any data pertaining to an alien civilization."[16] Oppenheim's uneasiness with what he sees as the large-scale domestication of ancient Mesopotamia echoes concerns expressed three decades earlier by Benno Landsberger in his much-quoted essay "The Conceptual Autonomy of the Babylonian World."[17] "To what extent is it possible," Landsberger had then asked, "to reconstruct *vividly* and *faithfully* an ancient, alien civilization by philological means, without the help of a tradition continuing down to the present day?" (5) Any such attempt necessarily involves a construction of (partial, often tendentious) equivalences: "All understanding consists first of all in establishing some link between the alien world and our own. In the initial stage this is expressed by a number of simple equations, which are compiled in grammar and lexicon [...] but as such full equations are possible only to a limited extent, most often we have to content ourselves with partial equations of the type: part of the Babylonian concept x corresponds with part of our concept y" (6).

Landsberger's phrasing echoes discussions of equivalence in the fields of translation studies and bilingual lexicography alike. Indeed, if lexicography is

---

[16] Oppenheim: 418. In this essay, he argued in part the need for Assyriology to move into the social sciences and away from the humanities, whose "conceptual tools have been and still are geared for integration on their own terms and for assimilation along Western standards" (419).

[17] I am quoting here from the 1976 English translation by Jacobsen, Foster, and von Siebenthal of Landsberger's "*Die Eigenbegrifflichkeit der Babylonischen Welt*" (1926).

at heart a project rooted in "equivalence seeking," and a bilingual dictionary "the result of many separate equivalence acts performed by the lexicographer" (Hartmann 1987: 60), current-day discussions regarding the creation of such dictionaries would do well to consider the challenges to the notion of equivalence, and particularly lexical equivalence, that have shaped recent discussions among scholars of translation. Likewise, translators and scholars of translation (myself among them) who dismiss the idea of equivalence and its attendant conceptualization of translation as transfer would do well to recognize the ways in which paradigms of equivalence continue to structure the most basic tools of our trade, not to mention readers' expectations for what a translation will provide. For a long while, equivalence was in fact a conceptual cornerstone in writings about translation; practitioners and theorists proposed any number of criteria—lexical, functional, formal, dynamic, stylistic, communicative, ontological, and so on—by which a supposed equivalence between words, phrases, or entire texts in different languages might be determined or described.[18] Yet in the wake of poststructuralist arguments regarding the instability of meaning in language, scholars of translation, particularly those concerned with literary translation, increasingly moved away from discussions of equivalence toward an understanding of translation as an interpretive process in which the very notion of an "invariant" to be "transferred" was suspect. In an oft-cited early critique of equivalence as "unsuitable as a basic concept in translation theory," Mary Snell-Hornby argues that the term "presents an illusion of symmetry between languages which hardly exists beyond the level of vague approximations and which distorts the basic problems of translation" (1988: 22). Subsequently, scholars as wide-ranging in their approaches as James Holmes, Gideon Toury, Theo Hermans, Karin Littau, Dilek Dizdar, Anthony Pym, and Esperança Bielsa and Susan Bassnett have all challenged this paradigm from various angles.[19] Yet the very persistence of these arguments against equivalence shows the continued need for them, thus indicating the tenacity of the concept itself, even among translators: as Venuti points out, despite decades of theoretical challenges to equivalence, translators "nonetheless try to maintain a semantic similarity based on current dictionary definitions, or in other words a lexicographical equivalence" (2013: 36). Indeed, the dictionary is one of the primary sites where a concept of equivalence gives shape to the *creation* of translingual synonymity on the level of the word.

In *Translingual Practice,* Lydia Liu likewise interrogates the ways in

---

[18] See the entry on "Equivalence" in the *Routledge Encyclopedia of Translation Studies* (ed. Mona Baker) for a brief but fairly comprehensive overview of the history of the various usages and qualifications of this term.

[19] Representative texts for each are included in the Bibliography.

which bilingual dictionaries consolidate the belief in word-level equivalents. This idea, Liu notes, is merely "a common illusion that philosophers, linguists, and theorists of translation have tried in vain to dispel" (3)—yet the "thriving industry of bilingual dictionaries depends on the tenacity of this illusion," since bilingual dictionaries establish paradigms of lexical equivalence between, say, "the English word 'self' and the Chinese *ji, wo, ziwo.*" "Once such linkages are established," Liu concludes, "a text becomes 'translatable' in the ordinary sense of the word." (7)[20] For Snell-Hornby, the understanding regarding "translation equivalents" that such dictionaries put forward "clashes with the notion that cultures and concepts must be viewed in their own terms, demanding a heuristic method of discovery procedures" (1986: 216)—clashes, in other words, with Oppenheim's insistence that "the standard applicable to the world of ideas to be unraveled must be derived from [that world] itself" (6). Both Snell-Hornby and Liu are writing about the construction of linguistic and conceptual equivalents between cultures contemporaneous to one another. The potential imbalance of these structures of supposed exchange is dramatically heightened in the case of languages unspoken, unwritten, and unread for millennia. And yet bilingual word lists, featuring columns of Sumerian and Akkadian words treated as lexical equivalents for the purposes of scribal education, were in fact ubiquitous in ancient Mesopotamian culture, and proved instrumental both in deciphering languages written in cuneiform and in compiling the dictionaries students of these languages use today. Indeed, Snell-Hornby posits the Mesopotamian word lists as some of the earliest embodiments of "the mistaken assumption of interlingual lexical equivalence (the idea that a word 'is' another word in the foreign language)" (1986: 207).

It is both fitting and ironic, then, that Oppenheim and Landsberger were instrumental in shaping the twenty-one-volume *Chicago Assyrian Dictionary,* a massive lexicographical project that involved generations of scholars and took several decades to complete, from the mid-1950s to 2011. In keeping with Landsberger and Oppenheim's cautions against drawing too-easy parallels between the ancient experience and our own, the *Chicago Assyrian Dictionary* attempts to build an understanding of the Assyrian language and its culture from within. Erica Reiner, another of its key figures, notes how its entries go beyond what she calls "mere translation" (betraying an understanding of translation as word-level equivalence-seeking) to offer multiple meanings for a given word, drawing on both Akkadian and Sumerian evidence, citing lengthy passages from multiple recorded instances of given words, and providing information regarding

---

[20] See also Nappi (2015) on the creation of equivalences in miscellany in early modern China.

the social context of those sources (Adams and Reiner 2002: xiv). In these long, encyclopedia-style entries, the sheer number of potential "equivalents" undermines the sense that a singular translingual definition for any given set of cuneiform symbols could ever be precisely or confidently fixed; the entries document a process of linguistic and material excavation and lexicographical construction in which infinite layers could theoretically be added.

Yet this all-encompassing approach might in fact push the *Chicago Assyrian Dictionary* to a point beyond (or before) what qualifies *as* a dictionary: "the results were often only prolegomena to a dictionary," Reiner writes, "or rather a tool for future efforts to determine the words' meanings" (3). This statement reveals a fault line in the understanding of what a dictionary should be, and even in the meaning of the very word "meaning," as the editors attempt to escape the word-list mentality of assigning lexical equivalents even as the genre of the dictionary seems to require it. As indicative of this conundrum, Reiner also quotes a letter Landsberger wrote to another Assyriologist, which reveals this tension starkly, as well as tensions within the editorial team regarding the purposes of the project:

> However, in most cases determining [the meanings of words] is beyond our powers; true, if I were to work on it very intensively, perhaps a few meanings would come out. Leaving aside obscure plant names and the like, I can state that the meanings of 60% of the Akkadian words are unknown and that it is not even the aim of the Dictionary to establish them. If [I. J.] Gelb were again to obtain the exclusive directorship and find slaves for it, the Dictionary would turn into a mere (and bad!) word list. (3)

At this stage in the development of the field, "meanings" were to be gleaned by intense study of all known occurrences of a given word, and might change as new evidence arose; reducing the dictionary to a bilingual word list would create a false impression that equivalences had been fixed. Yet Landsberger also noted that the dictionary would be a tool "handed to the next generation for finding the meanings," suggesting that meanings would at some point be "found," and would likely be presented as a series of lexical equivalents, however contextualized or multiple.

The size and cost of the *Chicago Assyrian Dictionary* render it impractical for all but the most specialized users. Beginning learners are far more likely to turn to Jeremy Black and Andrew George's 450-page *Concise Dictionary of Akkadian* (2000), whose comparatively brief entries offer only a few possible translations for each word. While the *Chicago Assyrian Dictionary* presents meaning as a moving target to be understood only within a complex web of textual contexts, Black and George's dictionary lends itself more readily to an understanding of lexical meaning as relatively stable content that can be transferred or transported across languages. This impression is heightened by the fact that this dictionary is itself an abridged translation of Wolfram von Soden's three-volume, German-language *Akkadisches Handwörterbuch* (1958–1981). Like the commentators who suggested Oppert's translation of the Tiglath-Pileser inscription would have been easier to compare to Rawlinson's, Talbot's, and Hincks' had it been composed in his native French, the *Concise Dictionary of Akkadian* treats the meanings of these words as transferable both into and between modern European languages. In their introduction, Black and George note that their dictionary can replace neither the Chicago project nor von Soden's dictionary—at least not for serious Assyriologists, who will inevitably "end up reading German"—which more adequately reflect the "finer nuance of meanings" (ix). Yet the fact of the matter is that for many, particularly beginning learners of the language, this dictionary *does* replace those others, which might be available only to those with university libraries at their disposal.

These compact, affordable dictionaries intended for beginning learners and the more extensive dictionaries intended for advanced scholars thus reflect two fundamentally opposed philosophies of language and translation one based on equivalence and one that promotes instead a model of contextualization and supplementarity. Only on progressing to a more advanced level does a learner *un*learn the fixity of the assigned equivalents in which she had initially been taught to believe. In the case of an ancient work such as *Gilgamesh*, the division between pocket and encyclopedia-style dictionaries is echoed, too, by a division between translations that present unified, lacuna-free texts for popular audiences, and editions that strive to reflect the textual instability of the *Gilgamesh* "sources." If these dictionaries reflect different understandings of the relationship between language and meaning, so too do the many editions of ancient works reflect and promote different understandings of the relationship between story and source, between the work and its many textual manifestations.

What we talk about when we talk about *Gilgamesh*

The story of Gilgamesh refracts many of the issues its rediscovery could be said to raise. It is a story about losing and finding, about failed attempts to achieve immortality, and about the partial recovery of meanings and messages from earlier eras, full of doublings and couplings that complicate attempts to distinguish originals from copies. Gilgamesh, ruler of Uruk, has become a tyrant. The goddess Aruru takes a pinch of clay and creates a wild man, Enkidu, to confront Gilgamesh and bring him under control. First, however, Enkidu himself—who runs with the gazelle, grazes on grass, and frees animals from hunters' traps—must be civilized, a task accomplished by the harlot Shamhat, who is sent to couple with him. Enkidu, made (in one of Andrew George's two translations) in "the image of Gilgamesh, but shorter in stature and bigger of bone," then challenges the ruler and proves himself his "equal" (2003b: 15; 10); they become inseparable companions and embark on a series of adventures that bring them to faraway lands. They slay the Bull of Heaven and the giant Humbaba, who calls down death upon Enkidu and consigns Gilgamesh to a consequent mourning. In deep grief at the loss of his friend and terrified by the thought of his own mortality, Gilgamesh sets off again in search of Uta-napishti, survivor of a great flood, in hopes of learning the secret of eternal life; instead, he learns only that death is inevitable. Himself now a wild man with matted hair, transformed by grief into a physical echo of Enkidu prior to his taming, Gilgamesh is bathed by Uta-napishti's wife and returns to Uruk a restored man, no younger but a good deal wiser. There he stands and surveys his realm: the date grove, the temple, and the clay pit, source of the material that enables both building and writing—two activities whose products, as the survival of the tale itself shows, can far outlast a human life.

This is the *story* of Gilgamesh—or rather, a condensed version, a capsule paraphrase based on a long string of previous rewritings, from illustrated books for children to scholarly editions. But where are we to find the epic itself? *Is* there an "epic itself"? If texts about this legendary king and his companion have been discovered all over the Near East, always in fragmentary form, and composed in several languages over two millennia, what are we really talking about when we refer to the "epic of Gilgamesh"? What is the work that goes by this name, and what is the relationship between it and its many textual manifestations, not to mention rewritings of other sorts?

One of the finest analyses of the theoretical issues involved in presenting works and texts from ancient Mesopotamia comes in Jeremy Black's 1998 *Reading Sumerian Poetry*. The volume, which includes Black's edition of the Sumerian poem *Lugulbanda* (about Gilgamesh's mythical father), is largely dedicated to a discussion of the multiply mediated forms by which cuneiform texts reach contemporary readers.[21] Each stage in moving from a multitude of clay fragments to composite transliterated and then translated texts involves

---

[21] As I mentioned in footnote 2, the appendix to George's Penguin Classics edition also offers an excellent account of how scholars have moved from tablet fragments to translated text—though his account interestingly elides the process by which meanings were assigned to words, moving on 220 from a normalized translation to an English translation without discussion of the intermediary step of semantic rather than syllabic decipherment.

significant interpretive labor, undertaken on the assumption that fragments found at different times, in distant places, even composed in different languages, can be understood as manifestations of a single work. The texts presented are invariably collated from multiple witnesses, while images of fragments, either photographic or hand-drawn, are usually offered only selectively, even in scholarly editions, as a gesture to the material condition of the textual witnesses.[22] In the words of Sumerologist Piotr Michalowski, a reader can "be quite certain that a text such as the one presented [in a scholarly edition] has never existed" before (quoted in Black: 35). Black stresses the need to formulate new methodologies of reading, discussing, and teaching commensurate to the particular challenges presented by what he calls "reconstructed" ancient texts (a term whose implications I myself would contest). "How is the critic to approach such a text?" he asks. "Virtually all the critical techniques and procedures that make up literary critical practice"— including, I would add, our practice as translators and teachers—"rely on the existence of a text" to serve as the object of enquiry (Black: 35–6).

For the Gilgamesh epic, as for other ancient works, the text or texts on which we base our interpretations as casual readers, literary scholars, or students of Babylonian culture will inevitably be the editorial product of others' prior interpretive labor. In the decades since Jeffrey Tigay's 1982 *The Evolution of the Gilgamesh Epic*, most scholars have posited the existence of three stages of the work. The Sumerian tales about Bilgamesh in circulation in the region during the late third and early second millennia B.C.E., while recognized as precursors, are generally excluded from consideration of the work as such. The Babylonian texts inscribed over the course of nearly two millennia are separated into the Old Babylonian version, dating to the second millennium; a number of Middle Babylonian versions which spread as part of a scribal curriculum and gave rise to local versions and translations throughout the Mesopotamian region; and the Standard Babylonian version, which took shape between 1300 and 1000 B.C.E. and was consolidated during the reign of Ashurbanipal in the 600s into "a single, integrated composition with episodes arranged in meaningful sequence and held together by recurrent themes" (Tigay: 43). Most translations of the epic into modern languages, and certainly those intended for a nonspecialist audience, focus on the Standard Babylonian version, which conforms most neatly to our understanding of what a literary work should be. (Indeed, many editions choose to exclude the twelfth tablet, a direct translation of a

---

[22] One exception is George's extraordinary two-volume scholarly edition of 2003, which, as I note below, offers hand-drawn images of every available fragment, as well as transliterations and translations.

Sumerian source that exhibits both narrative and stylistic differences from the other eleven tablets.)[23] Given the incomplete nature of the available textual witnesses, translations as well as cuneiform editions must decide what amount of fragmentariness they are willing to sustain, and whether to fill the gaps with plot summaries or material from other versions.

For most of the twentieth century, the only published edition of the cuneiform texts was R. Campbell Thompson's 1930 Oxford edition, which included both hand drawings and a transliteration of reconstructed tablets. Thompson compiled his texts primarily from witnesses to the Standard Babylonian version. In the interest of communicating the story more adequately, however, he often included fragments from Old and Middle Babylonian texts when a Standard Babylonian fragment could not be found to complete a particular tablet. Many scholars subsequently took issue with Thompson's approach, and ongoing archaeological discoveries quickly rendered his edition "hopelessly out of date," as Simo Parpola wrote in the introduction to his own 1997 edition of the Standard Babylonian version, published as part of the University of Helsinki's Neo-Assyrian Text Corpus Project. Parpola's slim edition offers composite texts in a cuneiform font, as well as transliterations that register the specific material source or sources for each line, with variants from other clay fragments noted in a textual apparatus at the bottom of each page. Parpola intended his edition primarily as a teaching tool, since "every Assyriologist studying or teaching the Epic has in practice been compelled to produce an updated edition [of Thompson's 1930 version] on his [*sic*] own" (ix), a note that testifies to the many divergent cuneiform versions being distributed in scholarly circles, and also suggests a curious parallel between the labor of modern Assyriologists and that of ancient Mesopotamian scribes. (Indeed, since many consider pen-and-ink drawings more accurate representations of the three-dimensional tablets than photographic reproductions, committed scholars continue even today to copy Akkadian texts by hand, becoming modern-day scribes of sorts, the most recent links in a long, if broken, tradition of manual reproduction of cuneiform texts.)

In the introduction to his volume, Parpola mentions the much anticipated publication of George's *The Babylonian Gilgamesh Epic: Introduction, Critical Edition and Cuneiform Texts*, which was released a few years after Parpola's,

---

[23] Consider, as one example, David Ferry's contention in the notes to his translation that "to include [Tablet XII] as an organic part of the main poem would cause a number of problems, the most obvious of which is that it would spoil the effect of Tablet XI's conclusion, which returns to the language of the opening passage of the poem" (94). In other words, this decision marks an aesthetic preference for a certain kind of closure or structural return. Kovacs, too, notes that "the decision to eliminate Tablet XII" from her own translation "was a matter of personal judgment, shared by many others, that though Tablet XII may be literally a part of the Epic […] it is not part of it in literary terms" (116).

in 2003. George's massive, two-volume scholarly edition includes hand-drawn images and transliterations of all extant cuneiform witnesses to the Standard Babylonian version, as well as composite texts and translations representing the three stages Tigay proposed in the epic's evolution. It is a magnificent scholarly achievement, and the form of the edition includes a dazzling amount of information about the extant fragments and about the editorial methodology that has been followed, such that a reader desiring to create a competing edition or translation could certainly do so on the basis of the materials provided. There is, though, some degree of tension between the range of treatments to which these two volumes submit their materials, from the images and transcriptions to the composite texts, which George forthrightly declares "a work of textual reconstruction" incorporating "every available piece of the Babylonian Gilgameş" (2003b: v; vii). Elsewhere, he has acknowledged that the results of this latter editorial procedure "are essentially idealized texts, in Michalowski's words 'intellectual constructs.'" He also suggests that persistence in this approach will eventually result in the (re)creation of a stable, reliable composite text, at least for the Standard Babylonian version: "with the continuing discovery of new pieces in museum storerooms and archaeological digs there is no doubt in my mind that eventually the whole text of the Standard Babylonian Epic of Gilgamesh will be recovered and the poem reconstructed much as it last was more than two thousand years ago."[24]

This sentence, with its focus on completion and singularity, stands in contrast not only with the mediated nature of the many ways in which modern readers come into contact with these ancient works, but also with the comparative flexibility of modes of textual reproduction George himself describes in his account of ancient Mesopotamian scribal culture. Indeed, it is worth considering whether the very notion that we even *need* a single composite text to serve as a stable object of interpretation may be a product of the age of print, or at least profoundly historically contingent. Martin Worthington is one scholar who has invoked the more fluid notions of "fidelity" at work in ancient Mesopotamia in order to destabilize our modern preoccupation with textual fixity. Noting how accustomed contemporary readers are to the idea of mass reproducibility, Worthington warns us not to allow this to condition our view of how texts were copied and circulated in the ancient world: "In cultures where identical reproduction is difficult, the notion of exactitude is relativised, or even de-prioritised" (21). Minor or even major disparities in wording, grammar, and the ordering of lines in different textual manifestations of a work like the Standard Babylonian

---

[24] George. "Shattered tablets and tangled threads: Editing Gilgamesh, then and now." Published on the SOAS website in PDF form: http://eprints.soas.ac.uk/7497/ (last accessed 7 May 2017).

Gilgamesh may well have been understood by ancient readers and audiences as entirely acceptable variation, just as the many translations contemporary readers might encounter are usually considered acceptable manifestations of the same work, though some might be preferred over others. And yet while modern scholars recognize the flexibility by which one witness to the abstract entities we call "Tablet I" or "Tablet II" inevitably differs from all others, the practice and ideology of textual reproduction that has prevailed since the rediscovery of Akkadian texts in the mid-nineteenth century has been bound up in the codex form, shaped by the technological promise of relatively exact reproduction. Translation scholar Anthony Pym has suggested that even our modern notions of equivalence in translation might be a product of the age of print. "[T]he conceptual geometry of equivalence," Pym notes, "was difficult to maintain prior to the age of the printing press, since printing reinforced notions of a fixed source text to which a translation could be equivalent. Before that fixing, textuality tended to involve constant incremental changes in the process of copying, such that translation was often just further extension of that process."[25]

Cuneiform editions, transliterations, and translations intended for scholarly and nonscholarly audiences follow a range of methodologies in presenting these fragmentary ancient texts: some account typographically for the process of reconstruction but, in doing so, create challenges for untrained readers; others silently fill in lacunae with material from other versions but, in doing so, give the impression that scholars' knowledge about a particular work is more complete than it actually is. It is by now a commonplace that any two translators will produce different translations of a given text. In fact, as the twin epigraphs to this chapter reveal, even the same translator working with the same material may translate a text differently for different audiences, in different contexts, or to stress different aspects of the work in question. Moreover, with a work like *Gilgamesh*, for which new material is always being discovered, translators are *not* always working with the same "source." Many recent translators of this work have not been specialists, and tend to base their translations not on the cuneiform text but on previous translations by trusted Assyriologists: in preparing his 2004 version Stephen Mitchell consulted seven scholarly and two popular editions, all in English; N. K. Sandars' 1960 prose translation—which had sold over a million copies by the turn of the twenty-first century, and remains in print to this day—was based on scholarly editions in English, French, and German; David Ferry's 2001 version also relies upon prior translations by specialists, and even incorporates a variant reading of one line in

---

[25] Pym (2009: 83). Pym also suggests that the advent of digital technology may affect our notions of equivalence, as its variability supplants the seeming fixity of print.

a witty nod to ongoing scholarly debates about the meaning of a particular Akkadian word.[26] For all their differences, these translators clearly all prize narrative continuity, some more so than others. In order to move the story forward, they often incorporate elements from multiple stages of the epic's textual history, even from different languages, or choose not to include parts of a text that seem irrelevant to the plot.

Take the opening passage of Tablet VII, which describes Enkidu's death. The opening line has survived, but the following twenty-six are entirely missing; several subsequent lines exist only in extremely fragmentary form. When we once again pick up the narrative thread, Enkidu is cursing both himself and a wooden door he and Gilgamesh built as a gift to Enlil, which failed to appease the god and therefore also to save Enkidu from death. George's 2003 scholarly edition of this passage offers a transliterated composite text and *en face* translation for all available lines, marking lacunae both across and within lines; he also notes alternate readings in the critical apparatus at the bottom of the page. In his edition for Penguin Classics, first published in 1999, George prefaces the translation of this (and every) tablet with a synopsis of the action, and fills in the missing episode with a translation from "a fragmentary prose paraphrase, written in Hittite, which was based on an older version of the epic" (2003a: 54). Benjamin Forster similarly offers a synopsis of the Hittite version at the beginning of his text for Tablet VII, as does Kovacs, and John Gardner and John Maier, as well, in a translation published in movingly unfinished form a few years after Gardner's untimely death. Ferry, whose translator's note declares that a "'true original' is always unrecoverable, even for the most faithfully literal [*sic*] translation," treats the gaps as "both problems and opportunities" (94). In his version of this passage, Ferry rearranges the lines, condensing Enkidu's elaborate series of curses and folding them into his retelling to Gilgamesh of his dream of the previous night. Mitchell likewise notes that even scholarly versions interpolate text, and takes that as license to "add lines or short passages to bridge the gaps and clarify the story" (60). Here, however, he does not add but actually removes a large portion of Enkidu's curse, presumably viewing it as incidental to the forward momentum of the narrative.

[26] In his translator's note, Ferry writes, "There are places where I have exploited scholarly disagreements. Some scholars think that Ishtar, in Tablet VI, turned Ishullanu into a mole; others think he was turned into a frog. I like both possibilities, so I turned the scholars into ancient gossips whose stories, as usual with gossips, don't quite match" (94). The lines in question are: "Some say the goddess turned him into a frog / among the reeds, with haunted frog voice chanting, / / beseeching what he no longer knows he longs for; / some say into a mole whose blind foot pushes / / over and over again against the loam / in the dark of the tunnel, baffled and silent, forever. / / And you would do with me as you did with them." (32)

Yet the substance of Enkidu's curse is arguably crucial to a reading that seeks to trace fault lines in the epic's recuperative tale of learning through suffering and the return of power into the hands of a single ruler. Enkidu's curse destabilizes the supposed durability of the epic that contains it; his curse challenges the sacrosanct nature of the "message from the antediluvian age" tucked away in the cedar (or copper) box, by pointing to the possibility that another tale could have been told—a tale that was both written and ultimately silenced by Enkidu himself. Just as Gilgamesh's inscription is embedded in the walls of Uruk, and his story recorded also on a set of clay tablets, this door bears Enkidu's inscription, yet is chided for not being able to understand the inscription's message: "O door of the woodland, that has no [sense]" (George 1999: 55); "stupid wooden door that does not hear" (Ferry: 38); "Bosky door, insensate, which lends an ear that is not there" (Forster: 53). The closing lines of this passage, Forster writes in his introduction, parody "traditional Mesopotamian inscriptions affixed to monuments, which called the wrath of the gods upon anyone who damaged, removed, or usurped the monument" (53)—the very sort of curse we saw in the Tiglath-Pileser inscription above. Yet in a reverse of Tiglath-Pileser's railing against future despoilers, Enkidu curses not an interloper but the door, himself, and his tale to obscurity: "May a king who comes after me reject you, / May the god ... / May he remove my name and set his own there!" (Kovacs: 61)—or, in Forster, "May [...] conceal you, / May he alter my inscription and put on his own!" (54). Gilgamesh's message may remain for future generations to read, but Enkidu's is consigned—by Enkidu himself—to silence.

This replacing, rejection, or alteration of the text is, arguably, what translation does: each new translation replaces one text with another that both represents and obscures what has come before. But if the discovery of *Gilgamesh* enabled a sudden encounter with deep time, with the sublimity of a human history far longer than anyone had yet imagined, we might also consider this gesture to Enkidu's lost story as embodying the potential for a different kind of "encounter with the deep" that parallels yet contests Gilgamesh's own—for an encounter, that is, with our ultimate inability to arrive not at *the* meaning but at any one meaning, or even any one textual configuration of the work. It could be that the proliferation of modern translations, paraphrases, and other rewritings of the tale is far more in keeping with an ancient understanding of textual production and reproduction than the attempt to arrive at a single cuneiform text to represent this long-lost work. Acknowledging the inevitable textual proliferation involved in the contested reconstruction, decipherment, and translation of this epic may help us move discussions of translation firmly away from equivalence and into a realm of iteration to which works such as *Gilgamesh* may point the way.

2

"Monuments of the Word": Translation and the Textualization of Modern Greek Folk Songs

She bewitched the ships, they won't set sail
She bewitched me too, I cannot go home.
When I try to leave, there's snow and rain
When I turn back, sun and starry skies.
I don my armor, it drops to the ground,
I write and the writing comes unwritten.

—Greek folk song[1]

This book already contains one origin story for its preoccupations: in my Introduction, I cite the experience of translating a novel by Vassilis Vassilikos as the origin of my interest in the relationship between textual instability and translation. Yet in a book that challenges the notion of stable, singular origins, it seems hardly suitable to offer only one such story. Here, then, is another.

Several years ago I was invited to translate a handful of poems for an anthology that was to represent, in English, three millennia's worth of poetry composed in various historical and geographical varieties of Greek. Among the poems was the well-known folk song "Το γεφύρι της Άρτας" or "Το γιοφύρι της Άρτας" ("The bridge of Arta"), as published in Nikolaos Politis's 1914 *Εκλογαί από τα τραγούδια του ελληνικού λαού* (*Selection of the Songs of the Greek Folk*), the most widely available and arguably most influential collection of its kind. Politis's volume opens with a declaration, which I translate here from his *katharevousa* Greek (a formal, archaizing register of the modern language whose history I will touch on later), that

[1] *The Greek Poets: Homer to the Present* contains another translation of this song, by Pavlos Avlamis and Edmund Keeley. I chose to offer my own translation in order to highlight some of the arguments I am making in my chapter. Both translations are based on the Greek text numbered 172 in Politis's collection. It can be found in Nikolaos Politis (2009: 332), a reprint of the 1914 edition.

the roughly 250 songs he presents "hold an undeniably special place among the monuments of the word produced by our folk," as the truest bearers of the "particular character" of the Greek ethnos. His goal in collecting and publishing these songs is explicitly nationalistic: he wants to turn the "demotic poetry" of these songs into a "solid foundation" for a national literature. In order to do so, he must make them available as texts, as a body of "common reading" which—brought together from all regions of the nascent Greek state, and even from lands that still lie beyond it—will be "distributed to the whole ethnos" by way of this volume. In his goal of wide distribution, at least, Politis had remarkable success. Still in print a century after its initial publication, his collection has in fact been reissued by at least five publishing houses in the past fifteen years. Its texts—creations of an anonymous "folk" and therefore not eligible for intellectual property protections—have also been widely reproduced in countless anthologies and school textbooks, in sound recordings by popular musicians, and on websites and blogs.

Although he is generally considered the founder of folklore studies in Greece, Politis's methods have not been immune to criticism.[2] Unlike his contemporaries elsewhere who sought to encounter songs in performance contexts, Politis relied solely upon a preexisting print tradition in compiling his anthology. He also approached his task as an editor of ancient, written texts might: he treated each manifestation of a song as an incomplete or faulty rendering of an ideal, inaccessible "original." His methodology followed a philological model of textual recension formulated by European scholars hoping to reconstruct the lost Ur-texts of ancient works that survived only in fragmentary forms. Politis's notes for "The Bridge of Arta," for instance— tucked away at the back of the volume, leaving the song itself to stand on its own on the page—name over two dozen published sources, many exhibiting elements of regional dialect, from which he shaped a single composite text that he deemed suitable for distribution throughout Greece. To be sure, the variation that characterizes the oral tradition is difficult to register in print— yet even at this early date in the history of folklore studies, other models were available for how Politis might have presented these songs.[3] He could in fact

---

[2] See Apostolakis (1929), Beaton (1980), and Moullas (1994) for representative critiques.

[3] For instance, one major source for Politis's texts was a collection published in Leipzig in 1860 by German scholar Arnold Passow. Like Politis, Passow, who never visited Greece, drew extensively on an existing print tradition, but he also had at his disposal a large collection of manuscript texts that passed into his hands after the death of his father-in-law, Heinrich Ulrich, a professor at Othonian University in Athens who had been planning a collection of his own. Passow's massive collection often includes several versions of a given song, or offers extensive notes regarding regional or other variants. He also explicitly identifies his sources immediately below the title he assigns to each song. Politis, on the other hand, leaves his (often incomplete) information about sources

have treated his texts as contingent and multiple, rather than consolidating a textualized canon of songs deemed most worthy of forming the backbone of a new national literature—an enterprise for which gestures to the songs' mutability and regional variance may have seemed to pose a threat.

As a commissioned translator for Norton's *The Greek Poets: Homer to the Present*, I wasn't in a position to question the editors' decision to include only a single translation of the single version of "The Bridge of Arta," or their choice of this particular text as my "source." Yet I found the usual practical questions about how to translate that text compounded by more persistent theoretical questions regarding the provenance and textual configuration of the manifestly *non*-original "original" I was working with. How had Politis adjudicated between the several published sources available to him? How did those earlier print versions relate to one another, and to the oral tradition? Given that songs of this sort can be sung differently in each new performance context, and given the frequent repetition of formulaic language and motifs not only within but *across* songs, how can we say for sure what counts as a particular song, or where one ends and the next begins? Are there better and worse ways of denoting in print the fluidity, variability, and continual production of difference that characterizes this genre? Would, for instance, an edition that compiled variants really gesture more adequately to the oral nature of the genre these texts purport to represent? After all, as Roderick Beaton points out, "[t]he whole idea of 'variants' is apt to be misleading" (21) in the case of folk songs: "to speak of variants presupposes a belief that there exists an archetypal or original version of each song, from which individual versions diverge" (30). In that case, one could also argue that any oral or textual manifestation (including, potentially, those in other languages) could be understood as simply another iteration, equally capable of representing the song in question. In that case, when preparing an anthology whose texts may indeed become "monuments of the word," in or out of a national(ized) language, how does one choose? And what difference does translation make?

This chapter takes these questions as its starting point. It focuses not on Politis's efforts but on the instability of even the textual sources, an instability that made his attempts at monumentalization so necessary. Jumping back nearly a century before the publication of his volume, I explore the early history of efforts to collect Greek folk songs in the context of nation-building efforts of the time as well as the rise of interest in folklore across Europe. I begin with the first printed collection of Greek songs, Claude Fauriel's *Chants*

---

for the end of the volume: eclectically edited texts for each song are presented entirely free of variants. These two collections thus both embody and foster very different conceptions of the status of the texts they include.

populaires de la Grèce moderne (*Popular Songs of Modern Greece*, 1824), and trace the movement of these texts through space and time, and between languages, in Europe, Britain, and Greece. Fauriel was a Frenchman who never visited the lands that would later become Greece. He received most of his texts from literate Greeks living in Europe, who would have had little contact with the hypothesized folk about whom Fauriel and others were so curious—a folk that may, in the end, be as much an invention of these scholars' discourse as anything. The multiply mediated texts in Fauriel's collection were destined to become "originals" for a spate of further editions in a range of languages: 1825 alone saw a version in French verse, as well as translations into Russian, German, and English. His work subsequently became a resource for Greek editors, as well: in the 1850s, *Chants populaires* became the central source for the first collections of folk songs to be published in the Ionian islands, which would join the fledgling Greek state a decade later. In the course of my examinations of this series of motivated rewritings, I treat Greek folk songs as exemplary of the textualized history of folk songs in nineteenth-century Europe. I demonstrate the impossibility of ever arriving at an originary moment of oral performance that might precede this textualization. I also argue, most importantly, that while the modes of presentation in each new context project an image of these songs as distinctly Greek, this translingual dissemination of texts implicitly resists the attempt to turn them into national "monuments of the word." On the contrary, at least for those who felt it to be an ideological threat, the instability of these texts is precisely what calls out for their stabilization.

Both before and after the revolution, both outside and inside this nation in the process of becoming, these songs were used to support ideological arguments about what Greece was and what it should aspire to be. Tracing the circulation of Greek folks songs in these multiple languages, in collections whose paratexts often conflate ancient and modern Greece—or, with equal frequency, contrast them, always to the detriment of the modern—also allows us to see how the songs have been mobilized for a variety of social and political purposes. In the case of Greece, as with so many other modern states, the narrative of a nationalized, emphatically monolingual literature aided the creation of a social imaginary and a political reality whose continued legitimacy came to depend on the very stories it told.[4] What was

---

[4] By "monolingual," here, I am referring rather imprecisely to Greek in all of its modern guises. As I will discuss later in the chapter, the issue of what language should prevail as the national language of the nascent Greek state gave rise to an extremely heated debate in the years even before the revolution of 1821. The varieties of Greek spoken, then and now, are numerous. But my point here is that, in Greece as elsewhere, the formation of the state brought also an effort to settle on a single language to unify the nation, among

at stake in the stabilization and reification of these "monuments of the word" was less the return to an originary oral performance than the creation of an origin story for Greece itself. That origin story, at first invested in the creation of the Greek state, continued after the revolution to be employed to shore up projects of cultural nationalism. This is true even of the Norton anthology to which I was asked to contribute: its inclusion of material from Homer to the present constructs an implicit narrative of linguistic and even cultural continuity similar to those that proved instrumental, in the early nineteenth century, in legitimizing the Greek revolution on an international stage.

Yet as vernacular literature that respects neither linguistic nor national divides, folk songs also resist such projects from within: the inclusion in these collections of wide-traveling songs claimed by (or, at any rate, for) the "folk" of many places and languages challenges the nationalizing narratives such anthologies are designed in part to promote. Songs similar to "The Bridge of Arta"—whose story, about a bridge that will only stand if the master builder sacrifices his wife in its foundations, could be understood as a disturbing allegory for the national project itself—have long circulated not just in Greece but across the Balkans, and have been drawn upon by numerous modern and contemporary writers, including Albanian Nobel laureate Ismail Kadare.[5] This doesn't make it any less a Greek song—or, at least, a Greek poem, in the textualized form presented in an anthology of poetry. But its Greekness also can't be held to contradict the Serbianness or the Albanianness of those other versions. In his collection, Politis treats "The Bridge of Arta" as a foundational text of the Greek tradition, claiming that the song was Greek first, and only subsequently "received" by the "other people [laoi] of the Greek peninsula (Romanians, Albanians, Serbs, and Bulgarians)" (214). Yet this was more the wishful thinking of a scholar with strong nationalist impulses—writing in 1914, just after the Balkan Wars and during a time of expansionist Greek politics—than an established truth.

One could argue that it is precisely the structural propensity of orature to frustrate the quest for origins and to resist closure—to continually come unwritten, as the song quoted in my epigraph would have it—that makes such attempts at monumentalization necessary for those working within a nationalizing framework. The genre of folk poetry, with its continual reartic-ulation of preexisting material both within and across songs, undermines

the many—Aromanian, Albanian, Turkish, Vlach, and so on—that were spoken in those territories at the time. See Mackridge (2009) for more on this issue.

5 See Armistead and Silverman (1963) for a discussion of the breadth of this song's occurrence throughout the region. For a discussion of the thematic importance of this song and the metaphor of the bridge to the literature of Greece and the Balkans, see Calotychos (2005; 2013: 93–120).

the very search for origins that these early collections presupposed. And it is not only the oral "origins" of these songs that makes them so difficult to pin down. On the contrary, as I argue in this chapter and in the book more broadly, transitioning from the oral to the written realm does not necessarily move a work from a condition of instability to one of stability: the textual condition, too, is one of iteration and variability. The gesture of containment represented by the reification of a particular set of texts remains in tension with the disseminating flux not only of the oral tradition, but of a print tradition as well—particularly a print tradition as translingual as the one these songs have known.

Romancing the nation: Nationalism and the philology of vernacular literature

There is some irony to the fervor with which ideas regarding nation formation, efforts to cultivate national literary production, and the rise of interest in folk culture spread through Europe in the late eighteenth and early nineteenth centuries: the interest in defining the borders of a nation, and in aligning those borders with the geographic reach of a peasantry who spoke versions of a particular language, was an indisputably international trend. From James Macpherson's pseudotranslations of the fabricated ancient Celtic poet Ossian during the 1760s, based partly on vernacular poetry but much more on material of his own invention, to Johann Gottfried von Herder's conceptualization of *das Volk* in his 1774 *Volkslieder* (*Folk Songs*), to Walter Scott's 1802 *Minstrelsy of the Scottish Border*, to Jacob and Wilhelm Grimm's 1812 *Kinder- und Haus-märchen* (*Childrens' and Household Tales*), to Théodore Hersart de La Villemarqué's 1839 collection of Breton folk songs *Barzaz Breiz* (*Ballads of Brittany*), intellectuals across Europe were formulating and promoting ideas concerning the link between language, the peasantry, and an often ill-defined territorial expanse.

All of these figures were educated. Many were multilingual. They read, translated, and responded to one another's work, and saw their writings and collections rapidly translated and imitated in turn. The national literatures whose development they fostered, however, were to be monolingual in languages codified and stabilized, in part, *by* these new literatures, while the folk they wrote about were understood and presented as a collective whose tales and songs sprung from nature rather than individual creativity: the voice they sang with was communal, timeless, and tied to the land on which they toiled. "As with ruins or manuscripts," writes Roger Abrahams of this newly imagined group, "their lives served as a palimpsest through which the past still might be dimly observed, perhaps even recovered." The peasantry, thus constructed, offered a prime ideological receptacle both for Romantic ideas about nature and for a sense of historical continuity that fed arguments for national sovereignty based on shared language and ethnic identity. By distributing the orature of this presumed folk—fairy tales, stories, jokes, songs, and the like—in highly mediated textual forms, learned elites drew on these rhetorical ties to nature, history, and the land, either to consolidate the gains of recent revolutions or to imagine the communities they hoped would soon take shape as political realities. "Thus," Abrahams continues, "the folk and their lore were enlisted in the nation-building cause, and the fact that the folk and their lore were the result of elitist social and cultural constructions was disregarded" (10).

In the interests of establishing national literatures for their languages, many European philologists went in search not just of folklore but of a national epic. Some in fact turned to orature as part of that latter search, or framed their finds in paratexts that presented folk poetry as a sort of fallen epic voice. Of Elias Lönnrot's construction of the *Kalevala*, the national epic of Finland, in the mid-nineteenth century, largely on the basis of oral poetry, André Lefevere writes that since "the dominant concept of 'world literature' of his time demanded that all literatures should begin with epics, Lönnrot did what he could to oblige within the context of Finnish language and culture, by creating a passable analogue" (1998: 82). (Lönnrot's resulting epic was not always treated as sacrosanct "original": subsequent translations, which ushered the *Kalevala* into a canon of world literature by prefacing it with introductions that compared it to the Homeric epics, felt free to significantly modify the text. Similarly, Jón Karl Helgason has shown how nineteenth- and even twentieth-century translators of Icelandic sagas—for which no "original," he argues, could ever really be identified—tailored them to suit a broader definition of what an epic should be, thus enabling their integration into a transnational literary canon (69).) Macpherson, who fabricated the figure of Ossian as a "Homer of the north," produced not one but two Ossianic epics for Scotland, and also translated the *Iliad* into "'Ossianic' prose-poetry."[6] In response to readers who challenged whether manuscripts for these poems really existed, he began translating his pseudotranslations into Gaelic in hopes of producing a believable set of pseudo-originals. These Gaelic

---

[6] Ruthven (2001: 9). Macpherson's first Ossianic work was the *Fragments of ancient poetry, collected in the Highlands of Scotland, and translated from the Gaelic or Erse language* (1760). Two Ossianic epics followed: *Finegal, an Ancient Epic Poem, in Six Books* (1762) and *Tomera* (1763); all three were collected as *The Works of Ossian* in 1765. His *Iliad of Homer* appeared in 1773.

translations were finished by friends after Macpherson's death and published in 1807, accompanied by a Latin translation—thus rendering Macpherson's pseudotranslations the originals for two translations at once, and making his fictional ancient Scottish bard speak the language of Virgil and Ovid. Macpherson's Ossian, while an extreme case, is not the only one in which philological material was concocted in support of a nationalist cause. Even literary products that were in fact largely based on actual vernacular materials were often an amalgam of invented and found material, with the latter shaped to accord with current literary or proto-ethnographic conventions.[7]

Some of this invention may have been prompted by the distance between collectors and their supposed folk subjects, which may have made some degree of elaboration seem necessary. While Herder, Scott, and the Grimms could all claim to belong to the language community (though certainly not the social class) of their respective folk, many of these early forays into folklore were conducted from afar, by Europeans living in countries distant from and writing in languages other than those they were writing about—a mode of philological work that, as Edward Said famously argued, was also fundamental to the Orientalist project.[8] In *National Dreams: The Remaking of Fairy Tales in Nineteenth-Century England*, Jennifer Schacker examines the confluence of literary translation and ethnography in the popularization of fairytales from other languages and places in nineteenth-century England. Schacker argues that these English versions of contemporaneous tales from elsewhere were treated even in the paratext to these volumes as "translations across time," encouraging readers to see literary and cultural differences "in progressive and chronological terms" (6). We see this approach most clearly in the frequent presentation of these supposedly lesser cultural specimens as children's literature in English. Moreover, the tales were taken not just as literature, but as informative pieces offering ethnographic details about the lives and customs of distant populations. This attitude helped consolidate an English middle-class sense of a collective self in opposition to groups of imagined, exotic others. Schacker notes, for instance, the oddity of Edward Lane's inclusion of notes in his *Arabian Nights* (1839–41) describing the Egyptians among whom he had briefly lived, as if this anecdotal information about current-day Egypt would provide readers a better understanding of the early modern Arabic culture that the tales were assumed to represent.

[7]   Mary-Ann Constantine, who writes about the admixture of found and invented material in early collections of Breton folk songs, points out that "literary works purporting to be in some sense primitive (either popular or very ancient) appeared in Sweden, England, Scotland, Wales, Russia, Czechoslovakia (in both Czech and Slovak), Bulgaria and Frisia; the list is by no means complete" (1996: 7).

[8]   See my discussion of Orientalism and the philological project of Assyriology in Chapter 1.

In many cases, the nationalist attempt to consolidate a corpus of folk poetry preceded the translation of those materials for consumption among speakers of other languages. In the case of Greece, however, European intellectuals with limited knowledge of modern Greek were the first to embrace a philological project of collecting and distributing folklore from the Greek-speaking people of the Ottoman Empire. The earliest publications of Greek folk songs came in the form of foreign translations and editions compiled by individuals at a geographical remove from any presumed folk subjects; these editions offered only the most general descriptions of oral performances, and almost never included musical notation.[9] The oral tradition thus begot a written one—and in fact a continually rewritten one, which spread via a series of translations that continued to circulate the songs far from their supposedly native linguistic, cultural, and even natural setting. The European discursive construction of Greece and the Greek folk also partook wholeheartedly in what Stathis Gourgouris has described as the "secular magic" of philhellenism, "perhaps one of the most audacious tricks of nineteenth-century European history, drawing extensively (but also furtively) upon the most characteristic ideological industries of the period (Orientalism and philology) to constitute its discursive order" (1996: 128). For the rest of Europe, Greece was significant primarily for its perceived relationship to *ancient* Greece; it was the protection of this imagined topos that encouraged their support of the Greek revolution. The philhellenist imagination celebrated an ancient Greek past and promoted the creation of a modern Greek state while simultaneously denigrating the current inhabitants of the land, whose long period of subjugation to the "Ottoman yoke" (an Orientalizing metaphor common in accounts of that time) had brought it too much under the sway of Eastern habits for European tastes. One of the primary loci of interest was in Greek folk poetry, understood as a living link between Homeric times and the debased current inhabitants of Greek lands, who were themselves remnants of an earlier, purer, but also more barbaric age. Greece stood both as the place of origin for European civilization, and as a battered, tainted land whose future depended on a resurrection of its past glory.

Of course even to speak of Greece, of Greeks, or of Greek in the early nineteenth century is arguably anachronistic, and certainly imprecise: where Greece was and where it should be, as well as what language its people should speak, was a matter of intense debate in the nineteenth and even well into the twentieth century. The Greek War of Independence against the Ottoman Empire began in 1821, with uprisings in the Peloponnese, the Danubian

---

[9] For an account of early collections of harmonized Greek folk songs, see Vlagopoulos (2016).

Principalities, Crete, and parts of the current Greek mainland; the 1832 Treaty of Constantinople resulted in a modern Greek state whose territory was quite limited, comprising less than a third of what it does now. As late as 1885, over half a century after the creation of the Greek state, the title and paratext of Lucy Garnett's *Greek Folk-Songs from the Turkish Provinces of Greece, Η δούλη Ἑλλάς [Enslaved Greece]: Albania, Thessaly, (Not yet Wholly Free,) and Macedonia* made irredentist claims, on behalf of Greece, to regions still outside the Greek state. Garnett's volume bore an impassioned dedication to the very people from whom the texts supposedly originated: to the "Hellenes of Enslaved Greece," with the wish that the act of translating these songs into English, "in giving some better knowledge of, and keener sympathy with, a people whose spirit and sentiment are still classical—may gain help for a last and successful struggle for the completion of Hellenic Independence."[10] The investment in the past in hopes of realizing a glorious future involved the invocation of a present Greek *laos*—Herder's *Volk*, or Garnett's "people," whose essentially classical spirit and sentiment had long been enslaved by an Eastern externality—as bearer of a historical continuity upon which that very resurrection depended. What was at stake for philhellenes was not only an origin story for Greece, but the conceptual shoring up of both revolutionary and national projects across Europe, understood here in opposition to the non-Christian, orientalized Ottoman Empire to the east.

Claude Fauriel and the making of modern Greek folk songs

The very first independent collection of modern Greek folk songs ever published in any place or language, and therefore an "original" in that sense, was Claude Fauriel's 1824 *Chants populaires de la Grèce moderne*, in two volumes that appeared some months apart. Fauriel's collection contributed to the cause of the Greek revolution by fueling interest across Europe in the habits, character, and heroic roots of the Greek people. It also contributed to the development of folklore studies, comparative philology, and ethnography (though Fauriel's approach was far removed from anything resembling what we would consider ethnographic research today). As one of the earliest collections of its kind, it also helped shape the form in which popular poetry translated from various languages was presented in France and beyond: Mary-Ann Constantine describes La Villemarqué's 1839 collection of Breton ballads as a "visual replica" of Fauriel's 1824 *Chants populaires* (187).

[10] Garnett (1885: n.p.)

Chants populaires de la Grèce moderne, whose title identifies the geographic source of these songs as a Greece that was still primarily a place of the imagination, contains roughly 125 texts in Greek, accompanied by prose translations in French. Its 137-page introduction describes the Greek peasantry's dress, agricultural methods, customs, wedding rituals, funeral rites, and so on, praising above all the habits and bravery of the klephts and armatoles, whose feats form the subject of many of the songs the collection presents. These armed, mountain-dwelling bands of men had been pockets of resistance against the Ottoman forces since the fifteenth century, and came to be identified with the Greek freedom fighters whose participation in the revolution of 1821 was crucial to its success. Fauriel himself had never visited the lands that would later become Greece, nor was he a terribly advanced speaker of modern Greek when he undertook this project, though like many in his cultural milieu he had excellent command of ancient Greek. In fact, both his study of modern Greek and his interest in Greek folk songs were born out of his research into the history of the epic: Fauriel collected, read, translated, and edited these texts as a way of learning modern Greek, and did so as part of a project that sought to draw an explicit link between ancient and modern Greek literary production—a goal that, we will see, colored the tone of his introduction, and encouraged a conflation of the ancient and modern inhabitants of these lands in an implicit and sometimes explicit narrative of continuity.

In his masterful study *H ανακάλυψη των ελληνικών δημοτικών τραγουδιών* (*The Discovery of the Greek Folk Songs*, 1984), Alexis Politis (grandson of Nikolaos Politis, and one of the most knowledgeable scholars working on Greek folk songs today) traces Fauriel's construction of his edition on the basis of earlier, unpublished collections, including a small compilation of songs by Swiss social scientist J. C. L. Simonde de Sismondi that circulated in manuscript beginning in the early nineteenth century, and a more extensive one that Prussian lawyer, scholar, and nobleman August von Haxthausen compiled shortly after. Fauriel, Sismondi, von Haxthausen, and other collectors of their time had some limited contact with Greek migrants in Europe, whose profile might have been made to match that of an imagined Greek folk. They also made use of songs written down by European travelers to Greece—or, rather, to regions of the Ottoman Empire that would later *become* Greece, where Greek was a dominant but by no means the only language.[11] Many such travelers published accounts of their

---

[11] See Mackridge (2009) for an account of the ethnic and linguistic makeup of these lands before the revolution, and the linguistic policy that shaped the nation going forward. See also footnote 4.

journeys, describing the shocking juxtaposition of the beautiful ruins of the ancient world and the fallen state of the region's current inhabitants. A fair number of these narratives included at least a handful of translated songs. Yet most of the early collectors' sources were ethnic Greeks of the merchant class living in Europe and the Mediterranean, who assisted in the production of these collections with what one might generously describe as mixed feelings. In 1804 when a French publisher planning to publish a travel memoir asked Smyrna-born Parisian scholar Adamantios Korais to correct the Greek texts of a handful of songs that would appear in the book, Korais obliged, but also responded (in my translation from Korais's French), "I only regret that they are not more worthy of being translated, for as you see, they are quite detestable."[12] Over fifteen years earlier, in 1788, when another French acquaintance asked Korais to provide him with a few songs, Korais wrote to a friend in Smyrna, this time in Greek: "Please send me three or four songs, the best you can find; it would be preferable if they had no Turkish words, or at least very few [...] and please make sure everything is properly spelled."[13]

Korais, whom Fauriel acknowledges in his preface as a source for many of the songs, played a crucial role in the prolonged debate known as the "language controversy" regarding what should be used as the official language of the Greek state. Some argued for a modified form of the demotic Greek then spoken by ordinary (or educated) people; others argued for an archaizing form called *katharevousa*, which would cleanse the language of Turkish influence while reviving elements of ancient Greek grammar, syntax, and vocabulary. Korais is famous for promoting a "middle way" between these two camps. Given the regional, dialect character of many folk songs, Korais's distaste for them is not surprising, nor is his insistence on "proper" spelling and his desire for texts free of Turkish words. Korais's attempts to shape this material in order to make a good impression on European audiences could be considered a form of soft censorship, on linguistic and aesthetic grounds but with political consequences, since European governments would certainly play a role in shaping Greece's fate. Informants such as Korais were thus selective about what material they shared. As diasporic merchants and intellectuals, they were also at a significant remove from any potential scene of folk cultural production. Even those informants living in lands where Greek was spoken sometimes offered texts for songs they had probably never heard performed: another of Fauriel's primary collaborators, the Corfiot Andreas Mustoxidis (whose primary language was Italian, not

---

[12] Quoted in Politis (1984: 73). The memoir was by François Pocqueville, and was subsequently translated into English in 1806.
[13] Quoted in Politis (2010: 241).

Greek), willingly provided Sismondi with a text of a song from Mani at Sismondi's particular request, though Mustoxidis had likely never been to that remote region of the Peloponnese.[14]

In short, the texts in Fauriel's collection are several degrees removed from anything that might pass as an "authentic" song as performed by a member of the Greek *laos*—if we can even assume the existence of this folk to precede the moment of its discursive formation. Fauriel's own editing of the songs, moreover, was not insignificant. Neither Fauriel nor others of his time, Alexis Politis writes, "seem to have been aware of the problem of presenting oral literature"—a term that already divorces the songs from their musical component—"in a textual form." On the contrary, "supplementing one version with parts of another, choosing eclectically between two different 'readings' (*leçon* is the word he uses), correcting perceived errors on the part of the speaker, converting an idiomatic text into standard modern Greek, and generally fixing up the text before it is handed over to the user, were all more than self-evident in those days" (1984: 290). For instance, in his introduction, Fauriel notes that Greeks tend not to pronounce the final "n" on nouns and verbs. "My intention," he writes, "was likewise to omit the 'n' in my printed texts, and to follow exactly the spelling of the vulgar pronunciation. However, as most Greeks whom I consulted concerning my project assured me that this spelling, entirely uncommon both in writing and in books, would shock their compatriots, I necessarily deferred to their opinion" (Fauriel 1824, iii). This statement points again to the class division between supposed producers and procurers of these songs: the compatriots who would be shocked by the absence of a final "n" from the Greek texts in a Frenchman's edition of folk songs could only be learned Greeks of the class who provided these texts, as opposed to the peasants (presumably illiterate, and not likely to come across Fauriel's Parisian publication) who would swallow their "n"s to begin with. In the end, Fauriel's stated early intention to "follow exactly the spelling of the vulgar pronunciation" gives way to Korais's (and others') insistence that "everything is properly spelled"—*properly* referring, here, to an adherence to an ideologically weighted orthographic system, rather than a reproduction of the sound of a (hypothesized) oral performance.

In other words, Fauriel modified the songs in order to make them accord more closely to readerly expectations for written texts. He also framed them as descriptive of the everyday lives of a Greek folk, present or past. We see this, first and foremost, in his organization of the songs into the sub-genres

---

[14] For a thorough account of Mustoxidis's involvement in the collection of Greek folk songs, see Politis (1984) as well as Konstantina Zanou's *Transnational Patriotism in the Mediterranean, 1800–1830: Stammering the Nation*, forthcoming from Oxford University Press.

"klephtic," "historical," "fictional," and "household": the "fictional" songs are separated out from the rest, which are treated as informative sources of historical or anthropological information about Greek life or history. At the same time, Fauriel recognized that the enjoyment of these texts also depended on some amount of prior knowledge regarding the places and people they depicted. Since the klephtic songs "refer to a social reality without the knowledge of which they would lose much of their clarity and nearly all of their interest" (Fauriel 1824, xliii), his introduction provides page after page of information about the armed bands of mountain-dwelling klephts: about their diet, their dress, their strength and courage, their place in the broader society as well as their internal social hierarchy. Again, these descriptions are not the result of ethnographic research in the field. Rather, his information was gathered from the same sorts of individuals who provided the songs: ethnic Greeks living in Europe and the Mediterranean, whose knowledge of the klephts was probably more the stuff of legend than anything else. Yet Fauriel seems not to have considered this distinction between legend and historical fact entirely relevant: "A collection such as this one, if it were complete, would be at the same time the true national history of modern Greece, and the most faithful depiction of the customs of her inhabitants. Whatever indefinite or mistaken element one song might have, other songs would correct or enlighten; such that the collective result would be clear and complete, even if each part were partial or dark" (Fauriel 1824, xxv).

The completion of this "true national history" is not merely a philological but also an obliquely political affair. Fauriel's primary reason for compiling his collection, he writes in the opening passage of his introduction, is to "offer certain new evidence that would help us evaluate more justly and accurately than is usually done, the customs, the character, and the genius of contemporary Greeks." This hint at the negative portrayals common in travelers' accounts becomes more explicit as the introduction progresses:

> For over four centuries now, European intellectuals speak of Greece only to mourn the loss of her ancient civilization, travel to Greece only in search of ruins... . As for the seven or eight million inhabitants, remnants to be sure, living remnants of the ancient inhabitants of this beloved land—there matters change. Intellectuals pay them no heed, or speak of them only in passing, to characterize them as a debased race, fallen so far as to deserve only the contempt or pity of cultured people. If one were to take seriously the arguments of most intellectuals, one might almost believe that the modern Greeks are something incongruous and unholy, tossed here and there among the holy relics

of ancient Greece, to ruin the view and the impression obtained by the rational admirers who visit her now and then.

Caught up as they are in a point of view so pedantic, the wise people of Europe did not simply commit an injustice against modern Greece. They also did something that goes entirely against their own most treasured desire: they denied themselves ways of coming to know ancient Greece more thoroughly, of better discovering the most exceptional, clean and indelible qualities contained in the character and spirit of these children of this happy land. (vii–viii)

Just a few years later, in his 1830 *Geschichte der Halbinsel Morea während des Mittelalters* (*History of the Morea Peninsula during the Middle Ages*), German historian Jakob Philipp Fallmerayer would crystalize many of the negative views of modern Greeks that were then in circulation. His widely influential treatise claimed that the modern inhabitants of these lands were descendants not of the ancient Greeks but of Slavs who migrated south sometime in the middle of the first millennium. For Fallmerayer and many other Europeans of the day, the presence of these barbarians in a landscape of prized ancient ruins was "incongruous and unholy" indeed.

While Fauriel is clearly writing against such views, and in support of a modern Greece that was at this point only a thing of the imagination, he also engages in some of the very rhetoric for which he criticizes other European intellectuals. In linking the people of Greece to a prior stage of development as well as to the land—as *enfants* of that *heureuse terre*—Fauriel both infantilizes and primitivizes the modern Greeks, positing them as objects of anthropological, even quasi-archaeological interest. He also describes them as interesting precisely because of the information they can provide about the ancients. Fauriel turns the inhabitants of Greece into a cultural missing link; travelers interested in visiting the ruins of ancient Greece are encouraged not to overlook the most curious ruin of all, the Greek people, those "living remnants of the ancient inhabitants of this beloved land." In presenting ancient Greece as the origin of modern Greece, and the ancient epic as the origin of the modern folk song, Fauriel is drawing on a philhellenic rhetorical strain that long predates him. Throughout his introduction, Fauriel's praise of the material he presents is also entirely in keeping with Romantic celebrations of the *Volk* in its many translingual guises: the songs represent "immediate and genuine expressions of a national character and national spirit, which every Greek feels with love, solely because he is Greek, plants his feet on the soil and breathes the air of Greece; a poetry that lives, not the false life of books, which often only appears to be a life, but within the people itself, and in the collective life of the people" (xxv). This "national spirit" both precedes and, he seems to suggest, will inevitably give rise to the nation itself. It is natural; it arises from the land; it passes inevitably from that land into the people connected metonymically to it, for whom living oral poetry is the primary mode of "immediate and pure expression," albeit presented here in the false form of a printed book.

Fauriel refers only obliquely to the armed struggle for independence underway at the time his collection was published. Yet, as Beaton has argued, "Whether or not the 1821 uprising provided the initial stimulus for Fauriel's work, it is certain that its prompt publication and instant success came largely as a consequence of political events in Greece" (6). And Fauriel was not alone in bringing folk songs into discussions of the social and political reality of revolutionary Greece. In 1826, Olivier Voutier, a French naval officer who had left his post to fight in the Greek War of Independance, published a collection of letters written during his time in Greece, recounting his experiences there; the volume ends with seven folk songs in Greek and in French translation, which Voutier presents in his letters as faithful depictions of the travails of the Greek fighters. "I have promised you war songs, madame," he writes in one letter from Missolonghi in 1824, "and am sending you an interesting one, which offers a complete picture of the siege which we have supported in this place in 1882."[15]

While the connections Fauriel draws between the songs and historical reality are not nearly as particular, he too shares in this understanding of the songs as, at heart, deeply descriptive of the Greek past and present alike, hearkening as well toward a future yet to come. A complete collection of songs, Fauriel claimed, would provide "a true history of Greece from since it was enslaved," through which "one would see that there was always a persecuted Greece in the mountains, worthy daughter of ancient Greece"; this collection would be "a true *Iliad* of modern Greece, which could stand by the side of the old" (Fauriel 1824, cxxxix). While the people of Greece may have been debased through their enslavement by the Turks, a true Greece worthy of her ancient forebear still persists in the mountains, gathering strength and preparing to reemerge. The *Iliad*, which supposedly records the far-distant facts of one great war, is rhetorically deployed in defense of the ongoing collection of folk songs, which will, with any luck, bolster the new war of which these songs are harbingers. In such a manner, following the release of Fauriel's volume, "the cause of Greek folk poetry and that of Greek nationalism became inseparably linked" (Beaton: 6). This linkage would become even more pronounced in the several translations based on Fauriel's collection that quickly followed.

---

[15] Voutier's *Lettres sur la Grèce, notes en chants populaires* was published in Paris in 1826, with profits intended to support the establishment of a new Greek state. 50.

Translations of versions of translations of versions: Charles Sheridan's *The Songs of Greece* (1825)

Within months of its publication in Paris,[16] Fauriel's *Chants populaires* had become the basis for several further editions in other languages. None was as extensive as Fauriel's two-volume edition, and most took a stronger stance in support of the revolution. (One exception is classical scholar Nikolai Gnedich, best known for his Russian verse translation of the *Iliad*. The paratext to his small volume of twelve klephtic songs, *Prostonarodnye pesni nyneshnikh grekov* (*Folk Songs of the Contemporary Greeks*), focuses on elucidating the Homeric epics and offering a foundation for the development of a Russian national literature—the former, of course, fully in keeping with Fauriel's original impetus for his project.)[17] Wilhelm Müller's *Neugriechiesche Volkslieder, Gesammelt und Herausgegeben von C. Fauriel* (*Modern Greek Folk Songs, Collected and Edited by C. Fauriel*) presented thirty-four klephtic songs in its first volume and another nineteen fictional songs in the second (in keeping with to Fauriel's classification). Müller's introduction places these texts squarely within the German Romantic discourse around *das Volk*, which he sees as not merely a national but an international phenomenon: he mentions Johann Wolfgang van Goethe on the first page and praises Fauriel's collection as "among the most important extensions of the poetic world horizon" (vii). While Müller, like Fauriel, does not explicitly discuss the Greek uprising in his paratext, his support of the Greek cause is visible elsewhere. A few years prior to the publication of Fauriel's volume, Müller had begun issuing a series of what would become six collections of his own poems, titled *Lieder der Griechen* (*Songs of the Greeks*, 1821–7), written from the points of view of various Greek figures, from an island boy to a mother in Mani to a Phanariot Greek of Constantinople. Some of Müller's persona poems openly attacked those in Germany who did not support the Greek cause, while his notes to these volumes were explicit to the point of courting censorship in their advocacy of German intervention into Greek affairs.[18] In France, just a few months after Fauriel's collection was published, Népomucène-Louis Lemercier used sixty-five of Fauriel's prose translations to produce his own versions in verse, again focusing on the klephtic songs, which were most easily enlisted in support of the Greek national struggle. At the end of the first volume, Lemercier expressed his hope that his "feeble pen

[16] The first volume appeared in June, the second in December of 1824, though the latter was dated 1825.
[17] For a description of Gneditch's volume and his work as a classical scholar, see Prousis (1994: 94–104).
[18] See Guthenke (2008: 116–40).

[might accelerate] the development of the spirit of Greek liberty" (190)—a spirit he sought to cultivate, of course, primarily in France, or at least in French.

Arguably the most extreme politicization of the songs came in Charles Brinsley Sheridan's *The Songs of Greece, From the Romaic Text, Edited by M. C. Fauriel, with Additions* (1825). Sheridan's vociferous support of the Greek revolutionary cause both preceded and prompted his interest in the folk culture of that language and land. Son of playwright and statesman Richard Brinsley Sheridan, the younger Sheridan had already published his *Thoughts on the Greek Revolution*, in which he encouraged British and European intervention in the struggle.[19] In 1823, he published a translation of the provisional 1822 constitution of rebelling Greece, along with "several spirited state papers," in a pamphlet which, as we glean from a comment in his preface to *The Songs of Greece*, had not exactly been flying off the shelves: "finding the edition too large," he writes, "I have now directed the publishers of these translations, to sell [the pamphlet] for three [shillings]" instead of five (1825: lxix). From start to finish, Sheridan's volume wears its political motivations on its sleeve. His introduction explicitly presents this volume as a collection "not so much of beautiful poems, as of historical documents, which prove the capacity of the Greeks to defend and govern their country, and, consequently, the injustice of shackling their freedom with the condition of receiving a foreign sovereign" (xviii). Sheridan is quite specific in his proposals regarding the possible terms of a treaty, the borders of the future Greek state, and the stance Britain should take toward it, both before and after independent statehood is achieved. But while he insists that Greeks are capable of defending and governing their country, they are certainly not to be left entirely to their own devices; *some* foreign hand is still needed. Sheridan promises, for that reason, to use the profits of his *Songs* to help found a Society for the Promotion of Education in Greece, whose aim will be to "diffus[e] the blessings of Christianity and education in Greece" (vi). "Instruction, and more explicitly religious instruction," he warns the members of the Greek Committee in London to whom his book is dedicated, "is the only means of preventing modern from being torn by factions like ancient Greece. If you now lose sight of Greece, you leave your task but half done" (viii)—rhetoric familiar to those in the U.S. from our own recent military embroilments. Both Sheridan's paratext and his translations are firmly oriented toward the twin goals of first liberating and

---

[19] This 1822 book is identified on the title page as a "second edition," but I can find no record of a first edition having preceded it; it was also included as number 24 of *The Pamphleteer* in 1824.

then re-forming the Greek people, preferably in the image of their more properly Christian (i.e., not Eastern Orthodox) British brethren. Even the pagan ancients, whose glorious culture is an inspiration, are not wholly free from censure; the modern Greeks must take instruction from their British contemporaries, too.

If Fauriel had only a novice's knowledge of modern Greek when he began collecting and translating his texts, Sheridan couldn't claim even that much. "I have been too much occupied in translating," he writes, "to find much time to learn [Greek]; and have been largely indebted to M. Fauriel's excellent version" (xxxix). If this offhanded admission of his ignorance of the language from which he is translating comes as a shock to contemporary readers, so too may his readiness to "remodell the songs" (xxxvi) on a textual level. Sheridan frequently edits out lengthy passages, seemingly in accordance with his understanding of how good poetry should read, rather than how good songs should sound—and, in particular, songs belonging to a tradition with a highly structured set of lexical and melodic conventions. His translations reduce repetition both within and across texts, removing in the process many of the formulaic elements that are hallmarks of an oral tradition. Sheridan has little patience for "that eternal bird" (85) that sings with a human voice in the opening lines of many songs, and generally cuts those passages from his texts. He compresses one song of 124 long lines into a version only half that length, and leaves out the last six lines of another, judging them "a worthless conceit unaccountably stuck there to spoil the whole" (132). His hand is equally free when it comes to adding material. While his notes preceding "Vevros and his War-Horse" admit that "the translation is not *quite* literal, being a *little* simplified" (149), he doesn't mention having added two stanzas to the text, nearly doubling its overall length and modifying its narrative progression. A close comparison of his texts with those of Fauriel proves that this approach is fairly consistent throughout Sheridan's collection.

It would be incongruous, however, for me to take Sheridan to task for his rather freewheeling approach to representing a set of texts that themselves are taken to represent the ever-changing products of an oral tradition. After all, one goal of this book is to challenge the notion that textuality brings stability, and the judgment that translations are necessarily wrong or bad simply because they refashion certain aspects of texts they are translating. What interests me here are the particular concerns that inspire Sheridan's rewritings—concerns that seem obviously political in nature. Take, for instance, his translation of "Stathas," a brief narrative poem describing a battle at sea between Greeks and Turks. In Fauriel's edition, the last stanza appears thus, accompanied by his French prose translation (and between the two, my English translation of the Greek):

Οι Τούρκοι βόλταν έρρηξαν, κ' εγύρισαν την πρώραν.
Πρώτος ο Ιάννης πέταξε με το σπαθί 'ς το χέρι.
'Σ τα βούνια τρέχουν αίματα, θάλασσα κοκκινίζει·
Αλλά! αλλά! οι άπιστοι κράζοντες, προσκυνούνε.

[The Turks fired a shot, and they turned the prow.
First Iannis jumped with sword in hand.
Blood flows in the drains, the sea turns red;
Crying Allah! Allah! the heathens pray.]

Les Turks virent de bord; ils tournent la proue. — Jean aborde le premier, le sabre à la main: — le sang court sur le lest; la mer devient rouge; — et les infidèles se rendent en criant: Alla! Alla! (14–15)

Sheridan's version, written in strong iambs with end rhymes on some lines, fleshes out this compact narrative and adds an ending as exuberant in its typography (a literate rather than oral device) as it is explicit in its attribution of victory to the Greeks—or, rather, to Hellas:

The Brig bore bravely up,
    And near'd her sable Foe.

They touch – the Grecians board –
    With Stathas at their head –
Carnage has choked the deck.
    And Ocean's self is red!

That bloody flag is *down*,
    That turban'd host are *slaves!*
Hellas has smote the Turk
    Upon her native waves! (12)

In the Greek text presented in Fauriel's edition, it is the Turks who fire a cannon and turn the prow of their ship; the Turks also have the last word, albeit one of mournful prayer. In Sheridan's version, all the action is reserved for the Greeks: there is no Turkish volley; the Greek rather than the Turkish ship bravely approaches the enemy vessel; the "Grecians" board that other ship, and a personified "Hellas" herself smites the Turk and regains control of her "native waters." Sheridan thus adds a decisive victory for Greece and silences altogether the interloping and now enslaved "turban'd host," removing the Turks' prayers to Allah that end the song in Fauriel's Greek and French versions.

    It is possible that Sheridan relied upon Lemercier's versions of Fauriel's translations in composing his own. The last lines of Lemercier's version of "Stathas" read as follows:

Les càbles, à la fois, lancés des deux vaisseaux,
De la proue à la proue enchainent ces rivaux.
Stathas vole; et déjà l'homicide abordage
Rougit de sang les ponts, les mâts, les flots amers.
Le Turc n'a de recours, dans l'horreur du carnage,
　　Que l'horreur des gouffres ouverts.
Alla! Son dernier cri signale son naufrage;
Et l'Hellène en vainqueur franchit les vastes mers. (66)

[The cables, thrown from both ships at once
String these rivals prow to prow.
Stathas flies; and the carnage on board
Bloodies the bridges, masts, and bitter waves.
The Turk is helpless, horrified by the carnage—
Let the horror of the open chasms.
Allah! His final cry signaled his shipwreck;
And the conquering Hellene crossed the vast seas.]

Here Lemercier, too, fleshes out the scene, outfitting the ships with cables and masts. He, too, chooses iambs and rhyme to represent the unrhymed fifteen-syllable lines of the Greek (the traditional meter used in most folk songs). He, too, sinks the Ottoman ship and has the Greeks traverse the vast seas. Regardless of whether we can ascertain lines of influence, one thing is certain: neither Lemercier nor Sheridan treats translation as a word-for-word or even phrase-for-phrase affair. Rather, they see their task as allowing for substantial expansion, including the drafting of entire stanzas that narrate events not accounted for in the text they purport to be translating. Both translators' additions also reflect an ideological or political desire to bestow liberty—if only a narrative liberty—on the Greek brigands. In fact, though the song was, he admits, "probably written a century since" (a choice of verb that textualizes the song, perhaps inadvertently), Sheridan explicitly tailors the nautical details of his amplified version of "Stathas" so as to make the action reflect the current conflict:

> The Greek vessel is, in the original, a Corvette (Κορβεία). This is probably not owing to the cacophony of Βριγ (Brig), for the details of all the songs in this class, belonging rather to history than poetry, are scrupulously true; but to the circumstances of the Greeks of that period not employing Brigs; to which they were driven by a heavy tax upon ships. Their largest craft are now Brigs, and I have substituted the word from a wish that this song should be applied to what is now passing on the waters of the Levant. (12)

As with other such texts, Sheridan takes the song as an accurate representation of an actual moment of combat, a "description of a naval engagement"
that belongs "rather to history than to poetry," and whose every detail is
"scrupulously true." At the same time, he feels free to abandon that scrupu-
lousness in his own version, gladly updating the brigands' gear so as to
incorporate the activity of the poem into the then-current moment of the
Greek revolutionary struggle.

If we judge Sheridan's text according to what Lawrence Venuti calls
the "canons of accuracy" (2013: 13) that currently obtain in the Anglo-
American sphere, his work will likely be found wanting: he routinely adds
narrative material, cuts freely, and alters countless details to make the songs
align more neatly with his political objectives. Yet what some might call
Sheridan's infidelities are motivated by an underlying sense of responsibility
to a different timeless "original": the Greek *laos* itself, inhabitants of a land
whose "soil and climate [...] are singularly favourable to the perfection of
man's physical and moral qualities," of that "hilly and arid speck" that stood
"the primary source of civilization over the entire globe" (ilxiv). Sheridan's
rewritings are best understood in the context of his broader attempt to
encourage his British readers (a group that, given his recently deceased
father's three decades in Parliament, likely included men of influence in
government affairs) to support, materially and otherwise, the formation of
a new Greek state. His translations are thus invested less in the "originals"
before him than in a hoped-for moment of future origination, a project
that colors his views both of the songs themselves and of his own task of
translation.

Sheridan's specific political objectives were not necessarily shared by
other collectors and translators of his day. Yet the politicization of Greek folk
songs continues to be a primary feature of subsequent collections, including
Greek-language editions that use these songs to support arguments about
the role of the modern Greek language in the nascent Greek state and the
relationship of contemporary Greeks to former inhabitants of the same
lands. These Greek editions display, I argue, a deepening tension between
the unstable nature of oral *and* print traditions and the use of these songs
to promote the stabilization of a Greek polity. We see, in fact, an attempt to
create the subjects of that polity via the dissemination of a nationalized story
of what these songs are, and of what role their language should play in a
Greek nation in the process of becoming.

Fauriel comes "home"

The first collections published by ethnic Greeks did not appear in print for another three decades: 1850 and 1852 saw Antonios Manousos's *Τραγούδια εθνικά* (*National Songs*) and Spyridon Zambelios's *Άσματα δημοτικά της Ελλάδος, Εκδοθέντα μετά μελέτης ιστορικής περί μεσαιωνικού ελληνισμού* (*Folk Songs of Greece, Published with a Historical Study Concerning Medieval Hellenism*) printed on the island of Corfu, which was then ruled by the British and joined the new nation only in 1862. While these volumes are quite different from one another in form and as regards their stance on the language controversy, they share both a nationalist interest in reevaluating Greek folk cultural production and a reliance on Fauriel's *Chants populaires*. It is perhaps understandable that Fauriel's Greek texts would repeatedly be used in these and later Greek collections, often without acknowledgment—after all, as folk material they belonged to no one in particular, and certainly not to a Frenchman. Yet Fauriel's critical apparatus was likewise mined for material, with extensive passages from his introduction and notes silently translated and incorporated into these Greek-language editions. Perhaps just as importantly, the very fact that Fauriel and other European intellectuals had taken an interest in Greek folk culture was often used to justify the printed circulation of these songs for an audience of ethnically Greek readers, and to mark their importance on a decidedly national(izing) stage.

Manousos's 1850 collection is a case in point. Published in the context of the intense debate among Greek intellectuals concerning what form of the Greek language should be used in the nascent state, Manousos's volume takes a strong and explicit stance in favor of the everyday language of the people, and presents these poems as the basis for a new national literature in demotic Greek. In keeping with his ideological support of the language of everyday spoken encounters, he opens not with a formal introduction but with the script of a fictional dialogue in demotic Greek, which begins as follows (presented, of course, in my translation):[20]

> *Man of the folk*: Excuse me, is it true that you are printing our songs?
> *Editor*: Well, I'm publishing them, through the press. Why? Do you want to make some complaint?

---

[20] See my discussion of Korais and the language controversy above. For an excellent English-language account of this debate, see Mackridge (2009). The form of the dialogue in Manousos's volume is undoubtedly influenced by the "Dialogue on Language" of Dionysios Solomos, his (Italian-speaking) contemporary on the Ionian islands who is now considered the national poet of Greece.

Other man of the folk: Of course not! How could you think it? We're
illiterate; that's none of our business!

Editor: You're wrong, my friends, these are your creations, it is the
overflowing of your souls, and no one is better able than you to hear
them, to correct their omissions and their flaws.

Other: That may be, but we didn't come here to correct you, only to do
our duty and thank you for making them public and praising songs
we sing during the sweetest hours of our lives, when we're relaxing,
a glass in one hand and an arm around our sweetheart, when we
forget our troubles and suffering and find solace and pleasure in
song.

Editor: I accept your thanks, as a kind gift rather than a duty. To be sure,
the duty is all mine, and that of all Greeks with some education and
breeding—who, if they love their nation with their hearts, should
study it, protect it, and not leave its glorious creations uncared for.
Italians, French, Germans, and Englishmen, all people of talent, have
recognized the great worth of these songs. Foreigners embrace our
Ethnos, and dedicate much effort and expense, attention and respect
to collecting, studying, and translating these songs, and have printed
them to resounding praise.

Other: He speaks wisely, and it breaks my heart to hear our dear
Father Gerasimus say that not only every foreign ethnos, but every
foreign nation has its history, its literature, biographies of its great
and talented men, and not just one or two, but ten or twenty, and
we still have nothing, or if we do, it's in foreign languages that we
can't read. They call us Greeks, or Hellenes, but we don't even know
what Greek means, what the Greeks did, or how much a Greek is
worth! (3–4)

I quote this passage at length because it embodies so clearly the issues I
have been discussing: the romanticization of orature as the outpouring
of natural peasant feeling; the class divisions between those who perform
these songs and those who print and circulate them; the gap between ethnos
and nation, which many ethnic Greeks sought to close, though not always
in the same way; and the rhetorical use of foreign interest to cultivate
local interest in Greek folk culture. The editor in this dialogue describes
his work as reflecting the duty of all learned Greeks—whose education,
of necessity, has taken place outside the newly formed Greece, among the
very Italians, French, Germans, and Englishmen he mentions as the first
to print these songs—to protect and care for the products of folk culture,
in part by promoting an interest in them among a class of literate Greeks.

Their task is to transform folk culture into a discursive field, cultivating a particular kind of Greekness in the process. Foreign collections, studies, and translations become a legitimizing force for Greek culture at home—a Greek culture that is called upon to imitate, in form if not in content, the cultural production of distant nations: histories, literatures, biographies of great and talented men.

The last statement attributed above to the second "man of the folk" is particularly ironic: he parrots the words of a priest, which dovetail with the opinions of the editor, which themselves rest on the pronouncements of foreigners. This presumably monolingual and self-proclaimedly illiterate "man of the folk"[21] is thus shown to have internalized the notion that a national literature or history, or even a sense of what Greekness is, can be consolidated only in written form—a form the supposed folk might have difficulty reading even were it to be published in demotic Greek. Meanwhile, this implicit rebuke of the Greek nation for not having a national culture is marshaled in support of a folk culture that will later be seen as needing not promotion but protection, as the nation continues to develop, acquiring educational institutions and a written literature of its own, which will in turn threaten the vitality of the oral poetry here celebrated.

Manousos's championing of demotic Greek in this introduction is not, then, a simple call to celebrate the everyday, spoken languge manifested in these songs. Rather, it represents an effort to incorporate an appreciation of folk cultural production into a written language and literature that are still in the process of becoming, along the model of other European national vernaculars. Manousos's paratext also gives space to an imagined ideological opponent: the remainder of his introductory dialogue consists of a debate between the editor and "wiser-than-thou Sir Swollen Tongue" (ο πανσοφωλογιώτατος Κυρ Πρησκολογάς), a caricatured supporter of the "purified" language of *katharevousa*. Sir Swollen Tongue—who speaks the most swollen of tongues, a comically exaggerated version of the archaizing syntax, grammar, and vocabulary of this invented form of Greek—arrives on the scene to praise the editor for his work, but also to chastise him for his belief that demotic Greek can become a language of learning and of national affairs. The editor, of course, has the last word. In his final speech, he

---

[21] The rhetorical construction of the Greek peasantry as monolingual, illiterate speakers of demotic Greek is a central feature of arguments in favor of the choice of that language as the official language of the new Greek state. See, again, Mackridge (2009) for an account of the many languages and dialects spoken in the region around the time of the revolution. The Ionian islands were a special case, given Venetian and then British rule; many inhabitants, particularly of the upper classes, used Italian as much as if not more than Greek as a language of everyday written and spoken interaction, and even peasants would have had exposure to Italian as well.

recognizes the relationship of modern to ancient Greek and the significance of the philhellenic spirit, while also arguing that the modern language must be nurtured into maturity rather than forced into the unnatural position of mimicking its linguistic progenitor: "Our language is naturally beautiful, because she is the daughter of the language that became beloved by all the enlightened nations of Europe, but she is still in her infancy. She can't yet show either her graces or her full stature, nor the shades of meaning that will ornament once she reaches her maturity" (Manousos 1850: 14).

The incorporation of this debate into the prefatory material to Manousos's collection shifts the terrain of these songs' reception into the locally politicized context of the language controversy. Manousos makes the case for a national literature based on demotic Greek, and in fact seeks to provide one of the foundational documents of this literature, both in the folk songs and in the quasiliterary form of his introduction. Strikingly, though Sir Swollen Tongue insists volubly on the fallen, debased nature of the Greek folk and the need to change their habits by strictly enforcing the use of an archaizing tongue, even he admits the importance of these songs, precisely because they have been praised by foreign writers and scholars: "Given that this is the opinion of foreign authors, I am consequently obliged to honor [the songs] and to praise the very idea of this valuable volume of the songs you have gathered from our ethnos" (7). Indeed, all four of these characters, from the representatives of the folk, to the learned editor, to the prating Sir Swollen Tongue, channel the praise of foreigners. This is not as surprising as it may at first seem, in a book so nationalist in its impulses. Just as arguments for the importance of demotic Greek found models in defenses of vernacular languages and literatures elsewhere, so too did proponents of *katharevousa* co-opt the rhetoric about ancient and modern Greece that we saw shaping the foreign editions of folk songs I discussed above. And of course the work of those foreign scholars is central to Manousos's enterprise: nearly all the texts in his volume are taken either from Fauriel's collection or from the fourth volume of Niccolò Tommaseo's *Canti Popolari toscani, corsi, illirici e greci* (*Popular Songs of Tuscany, Corsica, Illyria and Greece*, 1843), who likewise adopts many of Fauriel's texts.

Manousos doesn't rely only on the texts for these songs: his notes also make liberal use of these foreign scholars' paratextual materials. As when a student properly cites a passage or two to deflect a professor's attention from a far more pervasive plagiarism, Manousos's passing references to Fauriel and Tommaseo seem designed to conceal the fact that nearly every word in the volume is translated from one or the other—or, not infrequently, both. Yet, as with Sheridan, to chide Manousos for improper use of others' work might be to judge him on the basis of an anachronistic understanding of intellectual property. Manousos's appropriation of paratextual material from Fauriel and Tommaseo, while extreme, is not unprecedented. We have already seen above how other foreign scholars drew on the information offered in Fauriel's introduction—information that was, like the songs themselves, likewise culled from unnamed sources. Moreover, Fauriel's edition made similar use of the unpublished collections of Sismondi, von Haxthausen, and others, who may themselves have had prior manuscript collections at their disposal. Just as the oral tradition involves an iterative proliferation of versions both within and across languages, so too does the formation of a *print* tradition for these songs. In fact, one could argue that the patterns of print circulation of these songs reproduce, in a way, the iterative possibilities of the oral tradition, demonstrating a curious tension between the textual reification of particular versions and the fairly free hand with which editors and translators sometimes treat the materials they inherit or coopt.

In the opening dialogue in Manousos's collection, the editor invites the representatives of the Greek folk to "correct" any "omissions or errors" in the texts he presents. In declining that invitation, these fictional characters may articulate as well as anyone the divide between an oral and a literate understanding of what the songs are. The rhetoric of correction, omissions, and errors used by Manousos's fictional editor belongs to a literate world that presupposes a correct, complete, identifiable whole to which these texts could be compared. The oral circulation of songs in which the "men of the folk" participate, on the other hand, belongs to a cultural economy that recognizes variance as legitimate and in fact prizes improvisational flexibility. In this sense, the correction of texts is, indeed, "none of [their] business." But while these folk characters decline to edit the texts of "their" songs, and while Manousos himself uses largely unaltered texts from Fauriel and Tommaseo, similar texts did undergo editing by other, literate Greeks— including Zambelios, whose collection appeared a mere two years later. Like Manousos, Zambelios takes many of his texts from Fauriel and Tommaseo. Yet unlike Manousos, he substantially alters many of them, somewhat along the lines of Sheridan's interventions, emphasizing their folk nature while also underscoring the heroic aspect of the tales they tell. Even the titles he chooses highlight the bravery and fighting spirit of the Greeks: a poem Fauriel calls "Nanos's Lesson" becomes (once again, through the lens of my translation) "The Art of the Klephts"; "Stergios" is rendered "The Untamed Klepht"; "Mt. Olympos" becomes "Greek Freedom"; and "The Parting" becomes "The Brave Beloved."

Zambelios's altered versions were significant for the history of Greek folklore studies, given their popularity and frequent reproduction. For instance, in his 1860 Ρωμαίικα Τραγούδια (*Romaic Songs*), a critical edition that cross-references Greek versions from multiple print collections and later became a key source for Nikolaos Politis's 1914 collection, Arnold Passow tends to choose Zambelios's texts over Fauriel's for the clear reading texts of the songs.[22] This may have been due to the two men's respective places of origin: Zambelios, as a Greek of the Ionian islands, may have seemed a more authentic representative of the Greek people than the Frenchman Fauriel. Yet in 1929, literary scholar Giannis Apostolakis harshly criticized Zambelios for his treatment of these songs. While many "have remained the same as they are in the collections of Lambros, Fauriel, and Tommaseo," others have been substantially altered, such that "you can never quite know if you're dealing with folk songs or with songs by Zambelios [... .] The 'property of the people,'" Apostolakis fumes, "has ended up unrecognizable to its lawful owner" (32). Ironically, Apostolakis's rhetoric seems to suggest that the lawful owner is an owner only by proxy—that the correct versions of these songs are in fact to be found in the editions of foreign collectors. With regard to "The Brave Beloved," Apostolakis notes that what had been "both a love song and a song of exile" in Fauriel's collection "changed when it passed through Zambelios's hands and became a heroic song of war" (81). In noting Zambelios's altera-tions while declining to investigate whether Fauriel might have engaged in similar editorial activity, Apostolakis positions Fauriel's collection (and elsewhere Tommaseo's) as the proper "original" against which Zambelios's modifications are to be judged. In another context, Fauriel might have been criticized for the inauthenticities of his own texts—yet as the first published collection of its kind, produced by a foreign philhellene in support of Greek independence, his edition assumes the weight of a de facto original, even for those who later adapt his texts for purposes of their own.

In Zambelios's case, that purpose was clearly to support a particular kind of nation-building effort. His *Folk Songs of Greece, Published with a Historical Study Concerning Medieval Hellenism* might more accurately have been called a historical study accompanied by a selection of folk songs: the first 595 pages of this volume are devoted to a historical tract written in *kathar-evousa*, while the last 160 are given over to poetic texts.[23] Writing roughly twenty years after Fallmerayer's treatise concerning the Slavic background

---

[22] See footnote 3.

[23] Not all of these, moreover, are folk songs: Zambelios includes a generous sprinkling of poems written by learned figures including Dionysios Solomos and Ioulios Typaldos, none explicitly attributed to those poets but rather interspersed with the other texts as if they, too, were works by the anonymous folk. The second volume of Fauriel's *Chants populaires* also contains a poem by Rhigas Feraios as well as Stanislas Julien's translation of Dionysios Solomos's "Hymn to Liberty," each of which is marked as a poem and attributed to its respective author.

of the modern Greeks, Zambelios never mentions the German historian by name, though he unquestionably crafts his argument in the shadow of that theory. While Fallmerayer sought to debunk the notion that the modern inhabitants of Greece were the direct descendants of the ancient Greeks, Zambelios's historical tract wages an explicit defense of this idea. He claims, more specifically, that proof of the continuity of the Greek people, and of their language, lies in Greece's under-studied medieval period, and argues that the "Helleno-Christian" nature of Greek civilization arises from the medieval reworking of its classical legacy. Zambelios presents the folk songs as one place we can look for vestiges of Greek medieval history: in them, "the life of the faceless and anonymous poet of the people"—singular and literate, a poet rather than a bard—"illuminates the shady passages taken by the race in its search for freedom" (5). Zambelios's defense of a narrative of continuity also takes the form of a literary and even linguistic isolationism: he urges Greek intellectuals to nurture the history, language, and literature of their land, while chiding "the majority of lovers of knowledge living in Greece, who overlook the history of their fatherland and, dressing in foreign clothes, squander their precious time translating shabby writings" (6). The irony here is twofold. First, Zambelios's volume imports into a Greek-speaking community a set of Greek texts on which foreign intellectuals had invested their *own* precious time, dressing them in the foreign clothes of their translations. Furthermore, while celebrated for the very tie to the history of the Greek language and land which Zambelios seeks to underscore, these texts were also seen both by outsiders and by ethnic Greeks such as Korais as shabby in comparison to the work of the ancients.

Zambelios's rhetoric and argument shift the discussion of the songs from the level of the folk to the level of the nation, a move that finds even clearer expression in Nikolaos Politis's edition of 1914. In his editor's prologue, Politis argues that, unlike proverbs, myths, fairytales, and jokes, in which "the numerous foreign elements make it difficult to determine what is native from what comes from elsewhere," the folk songs are a genre that displays "the particular character of the nation" in clear and undiluted form (5). Politis therefore contends that "all Greeks should know and study at least the best and more central of these specimens of folk literature" (6). In his long career as scholar and editor, Politis was remarkably successful in promoting this agenda, and in spreading a textualized knowledge of folk songs throughout Greece, including in school curricula. Yet in order to champion these songs as the "purest" form of Greek folk production, "untouched by foreign hands," Politis had to obscure their history of foreign mediation. Unlike Manousos, who uses foreign interest to spur local interest, Politis avoids mentioning foreign collectors in his introduction, and effaces as many signs as he can of their involvement in the construction of the texts he presents. While he includes two lists of sources at the back of his volume (one for the collection as a whole and another, more detailed, catalogue of sources for each individual song), he privileges Greek-language sources above others, even when those Greek editors were merely reprinting texts that first appeared in collections compiled by foreigners. At least twenty of Politis's songs can be traced back to Fauriel, yet neither he nor Tommaseo are even named in the general list of sources, while Fauriel is named only five times in the notes for individual songs. Politis's construction of his Greek corpus seems to have necessitated the elision of these foreign names—and of the complex, translingual, transnational history of the texts he places before his Greek readers' eyes.

In search of an end to origins

Many of the questions I raised in the opening paragraphs of this chapter concerned how to represent the fluidity and variability of orature in print—yet in the pages that followed I spoke only sparingly of the oral nature of the folk song, focusing instead on the fluidity and variability of these songs' translingual textual history. To some extent, this is a function of the available evidence: texts leave traces that oral performances do not. But it also reflects the central argument I am making in this book. The primary emphasis of this chapter has been on the textualized understanding of Greek folk songs that prevailed in the early days of their study, as the songs were submitted to textualizing practices that aimed not just at stabilizing them in books, but at creating a stable national entity that could shelter these books and songs alike. My goal has been to demonstrate the problematic assumptions behind such an endeavor—first and foremost the assumption that print confers stability, but also the assumption that a collective, recognizable "folk" existed prior to its discursive construction.

Across Europe, the practices of early collectors of folklore and folk songs diverged significantly from our current understanding of ethnographic methodology. In the Greek context, it was not until the mid-twentieth century that scholars of folklore began to produce recordings and transcriptions of folk songs from performance contexts, since the political turmoil that marked the early history of the modern state made recording in the field a difficult enterprise. The Center for Greek Folklore Research, which Politis founded in 1918, acquired its first recording equipment at the already late date of 1939, but was unable to make use of it until after 1950, due to the

Axis Occupation and the subsequent Civil War.[24] And of course even performances of folk songs are not, and have never been, the pure, unmediated outpourings of a collective voice that some would like to believe. Interaction between textual and oral spheres—between stories and songs that are told, sung, heard, retold, resung, written and rewritten, and continually adapted in new oral and written forms—has perhaps always been a feature of folk production. Certainly in the twentieth century, the dissemination of the texts made popular by Politis's edition had a strong effect on Greek oral tradition, as the dissemination of Fauriel's texts via editions such as those of Manousos and Zambelios may have had in an earlier era. American scholar Margaret Alexiou mentions one singer she met in the 1970s who claimed to be singing songs as she'd been taught them by her illiterate mother. "There is no reason to doubt the authenticity of her words," Alexiou writes, "yet her 'texts' reproduced almost verbatim those of N. G. Politis, demonstrably conflations of numerous regional variants." How was it that Politis's texts had infiltrated oral culture in this way? "Years later I discovered by chance," Alexiou continues, "that 'Politis' ballads' had been popularised to the very same tune on the radio and throughout northern Greece in the decades of the 1920s and 1930s" (11). Alexiou characterizes the effect that these sound recordings had on oral performances as a form of "radiophonic orality," an orality that assumes fixed sequences of words and tonal structures by virtue of modes of reproduction and dissemination that encourage replication rather than variance.

Despite the textualized early history of research into Greek folk songs, the rhetoric regarding these songs' oral origins was and remains strong. In 1999, Alexis Politis published a Greek translation of Fauriel's collection. Notwithstanding the borrowings I have described above, this translation was the first time the whole of Fauriel's paratext was made available to Greek readers. Yet instead of presenting the Greek texts for the songs offered in that 1824 edition, Politis chose to replace many of them with "the oldest surviving transcriptions" found in Fauriel's archives, including unpublished materials Fauriel collected during encounters with Greek migrants in Venice and Trieste, so as to allow readers "to come closer to the natural environment of the folk song and become better acquainted with the bearers of the tradition" (8). Politis's translation of this historic edition thus presents a set of song texts that have never before appeared in print, and articulates a goal for the songs very different from that put forward by the paratext of the collection he is translating. In one sense, Politis's swapping of one set of texts for another

---

[24] http://www.kentrolaografias.gr/el/content/εθνική-μουσική-συλλογή (last accessed 7 May 2017).

implicitly acknowledges the mutability of the songs even in their textualized form. Yet his editorial methodology rests, like his grandfather's before him, on a specifically print understanding of the nature of literary production: he, too, seeks a single, best text for each song, making his choice based on the belief that the earliest text will most closely approximate a transcription of a now-lost original. It may be that the best editions of folk songs are yet to come, and will be aided by new modes of distribution that are more attuned to textual variance, and less dependent on the medium of print. One can imagine, for instance, digital editions whose algorithms would allow a slightly different version of a song to appear each time a page is accessed, thus building textual instability into the very mode of textual dissemination.

If folk songs, a genre for which constant mutation is the norm, invite new modes of editorial practice that better embody that mutability, they also invite us to rethink some of our most basic ideas about how translation works. As Maria Tymoczko has argued, our discussions of literary translation, on both a practical and a theoretical level, "generally presuppose the presence of fixed source texts and the generation of fixed translated texts. In ignoring and failing to account for interlingual oral literary translation, the terms of our very discourse about literary translation presuppose a framework about literature and the workings of literature that fails to account for the position of literature in most of the world at present and the position of literature through most of human history." Concepts such as "literal" and "word-for-word" translation, for instance, are incompatible with orature, and with the oral translation *of* orature. What Tymoczko calls our "obsession with fixed texts" has shifted translation theory and practice towards various models of literalism that are incongruous with the way cultural products have been shared in most places and times. Thinking about translation in the context of an oral tradition therefore invites us to examine the limits of much Western translation theory and practice alike: "the dedication to a fixed text—a relatively recent development in human history, and a development still largely restricted worldwide—skews both theoretical and practical notions about translation."[25] Tymoczko's point is an invaluable one. Moreover, as this

---

[25] Tymoczko (1990: 53–4). The complicated oral *and* textual history of these folk songs also invites us to rethink notions of authorial originality that have tended to go hand-in-hand with the reification of fixed texts. If in the nineteenth century the creation of folklore was largely a project of national development, and folklore was seen as a tradition held in common, belonging to all and therefore to none, in the twentieth and twenty-first centuries, as Valdimir Hafstein argues, folk knowledge has increasingly become an object of appropriation by international capital. Hafstein has discussed efforts to protect traditional forms of knowledge that take recourse in the ideology of individual origi-nality: the head of the U.S. delegation for the World Intellectual Property Organization argued in 2002, for instance, that folklore is "always individually created and then

chapter and my book as a whole strive to show, this dedication to a fixed text not only ignores the reality of cultural production in oral contexts, but also stands in contradiction to the radically unstable nature of texts themselves.

Despite the attempts of countless scholars to shape stable texts that will best represent some originary moment of folk production, variability is part and parcel of the textual condition, as much as it is of the oral tradition. Considering the iterative translingual circulation of folk songs—both in printed form and in the oral versions that allowed songs such as "The Bridge of Arta" to spread through a multilingual region like the Balkans before the rise of mass literacy—allows us to challenge conventional thinking about translation in a variety of ways, by challenging first and foremost the notion that a stable original ever predated, or will ever postdate, a moment of textual mediation. It also allows us to challenge received narratives about the supposedly indissoluble national character of certain cultural products. Richard Bauman notes that most scholars have historically seen folklore as "a locally rooted, vernacular, face-to-face phenomenon," and view national-izing and internationalizing processes as "secondary and disjunctive uses (or abuses) to which folklore may be put." Bauman argues, on the contrary, that "a close critical examination of the textual ideologies and practices that have been employed ever since the concept of folklore was first invented [...] shows us ever more clearly that nationalizing and internationalizing forces have been *constitutive* of the very textual corpus on which the discipline—and the idea—of folklore are built" (267).

This is not to say that we should not try, as this chapter has tried, to trace some of the mechanisms by which various motivated rewriters have shaped the texts before us. It simply means that these investigations will never bring us to a moment *prior* to mediation and change; such a moment does not exist. In telling the story of the continual textual reconfiguration as well as recontextualization of Greek folk songs, I have also sought to *un*tell the story, to help the writing become unwritten (as my epigraph would have it)—not to return us to an originary moment, but rather to bring us forward to a moment when we will recognize that there is simply no origin to be found.

adopted by the community," and thus should be protected *as* individual creation, and eligible for copyright protection. Hafstein agrees with the need for protection, but disagrees with the particular rationale. "Instead of granting folklore a degree of origi-nality by postulating individual origination," he writes, "I propose that we recognize the cult and concept of originality for what it is: a Romantic relic and the ideological reflex of a particular economic order. Rather than claim a measure of originality for folklore, we should repudiate originality itself and embrace instead a social concept of creativity, along the lines of theories of intertextuality and distributed innovation" (2004: 309)—a concept that, in my reading, also leaves ample room for editing, writing, and translation as endeavors belonging to this nexus of collective creation.

3

On Manuscripts, Type-Translation, and Translation (Im?)proper: Emily Dickinson and the Translation of Scriptural Form

They shut me up in Prose –
As when a little Girl
They put me in the Closet –
Because they liked me "still" –

Still! Could themself have peeped –
And seen my Brain – go round –
They might as wise have lodged a Bird
For Treason – in the Pound –

Himself has but to will
And easy as a Star
Look down opon Captivity –
And laugh – No more have I –

11 Look down opon] Abolish his –

Division   *7 lodged |*

—*The Poems of Emily Dickinson*
(1998, ed. R. W. Franklin)

The history of reading Emily Dickinson (1830–86) is a history of editorial forms. The same could be said of countless writers, yet the case of Dickinson is more pronounced than most. Her remarkable body of work includes forty hand-sewn packets of handwritten poems and a far vaster number of loose-leaf sheets, fragments, and drafts, nearly all unpublished at the time of her death, and most exhibiting a slew of variants, alternate words or phrases between which the poet never chose. Thanks to this acute resistance to closure, Dickinson's work continually runs up against the limits of editorial theory and methodology, and continually invites editors to find new ways out of the presentational binds it reveals. The earliest print editions trimmed away her copious alternate forms and drastically changed the punctuation, lineation, capitalization, and spelling of her manuscript writings. Two later variorum editions accounted for the variants and tried to restore her punctuation, but continued to lineate the poems metrically. In 1981, a black-and-white facsimile edition of the packets, or "fascicles," gave many readers their first extensive view of her script. In doing so, it literally changed the way many *see* Dickinson's work, and encouraged a proliferation of print and digital editions that attempt to represent the visual details of her manuscripts. When quoting her work in their own, many scholars now try to account typographically for aspects of her script that earlier typeset editions did not treat as significant. Each of these several shifts in the mode of presenting Dickinson's poetry entails a concomitant shift in our perceptions not just of what but of *how* these poems (and others) can mean.

This impressive string of editorial reworkings has unfolded in conjunction with a lively discussion—in editors' introductions, but also in a number of scholarly articles and books—concerning better and worse ways of presenting Dickinson's challenging body of work. Many recent arguments in favor of increasing our attention to the visual and material aspects of her manuscripts are couched in the language of liberation. The poem that serves as my epigraph to this chapter has been coopted into those arguments, presented as an allegorical commentary on the ways in which many posthumous editions have betrayed the poet's wish for privacy and for control over the forms her work took: the early editions shut her poetry up in a conventionally typeset form, and the task of contemporary scholars and editors is to free it from the closet or pound of past editorial practice. Yet the poem is incisive in its irony. For all our rhetoric of freeing Dickinson from the strictures of print, the poem's speaker remains internally free throughout, notwithstanding external circumstances. In this sense, the "captivity" Dickinson's work seeks to abolish may be not hers but our own: her poetry continues to fly steadfastly around an ever-expanding editorial enclosure from the outside, tracing the shifting limits of our own print (and now digital) imagination. And as we continue to adapt our editorial modes, her poetry continues to expose their new limitations.

Dickinson's poetry may also expose, even more starkly, some limitations in our thinking about translation. As scholars and editors redraw the boundaries of Dickinson's work in English, translators remain focused on the language of her poems as presented in reading editions, forgoing the chance to engage with the variants, or with the potential significance of her script.[1] This makes sense, of course. Our tools as translators are other tools.

---

[1] While my research into the countless translations of Dickinson has not been exhaustive,

We are trained to deal in words, phrases, sentences—and these elements of Dickinson's work are already quite challenging as it is. Besides, if (for example) Millicent Todd Bingham's 1945 *Bolts of Melody* is the only book of Dickinson's poetry in English on the shelves of the Verdansky National Library, and others are equally difficult to find in bookstores, how is a Ukranian translator (particularly one working before widespread internet availability) supposed to know that later editions present the work differently, much less to imagine that a choice between "source" versions might be hers to make?[2] Yet given the widespread digitization of books and archival materials, and with information increasingly available concerning the textual history of this and other bodies of writing, the time seems ripe to invite translators of Dickinson to imagine other ways of going about their task—and to open the field of translation studies to discussions regarding visual and material form taking place among textual critics and literary scholars alike. This is one major goal of this chapter.

At the same time, I also want to question the widespread reliance on the *trope* of translation in scholarly discussions regarding the importance of Dickinson's script and the inadequacy of print to represent it. Ever since R. W. Franklin's 1981 facsimile edition of the fascicles, the term "translation" has been used time and again to refer to print editions of Dickinson's poetry—so frequently, particularly in the 1990s when this debate was at its peak, that Domnhall Mitchell pointed to an underlying assumption "that studying Dickinson in any standard typographic edition is effectively to read her in translation, at one remove from her actual practices" (1999: 39). Jerome McGann coined the term "type-translation" to refer to transcriptions

in writing this chapter I did examine dozens of translations in numerous languages— Russian, Bulgarian, Thai, Finnish, Norwegian, Chinese, French, Dutch—focusing when possible on translations produced in the 1990s and after, to give critical responses to Franklin's facsimile edition time to percolate into translators' work. Only a handful of the volumes contained a few representative images of the manuscripts, and almost none presented variants. Linguistically hampered as I was, I could perceive no attempt in any of the translations to experiment with the visual means of the language in question, or with the bibliographic possibilities of the codex form. Statements by translators in a 1997 special issue of *The Emily Dickinson Journal*, as well as many of the contributions to Domnhall Mitchell and Maria Scott's edited volume *The International Reception of Emily Dickinson*, whose chapters are devoted to translations of Dickinson in various national and linguistic contexts, reinforce the impression that translators have, by and large, not treated the visual and material aspects of Dickinson's work as meaningful to their own presentations of it in the way English-language editors have. For this reason, I chose not to engage with existing translations, but rather to hypothesize about some forms future translations might take. I very much welcome scholarly discussion of existing translations of Dickinson that engage the visual aspect of her work, or even the variants, from scholars with broader linguistic capabilities than my own.

[2]   See Chesnokova (2009) for an account of Ukranian versions of Dickinson.

of Dickinson's poems (1993: 27), and Paul Crumbley similarly speaks of "translating Dickinson's holographs into print" (1997: 8). Ellen Louise Hart and Martha Nell Smith, in introducing their edition of the poet's letters to her beloved sister-in-law Susan Dickinson, use the word "translate" four times in a single paragraph to describe transcriptions of her manuscripts (1998: xxiii). Marta Werner's review of Franklin's 1998 variorum edition notes how scholars fail to account in their respective editions for the "iconic value" of Dickinson's scripts; Werner argues that the poet's "dashes, pointings, strikeouts, pen tests, blurs and blank spaces" are (in the specialized vocabulary of textual scholarship) not accidentals but substantives, i.e., bearers of meaning that should be treated as such by an editor. "[T]he manuscript's refusal to disclose itself fully and at once," Werner continues, "is not evidence of its meaninglessness, but of the need for a method (and a theory) of translation attentive to the dialectics of writing (reading) and seeing" (1999: 272).

I agree wholeheartedly with this call for a new way of conceptualizing translation that would fold an attentiveness to the visual into the translator's purview. Yet Werner, like many others before and since, is referring not to translations in other languages, but to English-language print transcriptions of Dickinson's scripts. My unease with this rhetorical reliance on "translation" to refer to essentially monolingual practices arises from a suspicion that the term is being used at least in part for its unfortunate (and frankly unreasonable) connotations of loss. "The event of copying," Werner writes elsewhere, "constitutes a mysterious and sensuous form of translation in which *trans-*, the carrying across of a message, is also always a carrying away and an abandonment of that message in the arms of alterity's angel" (1995: 27). Here, the word "translation" is used to describe print transcription as a form of (failed) copying that in fact renders the poems radically changed; the etymology of the word is employed to shape a notion of translation not as interpretive iteration, but as the "abandonment" of a singular, quasi-mystical "message" to alterity. In other words, Werner is not in fact talking about what translation actually does, but using the term in a metaphorical sense to signal a belief in the radical untranslatability of Dickinson's manuscripts.

Werner and others who use "translation" as a code word for abandonment and loss are drawing on an outmoded, misleading conceptual framework that treats translation as transfer—a transfer that is, of course, doomed always to fail. Moreover, in asserting the primacy of her manuscripts as unique, inimitable "originals," scholars may in fact be imposing on Dickinson a conceptual captivity stricter than any that has come before. After all, keeping Dickinson in her own graphocentric idiolect would seem to mean keeping her in English—which means discounting the possibility of *actual* translation, and excluding the vast numbers of readers unable to read English at all, much less to decipher Dickinson's difficult scripts. Thus while scholars routinely treat early print editions as domesticating "translations" of Dickinson's work that shape her texts to suit the dominant poetic standards of the day, this visual turn in Dickinson scholarship ironically entails a different form of domestication, shaping our understanding of Dickinson's texts to suit a new set of poetic standards while also posing an implicit challenge to the legitimacy of their circulation in other languages.

This is a challenge I hope translators and theorists of translation will rise to meet. At the very least, the example of Dickinson suggests that we need to expand our conception of the translator's complex task to include an investigation of the editorial history of the works we translate, and a consideration of the potential significance of the nonlexical aspects of texts we take as our "sources." How might potential translators not abandon but convey the ever-changing, interpretively coded "message" of Dickinson's work in the alterity of another language, with its different modes of meaning, its different history of script and print, of private and public circulation? If a focus on Dickinson's scriptural form prohibits translation as it is currently understood, we have two choices: we can dismiss translation as impossible, or we can revise our current understanding of translation. And since proclamations of the impossibility of translation, even in their most interesting form, are lazy in their terminology (you can't define a process in terms of its failure to do what it clearly cannot do), Dickinson's work therefore invites us to elaborate new models of translation— ones that will embrace rather than sideline these other modes of meaning.

What translators and scholars of translation have to gain from this discussion is yet another defense against the misguided notion of untranslatability, and the equally misguided paradigm of equivalence on which it rests. If the borders of a work are constantly shifting even in its language of composition, one major shortcoming of the concept of equivalence becomes clear: there is simply no textually or bibliographically stable *there* there for a translation to be equivalent to. Translation becomes, on the contrary, an iterative process by which the borders of that work are reconfigured yet again, this time in another language. In telling the story of these changing (and competing) conceptual configurations of Dickinson's work in English, I invite us to rethink our modes of translating, too, particularly as regards certain aspects of texts that have generally been neglected by translators and scholars of translation. While acknowledging the difficulty translators face when dealing with even the early editions of Dickinson's poems, much less the later variorum or facsimile editions, I invite us to push beyond lexical meaning and imagine ways of accommodating more fully and more creatively the textual and bibliographic instability of literary works, as well as the visual and material aspects of the texts we translate.

"Explanation kind": Editing Emily Dickinson

Thanks in part to popular representations such as William Luce's 1976 one-act play *The Belle of Amherst* (widely translated and remarkably successful abroad),[3] Emily Dickinson may be as famous for her seclusion from the world as she is for her poetry. Second of three children in a prominent Amherst family, Dickinson traveled little, socialized mostly with family, and led an adult life of increasing seclusion. After returning home from a visit to a Boston eye specialist in 1865, she confined herself entirely to the house in which she was born and raised. Writing to Thomas Wentworth Higginson— the abolitionist minister and writer who would become one of her first posthumous editors—to decline his invitation to come and visit him, she penned this now-famous response: "could it please your convenience to come so far as Amherst, I should be very glad, but I do not cross my Father's ground to any House or town" (Dickinson 1958: 460). While reclusive, Dickinson nonetheless maintained a number of intimate relationships via an extensive correspondence that functioned, too, as an unconventional mode of controlled publication. Her letters to family and friends bristled with poems; indeed, the metrical nature of her prose often makes it difficult to know where "letter" ends and "poem" begins.[4] Higginson was one long-time correspondent and recipient of her work; Susan Dickinson, married to Emily's older brother Austin, was another. Letters to Sue, which had to travel only as far as the house next door, effaced generic boundaries perhaps more than any of Dickinson's other writing, with drafts of poems enclosed in the envelopes and lines of poetry woven into the letters themselves.

But even those closest to Dickinson were not aware of the staggering size of her body of work, and probably couldn't have conceived of it as an oeuvre until it was posthumously constructed as such. When, after the poet's death in 1886, her younger sister Lavinia decided to publish a volume from among the roughly 1,800 poems she had found in Dickinson's room, it was

---

[3] Several chapters in Mitchell and Scott's volume note the importance of Luce's play in shaping the reception of Dickinson's work in a number of countries and linguistic contexts.

[4] One of the first to note the blurring of prose and poetry in Dickinson's letters was Jack Spicer, the subject of Chapter 5 of this book. In his 1956 review of Thomas Johnson's variorum edition in the *Boston Review*, Spicer wrote, "The reason for the difficulty of drawing a line between the poetry and prose in Emily Dickinson's letters may be that she did not wish such a line to be drawn. If large portions of her correspondence are considered not as mere letters—and, indeed, they seldom communicate information, or have much to do with the person to whom they were written—but as experiments in a heightened prose combined with poetry, a new approach to both her letters and her poetry opens up." The review is included in Spicer (1998: 231–6).

clear to all involved that the texts would have to be reshaped in some way before *they* could cross her "Father's ground" to meet a wider public. Several decades later, Mabel Loomis Todd, a local writer (and Austin Dickinson's lover) who coedited the earliest volumes of the poems with Higginson and subsequently edited two more on her own, recalled her initial encounter with the manuscripts:

> In this box [Lavinia] discovered eight or nine hundred poems tied up in this way. They looked almost hopeless from a printer's point of view. The handwriting consisted of styles of three periods, absolutely different one from another. All were written in a hand which to most persons is exceedingly difficult to read, and many words were liable to be widely misconstrued. The poems were written on both sides of the paper, interlined, altered and the number of suggested changes was baffling. Almost every page had a number of crosses [before] many of the words. Each cross referred to a choice of several words at the bottom of the page which the author had thought equally good, and quite as expressive of her meaning as the word actually employed in the text. There was nothing whatever to indicate which word was supposed to fit into which place. The crosses were all alike. As there were frequently several sets of such changes on a page, no guide to assist in choosing could be relied upon except a sense of the working of the author's peculiar mind, by which the most characteristic word should be retained from the choice of several which she had indicated. It was of course necessary if anything were to be done about publishing the poems that they should be clearly and carefully copied and edited in copying, by choosing always the best of the author's own suggested changes, and putting the poems into such shape that they could be submitted to a publisher and easily read by him. (1945: 17–18)

Todd's description clearly conveys the overwhelming nature of her largely self-appointed task: to make legible, according to reading conventions of the time, a mass of manuscripts that struck her as profoundly unfinished, "almost hopeless" in their difference from then-current standards for poetry. (For readers who are not familiar with Dickinson's manuscripts, Figures 1 and 5 offer some sense of what Todd was dealing with.) Even in simply transcribing the texts into a clearer hand, and then into typewritten versions, variants and all, Todd was laying important groundwork for generations of editors and scholars to come.

Yet these same generations of editors and scholars have often taken Todd and Higginson to task for the assumption embodied in the "of course" in the last sentence above: that the poems needed to be fundamentally altered before they could be shared with a reading public. And Todd and Higginson did in fact intervene in substantial ways. In their 1890 and 1891 volumes, they assigned titles to the poems (usually borrowing from first lines), lineated them according to metrical convention, standardized capitalization, swapped out the poet's dashes for conventional punctuation, and chose between variants on the basis of seemingly aesthetic grounds ("the best of the author's own suggestions," selected according to the questionable claim to "a sense of the author's peculiar mind," supposedly afforded them by their social proximity to Dickinson during her lifetime). Many now see these alterations as invasive editorial techniques in need of correction or mitigation. For instance, where Todd saw "suggested changes," most contemporary scholars see supplements, variants between which no resolution was desired. Dickinson frequently tailored poems to fit specific circumstances—a poem might be sent to one recipient with one set of variants, and to another with a different set; her own copies recorded them all without deciding definitively among them. In some contemporary scholars' view, an edition without variants therefore misrepresents the radical instability even of poems for which we have only one extant manuscript.

The several major editions since Todd and Higginson's have increasingly accommodated aspects of Dickinson's work these earliest editors considered "hopeless" or "baffling." Volumes released by Dickinson's niece, Martha Dickinson Bianchi, including the 1914 *The Single Hound*, largely followed Todd and Higginson's approach, but assigned numbers rather than titles. The 1945 *Bolts of Melody*, edited by Millicent Todd Bingham, Todd's daughter, altered the punctuation and lineation of the manuscripts but retained their unusual syntax. Thomas Johnson's 1955 variorum edition offered the first systematic account of the variants, and honored Dickinson's irregular capitalization and use of dashes (for which he used long em dashes). Franklin's 1998 revised version of the variorum introduced only minor changes to most of Johnson's texts; he occasionally interpreted a word differently, or revised the order of lines or stanzas when markings on the manuscripts seemed to indicate a mistake on Johnson's part (and also replaced Johnson's em dashes with shorter en dashes throughout). But Franklin's variorum also included many more poems than Johnson's, and assigned the manuscripts new numbers according to a revised understanding of their dates of composition. (In the absence of titles, Dickinson's poems are now customarily referred to by a confusing set of double numbers, which gesture to the fact if not the substance of Franklin's and Johnson's interventions: the poem in my epigraph, for instance, goes by F445, J613, or both. Even our mode of identifying the poems is marked in this symbolic way by their editorial history.)

The edition that has arguably had the greatest influence on subsequent scholarship is Franklin's 1981 *The Manuscript Books of Emily Dickinson*, a two-volume facsimile edition of the hand-sewn packets the poet created at a furious rate during the early 1860s. Franklin's *Manuscript Books* made black-and-white images (including my Figure 5) of over a thousand of Dickinson's handwritten poems available to a far wider public than could ever gain access to the manuscripts in their archival homes. The edition also entirely reframed the debate over how to present Dickinson's work. Johnson's variorum had long been considered a welcome corrective to earlier editions. After the publication of Franklin's facsimile edition, a host of scholars came to feel that even the variorum went astray, because it "translated" her texts into the conventions of scholarly print publication, and no such "translation" could ever adequately represent the fully embodied meaning of those holograph forms. Jerome McGann, for instance, argued that Dickinson's scripts did not "[aspire] to a typographical existence," and thus "cannot be read (…) as if they were composed with an eye toward some state beyond their handcrafted textual condition. Her surviving manuscript texts urge us to take them at face value, to treat all her scriptural forms as potentially significant *at the aesthetic or expressive level*" (1993: 38, emphasis in text).

In addition to the visual details of individual manuscripts, there is also the question of Dickinson's intimate manner of sharing her poems with others. Many scholars, and particularly feminist scholars, see the fascicles as products of a private mode of book-making that reflects not timidity nor even a disinterest in publishing, but a flat-out rejection of print. Taking the poem "[Publication – is the Auction / Of the Mind of Man]" as an indication of (or at least an allegory for) that stance, they present the proliferation of variants in the poems written after 1881, as well as the shift from bound fascicles to loose-leaf sheets and from pen to pencil, as part of a witting defiance of the strictures and permanence of the codex form—strictures that the scholarship codes as masculine and patriarchal. To be sure, at least two of Dickinson's earliest and most invasive editors were women, who subsequently passed the editorial task to their daughters. Yet it is Johnson's work that comes under the greatest fire. Johnson, Susan Howe notes, "called his Introduction 'Creating the Poems,' then gave their creator a male muse-minister. […] By choosing a sovereign system for her line endings—*his* preappointed Plan—he established the constraints of a strained positivity. Copious footnotes, numbers, comparisons, and chronologies mask his authorial role" (1993: 135). For Howe, what Johnson saw as accidental breaks determined by the dimensions of the paper are in fact intentional line endings; Johnson's printing of the poems in hymn-like stanzas therefore obscures the poet's mode of metrical as well as visual experimentation. In other words, both scholarly editorial practice and print technology itself shut Dickinson up in the "Closet" or "Pound" of what Marta Werner calls the "carceral space of the book" (1995: 23).

The new focus on the visual aspect of Dickinson's work has resulted in a flurry of attempts to accommodate her script more fully. A number of print and digital editions offer high-resolution color images to supplement the black-and-white images of Franklin's *Manuscript Books*, while also expanding the corpus of poems available in facsimile far beyond the forty fascicles. The open-access *Emily Dickinson Archives*, launched in 2013, provides digital images, transcriptions, and information regarding the publication history of manuscripts held by numerous institutions, including Amherst College and Harvard University. Casual browsers all over the world are now able to compare print editions to Dickinson's handwritten forms. First released in 1999 (though on a subscription basis), Werner's *Radical Scatters*, a digital edition of Dickinson's late writings, expands our knowledge of Dickinson's writing to include drafts, notes, and fragments written on scraps of paper readily at hand. More recently, Werner collaborated with artist and poet Jen Bervin on *The Gorgeous Nothings: Emily Dickinson's Envelope Poems* (2013), which brings together fifty-two texts Dickinson jotted on envelopes, presented in color facsimiles with transcriptions in a font Bervin specially created to mimic the poet's handwriting. (This project has itself now been through multiple manifestations: a limited-edition artist's book; a large-format hardcover; and a more affordable, smaller-format hardcover; others may follow.) With facsimiles now increasingly available in forms such as these, many scholars feel compelled to provide images of the manuscripts when discussing particular poems, or to create new transcriptions that reproduce Dickinson's lineation and approximate her spacing, the slant of her dashes, and other visual elements of her script. At the very least, they choose carefully between existing editorial representations of the poems they treat. "[O]ne cannot even quote this poet," Cristanne Miller notes, "without identifying one's critical position as to what constitutes a Dickinson line or poem" (2004: 205).[5]

So often with Dickinson's work, when scholars speak about the poems, the poems seem to speak right back (though of course that "speaking back" is also a product of our interpretations). In my case, I read the poem "[Tell all the Truth / but – tell it slant]" as an impossibly prescient allegorical commentary on the increasing editorial accommodation of the idiosyncrasies of Dickinson's script. The manuscript, which can now be viewed online at the *Emily Dickinson Archive* (see Figure 1), differs in many respects

---

[5]   My policy in this chapter has been to provide images of manuscripts when talking about the visual aspect of these materials, and to offer transcriptions rather than images of editions that themselves transcribed Dickinson's work.

from Todd's account above. Written in pencil on a small slip of stationary in 1872, it contains very few variants; its clear, large, round letters are far more legible than those of later manuscripts produced when Dickinson's already bad eyesight had deteriorated further. And while Todd's description of variants crowded at the end of a poem—usually just beneath the rest of the poem, with only a series of cross-marks to indicate where in the text they belong—is true of many of her poems, here they are nestled within the body of the text itself. Yet even here, the experience of reading the poem in manuscript form could be described as one of delayed gratification. First, many readers will find even these relatively clear letters difficult to decipher. Second, the configuration of the lines, whether intentional or not, makes for nearly constant enjambment: "surprise" does in fact come as a surprise; "lies," which lies on a line of its own, resonates with the overtone of *telling a falsehood*, a meaning also encouraged by the triple occurrence of the word "truth" in this brief poem. And third, the circuitousness of the poem's inverted syntax is heightened by the way a reader's eye must continually circle back across these extremely short lines—a process that lengthens still further the time it takes to reach the end of any phrase. Cumulatively, these effects seem to necessitate, or at least encourage, the very easing-into that the poem describes.

Compare the image of the manuscript to its first published text, from Bingham's 1945 *Bolts of Melody*. Todd, Bingham's mother, died over a decade before the volume was produced, yet she is listed as coeditor because of her extensive work transcribing the poems—a useful reminder of the ultimately collaborative nature of the editorial process, even when later editions are shaped in explicit opposition to their forebears. I present my own transcription of Bingham's version here:

Tell all the truth but tell it slant,
Success in circuit lies,
Too bright for our infirm delight
The truth's superb surprise;

As lightning to the children eased
With explanation kind,
The truth must dazzle gradually
Or every man be blind.

(Dickinson 1945: 233)

Below are the versions from Johnson's 1955 variorum and Franklin's 1998 variorum; their respective popular editions of 1960 and 1999 use the clear reading texts presented here, only without the variants:

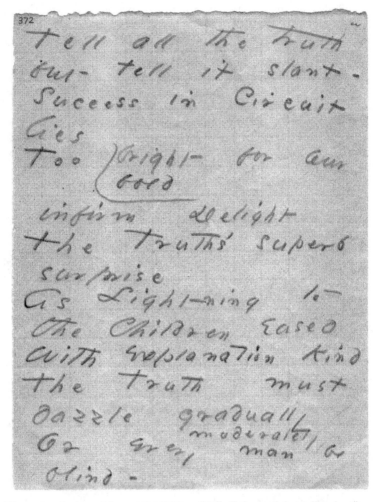

Figure 1   Amherst Manuscript #372 — "Tell all the truth but tell it slant."
The Emily Dickinson Collection, Amherst College Archives & Special
Collections.

Tell all the truth but tell it slant –
Success in Circuit lies
Too bright for our infirm Delight
The Truth's superb surprise
As Lightning to the Children eased
With explanation kind
The Truth must dazzle gradually
Or every man be blind –

3. bright] bold 7. gradually]
    moderately

Division 1 truth | 2 Circuit | 3 our |
4 superb | 5 to | 7 must | 8 be |

(Dickinson 1955: 792)

Tell all the truth but tell it slant -
Success in Circuit lies
Too bright for our infirm Delight
The Truth's superb surprise
As Lightning to the Children eased
With explanation kind
The Truth must dazzle gradually
Or every man be blind -

3 infirm] bold 7 gradually]
    moderately

Division 1 truth | 2 Circuit | 3 our |
4 superb | 5 to | 7 must | 8 be |

(Dickinson 1998: 1089)

In Bingham's version, any sense of circuity or slant must come not from the poem's form, but from its language and ideas. Bingham lineates the poem metrically rather than in accordance with the visual aspect of the manuscripts.[6] Bingham also punctuates the poem so as to clarify the grammatical relationship between clauses, and removes unexpected capital letters ("Circuit," "Delight," "Lightning," and so on) that might otherwise slow the eye and mind. Johnson's and Franklin's texts, meanwhile, are nearly identical, apart from the latter's contention that "bold" is a variant not of "bright" (directly above it in the manuscript) but of "infirm" (directly below). These versions make for a more challenging reading experience than Bingham's: in the absence of standard punctuation, readers must decide where to break the phrases, and must choose either to negotiate or to ignore information regarding variants and line division—information that complicates (or enriches) the labor of interpretation. Like Bingham, both Johnson and Franklin lineate metrically rather than visually, though they also both note where divisions fall in the manuscript. The digital facsimile presented in Figure 1 of course offers a far more immediate understanding of Dickinson's divisions—yet it does so at the expense of a certain kind of readability.

The publication history of this poem thus mimics the very process it describes. Yet the poem could be read as arguing not against but in favor of the early editorial interventions, as the "explanation kind" that allowed readers to be dazzled moderately or gradually, rather than struck blind to a beauty that

---

6   As some scholars have pointed out, the capitalization of many words that fall at the beginning of metrical lines suggests that Dickinson might in fact have arranged the lines thus had the size of the paper allowed. This does not hold for the particular poem under consideration here.

departed wildly from what was then recognizable as poetry. I have mentioned Jerome McGann as a scholar whose work on Dickinson is thoroughly invested in the significance of her visible language. In his *A Critique of Modern Textual Criticism* (1983), however, McGann argues for the important work editors, amanuenses, publishers, typesetters, and so on do in shaping a text for publication. "[A]n author's work possesses autonomy," he writes, "only when it remains an unheard melody. As soon as it begins its passage to publication it undergoes a series of interventions which some textual critics see as a process of contamination, but which may equally well be seen as a process of training the poem for its appearances in the world" (McGann 1983: 51). In keeping with McGann's understanding of literary production as a collective endeavor that shapes a work's representative texts to fit ever-changing practices of publication and circulation, not to mention ever-changing modes of reading, one could argue that Dickinson's earliest editors took a crucial first step toward accustoming the world to Dickinson's peculiar poetry. Its originality (as it were) could be experienced only gradually, lest it be dismissed altogether. The "superb surprise" of her work was therefore unwrapped slowly, over the course of decades, in doses readers could only just tolerate.

Yet to describe this editorial trajectory as a move from supposedly more to supposedly less invasive editorial forms—from editions that occlude the truth of her manuscripts to ones that reveal it more boldly or brightly—is to assume that there is, in fact, some solid, stable, identifiable truth about what and how these poems mean. This is precisely the assumption McGann, Howe, Werner, and others have made in arguing for visually oriented editions of Dickinson's poetry. While I value what such editions have to offer, I contest the assumption of authenticity that underlies this rhetoric. On the contrary, I see the history of successive editions of Dickinson as a history of successive constructions of an always mediated experience of her work. To my view, later editions partake just as strenuously in shaping Dickinson's oeuvre in accordance with shifting expectations of what poetry can or should look like; some of these "truths" are more compelling to us than others, depending on the position from which we approach the work. If, as I suggested in the opening sentence of this chapter, the history of reading Dickinson is a history of editorial forms, we might also describe the evolution of those forms as an embodied history of literary taste.

Domesticating Dickinson

Lawrence Venuti's now familiar distinction between domesticating and foreignizing modes of translation presents the former as one that "inscrib[es] the foreign-language text with values that are current in the receiving culture" (1995: 32), while the latter encourages the reader's awareness of the foreign origin of the translated text by disrupting the "hegemony of fluent discourse" and making the "receiving" language strange to itself. With the example of "[Tell all the Truth]" fresh in our minds, it is easy to see why so many scholars of Dickinson have adopted the trope of translation to describe print editions of her work. For many such scholars, Dickinson's writing appears as a quasi-foreign object within the English language; her poetry makes English already strange to itself. The editorial manipulation of her work, particularly in the early editions, presents a series of domesticating forms that reshape Dickinson's work to accord more easily with the dominant poetic discourses of their day. Yet what if the latest set of editorial preoccupations is simply another form of domestication, according to values newly current in the "receiving culture" of poetic production, of Dickinson scholarship, and of American literary scholarship more broadly? What if, by questioning the validity of "type-translations," this trend poses even greater theoretical as well as practical challenges to the circulation of Dickinson's work in other languages, thus limiting her readership to those able to read English, "domesticating" her in that far more crucial sense?

I see both of these concerns as warranted. To begin with, it is impossible to separate scholarly and editorial products from the intellectual context of their age. Contemporary scholars' interest in Dickinson's script is of a piece with the visual turn in U.S. literary scholarship in the last decades of the twentieth century; with feminist thinking about women's writing and alternate paradigms of textual circulation; and with new ways of conceptualizing literary meaning that have arisen with the advent of digital editing and archiving. Many see Dickinson's work as forerunner to a particular strain of poetic experimentation, arguing that the poet consciously explored a mode of expression that is inseparable from her visual and material forms. McGann, for instance, places her in a line of poets that includes Ezra Pound, Gertrude Stein, Laura Riding, and Bob Brown. Others read a feminist politics not only into her idiosyncratic syntax but also into her decision to absent herself from the print culture of her day. In *My Emily Dickinson*, Susan Howe describes Dickinson's work as a sustained, "skillful and ironic investigation of patriarchal authority over literary history," in which she "explored the implications of breaking the law just short of breaking off communication with a reader" (1985: 11). And the new wave of electronic archives and facsimile editions does indeed threaten to break off communication. Or, rather, they limit a certain kind of communication in favor of another: they exchange the ease of access to the lexical text afforded by Todd's or Bingham's editions, or even

Johnson's or Franklin's, for a very different kind of communication, in which the "information" or "message" offered is arguably more visual than linguistic.

Bervin and Werner's 2013 edition *The Gorgeous Nothings,* for instance, presents full-sized color facsimiles of fragments of text written on envelopes, those everyday enclosures that transported Dickinson's writing across her "Father's ground." Each page also exhibits a miniature outline of the manuscript in question, with a tiny transcription in blue ink, in a font designed to mimic Dickinson's hand while also regularizing the shapes of letters so as to make the transcribed texts more legible than the facsimiles themselves. In her afterword to the book, "Itineraries of Escape: Emily Dickinson's Envelope-Poems," Werner portrays those texts as aspiring to a freedom from fixity, and this editorial project as one of recuperative release. She lingers on one fragment in particular, the top fold of an envelope in whose shape she sees a bird's wings. Johnson's typeset versions of this and other "late ecstatic writings," she writes, are a form of "instantaneous trans-lation" that transports Dickinson's script from a condition of free flight into one of textualized fixity (Werner: 201). Whereas Johnson's typeset versions freeze Dickinson in immovable type, and even Franklin's facsimile version presents images only of those manuscripts that most resemble books, Bervin and Werner try to release the birds of these fragments into "a freer air" (207). The forms they offer are, of course, also transcribed, printed, mass-produced, and circulated in a codex form. Yet the editors express a hope that the volume they have designed will remain open to new modes of reading attentive to the details of Dickinson's script, and of the physical documents on which she wrote.

The Gorgeous Nothings is in fact a very gorgeous something; the slow deciphering of the manuscripts makes for incredibly rich encounters with these materials. As a reader, I find it beautiful and compelling. However, as a scholar whose reading habits were shaped in a post-poststructuralist moment in the U.S. academic sphere, I also find that the more strident arguments about Dickinson's visual and material experimentation give me pause, as being uncomfortably intentionalist in orientation. I also wonder to what extent my preference for editions that emphasize textual unfixedness is a product both of my training and of the historical juncture at which I am reading. The privileging of difficult poetry; the resistance to ease; the fascination with the materiality of literary production at a moment when modes of reading, writing, and publishing rely increasingly on digital tools and devices—these, too, may be historically conditioned preferences rather than inescapable truths about what Dickinson's poetry really is, or how it really means. Scholars have presented all editors through Johnson and even Franklin as having "domesticated and occluded" the poet's art (Howe 1993:

31). But these new editions, rather than unbinding the wings of Dickinson's manuscripts, may confine the work in a new "Closet" or "Pound," one simply more in keeping with current scholarly perspectives, or with the intellectual gestalt of our time. Miller reminds us that the focus on visual form is not only based on "a twentieth-century paradigm" anachronistic to Dickinson's moment of writing, but comes at the expense of other ways of encountering the poems. For instance, in a contemporary environment whose sound-scape is radically different from that of Dickinson's nineteenth-century New England, producing editions that privilege the visual might make it more difficult for readers to perceive the subtleties in the aural effect of Dickinson's manipulation of metrical form, an aspect of poetic texts that readers accus-tomed to free verse—or not accustomed to poetry at all—tend to find more challenging to begin with (Miller 2004: 203).

If editions that privilege the manuscript forms of Dickinson's poetry amplify rather than mitigate some of its most challenging aspects, this "fetishization of Dickinson's 'body' in holograph" (Miller 2000: 248) could also lead to what Miller elsewhere calls the reprivatization of the poetry, which would confine it once more to the domestic zone of her "Father's ground." Introducing a brief selection of poems by Dickinson in her 1998 anthology *Nineteenth-Century American Woman Poets*, Paula Bennett suggests that Dickinson's poems "cannot be fairly read apart from her letters, her 'fascicle bundles,' her cooking chocolate wrappers, her feathers, her roast chickens, her flowers, and her glasses of sherry—in short, apart from the material world in which she located and left them, a world as far apart from the sterility of the published page as one could possibly get" (quoted in Miller 2000: 244). Bennett focuses on what Jeanne Holland has called Dickinson's "domestic technologies of publication" (140), which involved both the circumscription of her readership to family and friends and her increasingly pronounced habit of writing on scraps of household paper. Bennett's list moves metonymically from the letters and fascicles to the raw materials that quite literally fueled Dickinson's poetic production; the chocolate wrappers on which Dickinson jotted lines act as a rhetorical hinge between the two. If we follow Bennett's argument to its logical conclusion, we not only reinscribe Dickinson into the old scene of writing—a room of cozy domesticity from which "every editor since Mabel Loomis Todd has tried to rescue her" (Dickie: 323)—but also threaten to make her work entirely inaccessible to readers unable to enter or to reproduce that scene.

Worries about the reprivatization of the poems are, to be sure, theoretical rather than practical: facsimiles of the manuscripts (including the Parisian chocolate wrapper in Figure 2, which bears the lines "necessitates / celerity

/ were better / nay were / immemorial / may / to duller / by duller / things")
are now widely available online; anyone with an internet connection or a
smartphone with a data plan can now view hundreds of Dickinson's texts
in high-resolution color images. Moreover, since Dickinson's work has long
been out of copyright, those forms that have been in circulation since the
late nineteenth century are fair game for use on tote bags and calendars or
in collections of inspirational writing. One troubling aspect of an argument
like Bennett's, that Dickinson cannot be "fairly read" without these domestic
accouterments, and certainly not on the sterile printed page, is that it
discounts the ways in which most people actually encounter Dickinson's
poetry. Relatively few readers will ever spend much time with variorum or
facsimile editions of Dickinson's writings, much less with the manuscripts
themselves; it is the early, heavily edited versions now in the public domain
that are most frequently reprinted in popular formats. To whom or to what
are these forms unfair? What is it that they betray?

Figure 2   Amherst Manuscript #540—"Necessitates celerity." The Emily
Dickinson Collection, Amherst College Archives & Special Collections.

Take the following poem, presented here in a form that no scholarly variorum would even consider an "edition" for possible inclusion:

Wild Nights

Wild nights! Wild nights! Were I with thee,
Wild nights should be Our luxury!

Futile the winds To a heart in port,—
Done with the compass, Done with the chart.

Rowing in Eden! Ah! the sea!
Might I but moor To-night in thee!

In 1891, this poem was risqué enough that Higginson hesitated even to include it in the first print collection of Dickinson's work; today, in an atmosphere of changed literary tastes, it is one of her most widely circulated poems. I have transcribed this particular version from the inside of a wrapper from a Chocolove chocolate bar (Figure 3), which brings the poem into the contemporary reader's domestic space, just as the bar of Meunier Lombart chocolate once entered the kitchen of the Dickinson household. In a critical study that borrows its title, *Rowing in Eden*, from this very poem, Martha Nell Smith reads its manuscript as a prime example of "Dickinson's extraordinary, somewhat seductive, calligraphy," and notes how any printed reproduction inevitably "levels the effects of letters" (1992: 65). The Chocolove version levels the effects of the script still further: while it approximates the lexical text of Todd and Higginson's version, it redraws their three quatrains into couplets of long lines, presumably in order to fit the poem into the printable space of the oblong wrapper, un-breaking once more the already un-broken lines of the 1891 edition. One could easily dismiss this text as a commercial bowdlerization of Dickinson's work. Yet the appearance of this version of the poem in 2014, in an "edition" that disregards recent scholarly discussions but likely has a far wider circulation than any scholarly version to date, suggests that a nonspecialist reader (and the nonspecialist "editors" of Chocolove's design team) have found things to savor in Dickinson's poetry other than its scriptural form.

There is certainly a degree of elitism in literary scholars' implicit rejection of these popular rewritings. What concerns me more, as a scholar of translation, is the potential linguistic elitism of insisting that the best way to encounter Dickinson's work is in manuscript or facsimile form—which, if it precludes "translation" into print, threatens even more to preclude translations in other languages. The assumption that language and meaning are inseparable is nothing new to discussions of translation: it is at the very

Figure 3   Chocolove chocolate wrapper—"Wild Nights."

heart of every claim that Dostoevsky can only be fairly read in Russian, or Aeschylus in fifth-century Greek, even if a historical majority of readers have encountered those works in other languages. Similarly, an insistence on reading Dickinson's poems in holograph implies that a manuscript's unique visual and material aspects are part and parcel of its mode of meaning, that the work is in fact *not* separable (or at least not satisfactorily so) from this single textual manifestation. Dickinson is thus made one of the purest examples of the supposed rule of untranslatability, and in fact presents yet another way in which translation is destined always to fail.

Yet this precluding of translation, like the reprivatization of the poems, remains only theoretical: given the existence of well over 100 book-length translations since 2000 alone, Dickinson's readership may be growing at a far more rapid clip abroad than at home. What, then, are we to make of the domesticating impulse of facsimile editions, in light of this competing impulse to make Dickinson's poetry available to ever-growing audiences further and further from her "Father's ground"? In my view, the well-documented "survival" of at least some aspects of Dickinson's work abroad should temper, or at least contextualize, some of the more forceful arguments about the irreducibility of Dickinson's scripts. In other words, translation is not impossible; it happens every day, and if we want to understand what it is, we would do well to attend to the *ways* in which it happens, instead of returning continually to discussions of things it manifestly isn't. At the same time, the ways in which translation happens may not account for all the ways it *could* happen, particularly as regards the visual and material aspects of works. Translators and scholars of translation, of course, bear some responsibility for failing to challenge these outdated conceptions of translation: even among translators, dominant modes of thinking about translation may be stuck in the Todd and Higginson era, focusing almost exclusively on lexical meaning. Perhaps the time has come to let these explorations of the visual and material aspects of Dickinson's poetry challenge what we have tended to accept as the limits of translation.

"Her translated faces": Hybrid Dickinsons

In 1967, long before he created his facsimile, variorum, and reading editions of Dickinson's work, R. W. Franklin published a scholarly study titled *The Editing of Emily Dickinson*. In it, he—like later scholars who subsequently folded Franklin's editions, too, into their critiques—outlined the treatment the poems experienced at the hands of a series of editors, and called for new editions that would take the poet's own forms more adequately into account. On the last page of this book, Franklin makes the following observation: "[W]e are not commonly organized in our pursuit of literature to talk about literature *per se*. Fortunately or unfortunately, authors are our categories, and there is little space for hybrid poems. We have no such category as Dickinson-Todd-Higginson, and the fact that we are not organized to talk about an altered poem as a poem shows how little the subject of our pursuit is poetry" (141). After the sustained critique of prior editions in which his book engages, this striking statement seems to recognize that each edition offers a newly rewritten form of a particular work; the result is a "hybrid poem" of shared responsibility, if not divided authorship. In this rather abrupt about-face from the sustained critique that has preceded this statement, Franklin ultimately accepts the validity of a Dickinson-Todd-Higginson or Dickinson-Johnson version, perhaps in the knowledge that some admixture is unavoidable: this is how works of literature enter the world. The important thing is an encounter with the "poetry"—which, for Franklin, resides elsewhere than in Dickinson's manuscripts, and not only is capable of surviving this process of editorial hybridization, but in some sense depends upon it.

In my introduction, I discussed the distinction textual scholars draw between a work and a text: a work is understood to be a quasi-metaphysical entity that is partly but never fully represented by a given text, or particular material manifestation. I invited us to expand the conceptual range of the work so as to encompass the ever-growing crowd of its actual and potential manifestations in translingual editions, as well. While textual scholars tend to focus on the editorial history of a work in a single language, if we stretch Franklin's discussion of "altered" or "hybrid" texts to include a poem's hybridization through translation, the insistence on the irreducibility of Dickinson's scripts may more easily give ground to an understanding of scriptural form as one mode of meaning among many. Rather than failed attempts to replicate a single, essential mode of meaning, editorial *and* translatorial projects may become varyingly successful attempts to embody the shifting significance of a literary work. Scriptural form thus becomes something that new versions in other forms, media, and languages can gesture toward, rather than attempt (and fail) to replicate. After all, if any typeset edition of Dickinson is an altered form, so too is any facsimile edition: like all prior editions, Bervin and Werner's edition gives us not Dickinson herself so much as Dickinson-Bervin-Werner. The search for an editorial mode that more adequately represents the manuscripts certainly foregrounds some fascinating aspects of Dickinson's writing—yet it will never result in the production of an unmediated original. All editing is mediation, just as all translating is.

What happens, then, when we think of these two activities together? If each edited version is a new hybrid form, shouldn't we encourage translators to develop a degree of conceptual rigor when negotiating between available editions? If a scholar's choice of what edition to quote reveals her critical position on "what constitutes a Dickinson line or poem" (Miller 2004: 205), a translator's choice of what and how to translate likewise reveals *her* critical position on this very same issue. Were I to translate Dickinson into Greek, say, the resulting poems might be Dickinson-Franklin-Emmerich or Dickinson-Bervin-Werner-Emmerich versions, depending on which form I chose as a basis for my translation. Perhaps I would take more than one edition into consideration, and create Dickinson-Franklin-Bervin-Werner-Emmerich versions. In the resulting Greek edition, I would take care to disclose to readers which editorial hybrid or hybrids I had taken as the basis for my own. Of course these lists of names could be expanded to include an infinite procession of other individuals involved in the socialized process of "altering" or "hybridizing" these poems: from the prior editors (Todd, Higginson, Bianchi, Bingham) whose conception of Dickinson's poetry helped shape our own; to the publishers, book designers, printers, and so on who labored on these textual representations; to the other Greek translators whose embodied interpretations I might consult; to the prior writers on whose foundations Dickinson herself built. After all, even Dickinson's most "original" writings are, in a sense, already hybrid texts; she too was an editor and alterer of a prior poetic tradition.

If "[Tell all the Truth]" can be read as an allegory for the publication history of Dickinson's work, the poem "[You see I cannot see]" speaks obliquely to the continually frustrated desire to arrive at an "original" Dickinson behind this series of editorial hybrids. It is also one of two poems in Dickinson's oeuvre that refer to translation (if not necessarily the linguistic variety). I present it on the left in its first published version, from Martha Dickinson Bianchi and Alfred Lee Hampson's 1929 *Further Poems of Emily Dickinson*, and on the right in Franklin's 1998 variorum version:

You see, I cannot see your lifetime,	You see I cannot see - your lifetime -
I must guess	I must guess -
How many times it ache	How many times it ache for me
For me today—confess	- today - Confess -
How many times for my far sake	How many times for my far sake
The brave eyes film.	The brave eyes film -
But I guess guessing hurts,	But I guess guessing hurts -
Mine get so dim!	Mine - get so dim!
Too vague the face	Too vague - the face
My own so patient covets,	My own - so patient - covers -
Too far the strength	Too far - the strength -
My timidness enfolds;	My timidness enfolds -
Haunting the heart	Haunting the Heart -
Like her transplanted faces,	Like her translated faces -
Teasing the want	Teazing the want -
It only can suffice. (162)	It - only - can suffice! (332)

Division 1 your 3 for 4 far

In Dickinson's manuscript, the poem has no variants. However, *editorial* variants have been introduced by the two different readings of a single word, as "covet" and "cover." Bianchi and Hampson also replace "translated" with "transplanted"—an ironically fitting substitution for a poem in which, as Virginia Jackson notes, "the representation of desire's object threatens to take the place of that object itself" (92). The collision or collusion of these two sets of terms speaks yet again to the synecdochic attempts in scholarly writing to reach back through the manuscripts to the poet's actual hand, and to the objects that comprised her scene of writing: her chocolate wrappers, her envelopes, the pencil stub (now belonging to the Amherst College library) that Dickinson once enclosed in a letter to Samuel Bowles, playfully encouraging a reply. There is a coveting of sorts, an enviousness of these manuscripts for having been there. This coveting begets, in turn, a series of editorial rewritings that continually cover over what layers of text we have, transplanting the poems yet again, in ever-changing forms, out of the drawing room or desk drawer and into the realm of mass production and distribution. In doing so, these rewritings usurp the place of any presumed "original," displacing it, transplanting it, transforming it into something quite other than what it may have been.

In the poem, however, there *is* no original. The desired face is vague and far; the speaker's present time and place offer only guessing, dim eyes, timidity, and want. Likewise, we may believe that the facsimile editions give us the clearest possible view—short of a visit to the archive—of Dickinson's "originals." Yet those facsimiles, so easy to see, are difficult to read. They, too, give most of us not a clear but a differently vague and distant view of Dickinson's poetry: unless properly trained, we can only guess what the words are, and will inevitably at times be wrong. Furthermore, whenever we read Dickinson, in whatever hybrid version, or even in the archive itself, we do so through filmed-over eyes, on a plane of historical and geographical distance from the desired "source," from Dickinson's time and place, from the fetishized homestead with its sherry and roast chickens and chocolate wrappers. Images of those wrappers may now be circulating far afield, in digital versions accessible in Amherst, in Bangkok, in Mumbai, in rural France—yet even within the space of Dickinson's supposed linguistic and cultural community, they have traveled to places where light *doesn't* slant on winter afternoons, where the flora and fauna are not the same, where very few would recognize an "Indian Pipe" as a flower, where the "unobtrusive mass" of a "minor Nation" humming in the summer grass is drowned out by the twenty-first-century sounds of lawn care. The poem is already changed, even without any intervention on the part of an editor or translator.[7] The longing for an original evinced by scholars' focus on Dickinson's

---

[7]   See Morris on the lack of homogeneity in readers of Dickinson even in her language of composition, as well as the survival of the poetry despite mistakes in hearing or reading her work. See also, Spicer's and Benjamin's comments in Chapter 5 on the inevitable change in language, as well as Schalkwyk's in the Introduction on time being a work's first translator. The rhetoric of change is one I use here with some degree of care because of its implication that there is a core essence there to *be* changed.

manuscripts, like the longing for an original evinced by discussions of untranslatability, is chimerical to the core, "teazing the want" which "only can suffice."

When a translator does engage with this poem, in the hopes of creating a successful version in another language—what then? The interpretation she produces will be affected, at least to a degree, by the editorial version(s) she has chosen or is able to consult. Again, "[You see I cannot see]" has no textual variants in the manuscripts. Yet the introduction of editorial variants makes a translator's choice of her editorial source(s) also a choice between divergent interpretations that encourage divergent renderings in other languages. This is, of course, true of translation in general, not just in the particular case of Dickinson. In telling the story of Dickinson's continual editorial hybridization in English, I hope to encourage a greater degree of rigor among translators when investigating the publication history of other works they set out to translate, and when helping to shape the editions that will embody their own hybridized forms. If any published translation is also an edition, the translator has no less theoretical leeway than an editor in English to make decisions regarding both her source and the bibliographic configuration of the text she presents (though she may, of course, have far less practical leeway, depending on the agency she can claim within the particular context of publication). Neither of these has generally been considered part of the translator's task or prerogative. I believe they should be—and that translators, editors, and publishers of texts in translation should develop a sufficient awareness of the fundamental issues in textual scholarship such that decisions regarding "sources" are made carefully and with purpose.

Similarly, if we draw the margins of Dickinson's work—or anyone else's—in such a way as to include scriptural form as one of its central modes of meaning, it seems odd to continue to translate in a way that excludes that element. In this regard, our conceptual and even practical tools as translators have not caught up with our tools as editors of work we consider visually experimental; translators remain largely untrained to consider and to work with the visual elements of texts. What would it look like if translators put visuality, materiality, or scriptural form on par with lexical meaning? Can we, as translators, learn to see differently, to expand our visual awareness of the texts we work with? Can we also learn to translate differently, imagining new forms for the translations we hope to see produced in our name?

"+ Risk [...] + could reach [...] + seraphic gain":
Seeing translation otherwise

Such questions regarding the translatability of visual form could be asked with regard to literary works from various places and times: Laurence Sterne's typographic flights of fancy in *The Life and Opinions of Tristram Shandy*;[8] the illuminated manuscripts of medieval Europe; William Blake's laborious technique of "illuminated printing," with its hand-colored etchings; Guillaume Apollinaire's calligrammes; Susan Howe's dense thickets of cross-hatched text; the illustrated, woodblock-printed books from nineteenth-century Japan. In each of these cases, an editor producing a new edition of the work in its language of composition must determine how significant certain visual elements are to the work, or to a particular textual manifestation of it, and how specific her edition's gesture to these elements needs to be. How closely, for instance, must a new typeset edition of Apollinaire's famous fountain poem follow the falling lines of the manuscript? Does the typographical "water" simply need to fall, or does it need to describe particular arcs, land in particular places? Likewise, a translator, who effectively edits a work in translation, will need to make such decisions anew in another linguistic context, helped (or hindered) by the added information of prior editors' and translators' approaches. In the absence of legal or practical constraints, a translator's task might involve investigating the editorial history of a work, considering how prior editorial versions (in and out of a work's initial language of composition) influence the reader's experience, and deciding how to treat various elements of those versions—including visual, material, and bibliographic elements—in translation. Again, this is not work translators are used to doing. Translators often consult previous translations of works to help them tease out the meaning of particularly thorny passages; they rarely look at multiple editions of works in the "original" language *or* in translation to see how editors and translators deal with these issues. But what if we were to take the example of Dickinson as a challenge to translation on this level, as well?

As a theoretical model for our engagement with the visual and the bibliographic in translation, we might look to Jen Bervin's *The Dickinson Composites*, a set of six quilts that offer visual responses to the ongoing editorial effacement of certain aspects of Dickinson's work.[9] They are

---

[8] See footnote 29 of the Introduction on Manuel Portela's Portuguese translation of Sterne's novel, which does in fact attempt to follow the typographic aspect of the book.

[9] I refer not to the artist book of the same name, published by Granary Books in 2010, but to the full-sized quilts themselves, images of which can be viewed on Bervin's website:

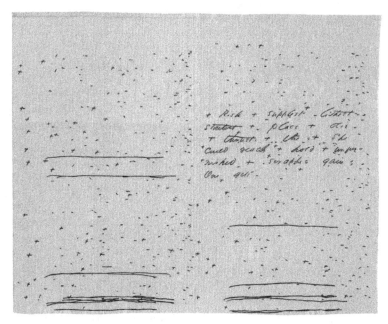

Figure 4   Jen Bervin, Fascicle 28 from *The Dickinson Composites*, 2008.
Cotton and silk thread on cotton batting backed with muslin, 6 × 8 ft.

large, oblong rectangles of cotton batting with muslin backing; some are
machine-ruled with blue thread to resemble composition paper; all are hand
embroidered in red. Four of the quilts contain no words, while the other two
present only a few lines of text. Instead of the language of the poems, Bervin's
quilts focus on the penned or penciled nonlexical marks that surround and
interrupt the text in her manuscripts: each quilt accumulates the markings
from one fascicle into a single composite image, presented as an open,
two-page spread. Figure 4 shows the quilt for Fascicle 28, which represents
not only dashes, commas, and the crosses that mark variants at the bottom
of the poem as well as their placement in the poems themselves, but also
the heavy lines Dickinson drew across the page at several points in this
particular fascicle, dividing one poem from the next or marking the end of
a poem at the bottom of a page. The words on the quilt are taken from "[My
first well Day]." Part of the poem was included in a letter to Samuel Bowles
and first published in Mabel Loomis Todd's 1894 *Letters of Emily Dickinson*;

http://jenbervin.com/projects/the-dickinson-composites-series (last accessed 7 May
2017).

the poem in its entirety subsequently appeared in Bianchi and Hampson's 1935 *Unpublished Poems of Emily Dickinson*, and has since been published in numerous other editorial versions.

Bervin, for her part, chooses to follow the visual details of the manuscript, and quotes a very specific part of the poem: while the words on the quilt seem to form a tight, compact stanza of their own, they are in fact the variants Dickinson recorded at the end of the poem in Fascicle 28. Figure 5 shows the relevant section of the manuscript. Compare that image to how Franklin presents the same variants in his variorum:

> 6 Chance] Risk *alt* 6 Risk] k *made from* h 8 strongest]
>] supplest – lithest – stoutest 11 stead] place 15 fade -]
> die – 15 held] thrust 17 a] the 21. that she met] she
> could reach 23 hide] hold 24 unfitted] unfurnished
> 26-27 Ethereal Gain One earns] seraphic gain, One gets

(1998, 308)

Here, Franklin doesn't simply reproduce the words on the page, but links each word or phrase to the line and even particular word for which he judges it serves as an alternate form. Each word or phrase thus becomes a "suggested change" (to borrow Todd's language) rather than a free-floating, unmoored alternate. Bervin's stitching, on the other hand, traces the shapes of the words as they appear in the manuscript. Her quilt doesn't just recuperate the variants, it recuperates *only* the variants, and does so in a very particular form: the visual form of Dickinson's holograph script. If we compare the manuscript to the quilt, meanwhile, we see that even the words in Bervin's piece become, in a way, *gestures* to words: far larger than their handwritten models, thickly embroidered, and overlaid by other markings, they are more difficult to decipher than those in the facsimile. And since their textual context has been entirely removed, a reader cannot look for help to the words of the preceding text. In other cases, the prior decipherments of print editions shape our understanding of what the manuscripts say; here, the facsimile helps us decipher the partial edition of this quilt.

What, then, of the actual "content" of the poem itself, to which Bervin's piece gestures mostly as an absence? The speaker of the poem has been ill for a long while. Finally feeling sufficiently recovered to venture outside, she hopes to see all the "things in Pod" that were just beginning to burst into early summer life when she was confined to home. Her illness has been grave, even life-threatening. Now, walking in the fresh air for the first time in weeks, she sees that the personified "she" of summer has faded: she "put some flowers away" and brought out "Redder cheeked ones – in their stead"; she "tied the Hoods to Seeds" and "dropped bright scraps of Tint,

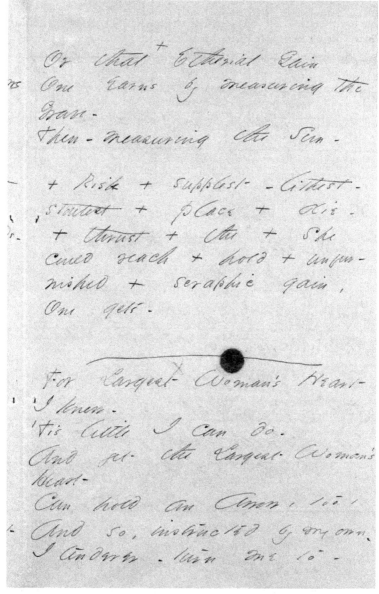

Figure 5 Fascicle 28, Houghton Library, Harvard University. By permission of the Houghton Library, Harvard University MS Am 1118.3 (139 a, b).

about"; she put up "both her Hands of Haze [...] to hide her parting Grace / From our unfitted eyes." Summer has advanced into fall, and is now rushing toward barren winter. In the final stanza, which I quote here in Franklin's variorum version (including the relevant variant), the speaker articulates less a sense of sadness at having missed the joys of summer than gratitude for the continued gift of life her recovery enables—and even more, for the heightened awareness of that gift:

> My loss, by sickness – Was it Loss?
> Or that Ethereal Gain
> One earns by measuring the Grave –
> Then – measuring the Sun –
>
> 26–7 Ethereal Gain One earns] seraphic gain, One gets

(1998: 308)

In the context of this chapter, the words "loss" and "gain" immediately suggest themselves as another allegory for the work of both translating and editing. Read thus, this question challenges the very notion that translation, or even type-translation, is loss and loss alone. Certainly, the summer is irretrievably gone. Yet those weeks of thinking she might not see the outdoors again, of contemplating the eternal darkness of the grave, has made the changed, autumnal sun on the speaker's hands feel like an ethereal (or seraphic) gain.

So, too, if we measure the manuscript of this poem against its type-translation, or against a translation in some other language, believing only the manuscript will suffice, we are likely to feel the sense of loss that recurs time and again in discussions about translation. But if we measure the light of the "Sunshine in [our] hands" provided even by an edition or translation we judge wanting against the total, unequivocal loss of *no* edition, *no* translation, what we have in our hands will feel like an incalculable gain. Dickinson's poem in the 1894 edition of her letters, in the 1935 *Unpublished Poems*, in Franklin's variorum, on a candy wrapper, or in a translation that doesn't do exactly what we, with our own interpretive biases, wish it would— all are gains, greater or lesser, but gains all the same.

This talk of gain stands in tension, of course, with the far more pervasive rhetoric of loss, damage, distortion, and destruction we find in popular and scholarly discussions of translation alike. It also stands in tension with the liberatory rhetoric used by many scholars of Dickinson who advocate a turn to the visual in editions of her work—the very turn that, I have argued, threatens to trap that work in English. It might even stand in tension with the recuperatory gesture of Bervin's quilts. And yet unlike facsimile editions that attempt to reproduce the scene of Dickinson's writing, Bervin's work seems to recognize that no gesture of recuperation can ever be total, nor should it seek to be. A gesture of this sort is conceptual in its very nature. Its task is not to represent but to remind. In Dickinson's poem, we cannot have the ethereal gain of autumn light without the passing of summer. In Bervin's quilts, we cannot have the words and the markings both—and we already have the words; they have been returned to us time and again, in myriad forms. Bervin's quilt for Fascicle 28 "loses" all but seventeen of them, retaining only the variants that have so long been effaced by editions of Dickinson's work, cut off from the context that supposedly gave them meaning. Yet Bervin gives them a different *kind* of meaning. First of all, her very choice to focus on these words, and in this form, is significant, for the reasons I have mentioned above. So, too, is her choice of medium, which gestures to the historically gendered component of this particular act of recuperation. Bervin uses fabric and batting to embody her interpretation of what matters to this work, and of how it has been made to matter by others. Likewise, her stitched script gestures to the words' materiality, giving space to the particular shape of the dashes, their upward or downward tilting, the clustering of crosses in certain parts of a spread, the crosswise sweep of the dividing lines, underlining absence. There is a kind of big data here, in the insistent focus on smallness.

Werner has called Dickinson's script "cometary"; others, too, see her manuscripts, and particularly the late ones, as records of stolen moments and flitting thoughts. Bervin's quilts, in contrast, are painstaking registers of time. They gesture, among other things, to a century and a half of prior reproductions of Dickinson's work. In offering composite images of the markings on Dickinson's fascicles, Bervin gives shape to those features that editors—and readers, and translators—have not seen, or have not seen as meaningful. In this, Bervin's quilts are scholarly objects, the result of a deep intellectual and practical engagement with how these poems mean, and with the history of their production and reproduction, the history of how they have been made to mean. *The Dickinson Composites* can, I contend, stand as a model for us as translators, less in their particulars than in their gestural stance. For if we are to locate meaning elsewhere than in lexical text, we must also admit the possibility of translating otherwise than purely lexically.

And we needn't be visual artists to do so, nor need our translations jettison lexical meaning altogether. We might, on the contrary, envision editions that present fairly conventional lexical forms for Dickinson's work in other languages while also incorporating an understanding of the manuscripts' visual or material aspect: bilingual editions that include as many facsimile images as possible, or translations that take typographically experimental transcriptions of the poems as their base and shape their own typographical experiments in another language. If we chose to focus on scriptural form as central to the poetry's mode of meaning, we might consider producing scriptural versions of the poems in other languages, other scripts. If we wanted to acknowledge the importance of Dickinson's quasi-private mode of circulation, we might envision a subscription service in the mail—with poems in Russian, in Finnish, in Thai, with or without accompanying facsimiles, with or without pressed flowers or pencils like the one the poet sent to Samuel Bowles. These more extreme forms might not seem like translation to some. They might also necessitate collaborative work of the sort that produced Bervin and Werner's *The Gorgeous Nothings*. Yet if our poets are creating visually-resonant work, we as translators might need to find other tools and develop other methods, or at least feel comfortable turning for help to others who have been differently trained than ourselves. It is a risky endeavor; it is also one that stands to achieve ethereal, seraphic gains.

The Unfinished Afterlives of C. P. Cavafy[1]

This was found among a poet's papers.
but difficult to read
There's a date, too, [[but half erased]].
then   then
The one barely shows. [[The]] eight, [[and the]] nine
the [fou]] fourth number [[s + +]] [[looks like a six]]
is crossed out

9
The 1 barely shows; then [[8]], [[nine]] then
1; the fourth number looks like a [[6.]] 9.
then nine, then
4 one; the fourth number looks like nine

—C. P. Cavafy (tr. Emmerich)

In the papers of a poet this was found.
It does have a date, but it's difficult to read.
The one is barely visible; then nine then
one; the fourth number looks like nine.

—C. P. Cavafy (tr. Mendelsohn)[2]

Though entirely untrustworthy as a source of biographical information about Constantine P. Cavafy (1863–1933), one of the best known and most widely translated modern Greek poets, Yannis Smaragdis's 1996 film Καβάφης

---

[1] This chapter draws on material published in "The Afterlives of C. P. Cavafy's Unfinished Poems." *Translation Studies* 4 (2) (2011).

[2] This quotation is from Daniel Mendelsohn's translation of Cavafy's unfinished poem "Το Ἔγκλημα" (The Crime). Mendelsohn, as I will discuss at length below, is translating from the clear reading portion of Renata Lavagnini's "last text" for this poem in her edition of Cavafy's unfinished poems. In my own translation above, I translate the "same" passage from her diplomatic transcription of Cavafy's manuscript. For more on these respective choices of a "source text," see my discussion in the chapter that follows, particularly pgs. 156–57.

(*Cavafy*) encapsulates many of the issues involved in the posthumous construction of Cavafy as a central figure in the Greek as well as the world literary canon.[3] Even before the opening credits we see an unnamed scholar step up to a podium in London in 1950 and begin to lecture about the poet in heavily accented English. The scene ends with the scholar reciting, in Greek, the last stanza of "Στα 200 π.Χ." (In the year 200 B.C.), which I quote here in a slightly modified form of John Mavrogordato's translation, published by the Hogarth Press just a year after this (fictional) lecture:

> We: the Alexandrians, the men of Antioch,
> The Seleucians, and the numerous
> Greeks over above of Aegypt and Syria,
> And those in Media, and those in Persia, and all the others.
> With our far-reaching dominations,
> With various influence prudently adapted.
> And our Greek Common Speech
> Into the midst of Bactria we carried it, even to the Indians.
> We, a new Greek world and great.[4]

The use of this poem implicitly frames scholar and poet as twin representatives both of and at the periphery, members of this new, great Greek world, charged with carrying that Greekness elsewhere. And the fact that a crowd has supposedly gathered in London for a lecture about Cavafy less than two decades after his death, and only two years after the first volume of his poetry was published in Greece,[5] suggests that this figure from the edges of the Greek world—who lived most of his life in Alexandria, wrote in his own idiolect of an already minor language, and whose sexual preferences kept him on the fringes of society even when he was at its center—has started to move outward into new lands and languages.

Smaragdis's use of this poem is multifaceted in its irony. There is, first of all, the historical irony in the poem itself, set not at the height but at the waning of the Hellenistic period—an irony intensified by the fact that in 1950, when this

---

[3] Current transliteration practice for Greek names would have me write Konstantinos P. Kavafis; I use "Cavafy" both because of prior convention, but also because this is how the poet himself signed his name in English and in French, the two languages other than Greek in which he wrote with ease.

[4] Cavafy (1951: 194). The last line of Mavrogordato's translation reads "A new Greek world and great"; I have modified it so as to include a first-person plural that appears elsewhere in his rendering. In addition, I have misquoted Mavrogordato's translation in keeping with Smaragdis's rearrangement of lines (see my discussion of the misquotation in the following paragraph).

[5] This edition, released by Ikaros in 1948, was not the first edition of Cavafy's work, only the first to be released in Greece. The first edition was edited by Rika Sengopoulou and privately printed in Alexandria in 1935, two years after his death.

scene takes place, the British Empire (and to some extent the Queen's English) had recently lost control of many of the places the poem mentions. Second, Cavafy's idiosyncratic Alexandrian Greek is taken to represent the "Greek Common Speech" before an English crowd presumably unable to understand the language at all (though the film's initial audience of 1990s cinema-going Greeks would certainly have been able to understand the scholar's few introductory phrases in English). And finally, a viewer with some knowledge of Cavafy's relatively small body of work might notice that the scholar *mis*quotes (or "prudently adapts") this poem: he swaps out its final line, which signals the speaker's willful blindness to the inevitable fact of historical decline, for a line that appears earlier in the poem, the grandiloquent "Εμείς, ελληνικός καινούριος κόσμος, μέγας" ("We, a new Greek world and great"), intoned to the accompaniment of swelling electronic music by Vangelis (of *Chariots of Fire* fame). This unnamed scholar thus creates a faulty oral "edition" of his own, tailored to the needs of the circumstance. Or, we might say, in selectively quoting and rearranging the lines of this poem, Smaragdis himself tailors the text to suit the image he seeks to create, in 1996, for this now canonical poet.

Smaragdis's film in fact takes the construction of images of Cavafy as a central theme. The film is anchored on the poet's seventieth birthday—famously also the day of his death from throat cancer in an Alexandria hospital—and unfolds in a series of flashbacks, each introduced by a voiceover quoting a fragment of his poetry. Throughout the film, the poet himself is silent: while the deathbed scenes show a Cavafy whose actual voice was silenced by a tracheotomy a few years earlier, even the flashbacks depict him not as actor but observer, silent voyeur onto his own biography. And if the poems in the voiceovers seem to speak for him, offering the deepest possible transformation of life into art, the film also gestures to the many ways in which Cavafy's biography has been shaped by others. The first scene after the credits shows us a boy still in infant's skirts, being photographed with his family. A series of popping flashbulbs, a closeup of his boyish eyes, then of an adult Cavafy's eyes in his distinctive tortoiseshell glasses, and we pan out to find ourselves in his hospital room on the day of his death. Reluctantly led in by a protective Alekos Sengopoulos (the poet's soon-to-be heir), the same scholar who twenty years later will be addressing the London crowd has come to fact-check his "Sketch on the Life and Work of C. P. Cavafy." On entering, he pulls a French magazine from his bag, exclaims, "Finally, Europe is recognizing your work," and begins to read, in French (a language Cavafy spoke fluently, along with Greek and English), a passage praising Cavafy as "an ultra-modern poet, a poet of future generations."[6] As the scholar places the

---

[6] My citation comes from the screenplay (Smaragdis 1997: 26). It is rumored though unproven that Cavafy himself was the author of this review.

magazine on the nightstand, his gaze falls on a small pile of papers lying on the bed, covered with the poet's scrawl—unfinished poems, presumably, on which the poet is still furiously at work. The scholar then pulls out his biographical text and invites the (mute) poet to make any necessary corrections or emendations. As he begins to read Cavafy the story of his own life, beginning with his childhood, the film follows him back to those years. Soon the scholar's voice gives way to the film's first voiceover, reciting lines from "Εκόμισα εις την τέχνην" ("I Brought to Art"), which likewise transport us once more to the past, as the poet "sit[s] and daydream[s]" the scenes that comprise the core of the film.

This opening sequence presents several themes central to my discussion: Cavafy's growing fame; his role as unlikely representative of the Greek-speaking world; the struggle for access to, even control over, the poet and his work; the fetishization of his manuscripts; the interpretation of his poetry as allegorical autobiography; and above all his silence, which seems to intensify others' need to extrapolate a poet from the poems. Smaragdis is no exception to this trend—yet he makes it clear from the start that the film will offer us not facts but mediation. While the film purports to awaken Cavafy's biography via an invocation of his poetry, it also shows the consolidation of the Cavafy myth taking place through scholarship: it is the scholar who inherits the task (or usurps the privilege) of telling Cavafy's story, and the film's imaginative biography is structured by his narrative—or at least his need for a narrative. A later scene returns us to the poet's deathbed, as the scholar momentarily interrupts his reading. "There's a gap here," he says, turning expectantly to the speechless poet for help.

The need to fill those gaps has in fact driven much scholarship about Cavafy: the attempt to decipher his "coded" diaries; the proliferation of biographical readings of the poems; the need to construct a solid oeuvre out of a mass of materials left unpublished (in any conventional sense) at the time of his death. Like Emily Dickinson, Cavafy chose not to make his work commercially available; rather, he circulated hand-compiled collections of printed poems among friends and acquaintances. Like Dickinson's, Cavafy's poetry therefore reaches a wide readership only in the mediated forms of posthumous editions. In the pages that follow, I offer an overview of Cavafy's habits of selectively sharing his poems, and discuss the editorial interventions of some of his posthumous editors. Both popular and scholarly engagements with his work show an ongoing interest in what we might call a search for origins—a search that encompasses not only a biographical impulse but a fixation on the materiality of Cavafy's poetic products. My analysis focuses primarily on what are arguably the most textually unstable works in his oeuvre, a set of unfinished poems found in the poet's archive after his death. I consider some of the ways translators have presented (and might present) these unfinished works in languages other than Greek. My chapter on Dickinson addressed the theoretical and practical challenges raised for editors and translators by the atypical visual and material aspects of her writing. While it hypothesized potential modes of engaging with her work in translation, it did not examine existing translations—primarily because most translators of Dickinson have yet to treat these elements as central to their task. This chapter, on the other hand, takes the comparison of existing translations as one of its basic methodological tools. It does so in order to focus on a key issue I bracketed in my discussion in Chapter 3: the translation of textual variants. In the process, I demonstrate how both in Cavafy's broader oeuvre and in the particular case of the unfinished poems, the "original" is always a singularly plural affair.

The editorial canonization of C. P. Cavafy

If one common trope in religious canonization is the veneration of a saint's relics, in Cavafy's case those relics are not the poet's corpse but his poetic corpus. In this regard, Smaragdis's film exhibits a noteworthy blind spot: it makes no reference to the poet's idiosyncratic habits of selective self-publication. Apart from two chapbook-sized volumes he had privately printed in very small runs in 1904 and 1910, Cavafy never produced a conventional edition of his work. Rather, he developed an idiosyncratic, extremely laborious system of what we might call semi-private publication: from 1912 until his death in 1933, Cavafy had individual poems printed at a local Alexandria print shop, then collated them by hand into makeshift collections and distributed them to readers, most of whom were personal friends or acquaintances.

About half of these collections were simply open folders containing sheaves of poems, often held together with a brass fastener. Scholar and editor George Savidis refers to them as "chronological" collections, since Cavafy ordered them by date of composition and added new poems as they were finished. Because these chronological collections included the latest poems to be printed, the composition of the volumes was ever shifting. Cavafy had covers printed when he set out to form a new collection, and would, when necessary, correct the dates on the covers by hand and write new titles into the printed table of contents he included at the end of each collection. When the folders became too unwieldy, he would remove some of the poems to form what Savidis calls "thematic" collections, which look, at least at first glance, like fairly conventional books. Yet they, too, are not printed in standard gatherings, but consist of single leaves pasted to thin strips of paper to form false bifolia. Textual scholars have long been aware that not all copies of a given edition are necessarily identical, since changes can be introduced even during the printing process. Cavafy's hand-compiled collections push this variance to an extreme: no two members of any one "edition" are likely ever to be entirely the same.[7] With Cavafy's so-called editions, variance (however subtle) is the norm, not the exception.

From the meticulous distribution lists Cavafy kept, we know he created an astounding total of approximately 2,200 such volumes, ranging between fifty and 200 a year.[8] His home on rue Lepsius was thus the site of what one scholar of Dickinson has called "domestic technologies of publication" (Holland: 139). Certainly Cavafy's recycling of materials—printed sheets from earlier collections, covers, and tables of contents—is reminiscent of Dickinson's reuse of scraps of household paper. But to a far greater extent than the remarkably prolific Dickinson, Cavafy "recycled" not just his writing materials but his poems themselves: all 2,200 of his handmade collections are cobbled together from a total pool of only 138 poems. Moreover, unlike other poets of his time, who may have produced unique books as special gifts in addition to conventionally published volumes, Cavafy produced *only* unique books. The handful of holograph books he presented to close friends may be valued more highly for the traces they contain of the poet's handwriting, but

---

[7] For instance, the two copies of *Poems 1916–1918* in the Rare Books and Manuscripts Collection at Princeton's Firestone Library display remarkable difference in bibliographic aspect. One is center-sewn, with a blue-specked, off-white cover, while the other is side-sewn, with a straight spine and salmon-colored cover. Many of the poems have been printed at different times, as we can tell from the dates in the colophons and, in at least one instance, from the texts themselves: the earlier of the two contains a 1927 printing of the poem "Ηδονή" ("Pleasure"), corrected by hand, while the one dated to 1930 contains a clean, undated copy whose printed text incorporates those handwritten changes. The latter of these two copies contains colophons dating from 1925 to 1930, while twenty of the twenty-eight page numbers have been either written or corrected by hand. A comparison of the crossed-out page numbers to those that appear with the same poems in the chrono-logical collection *Poems 1916–* suggests that Cavafy was using leftover copies from the printings done for that earlier collection, bodies of which may themselves have contained offprints from certain poems' publications in the periodicals *Nea Zoi* and *Grammata*, both of which were printed, like Cavafy's poems, in the Kasimatis and Ionas print shop.

[8] In 1920, for instance, Cavafy put into circulation at least twenty-eight collections of *Poems 1909–1911*, thirty-three of *Poems 1908–1914*, fifty of the chronological and thus open-ended *Poems 1912–*, and twenty-four of the likewise chronological and open-ended *Poems 1915–*, for an average of two and a half collections per week. The distribution lists from which this information can be gleaned are published as an appendix to Savidis's volume on Cavafy's editions (Savidis 1966: 215–83). This number does not correspond, however, either to the number of intended recipients or to the number of eventual readers these collections ultimately had: the former was much smaller, as Cavafy often gave multiple copies of a given edition to the same individuals, while the latter number may have been much larger, as copies may have been shared or circulated after they left the poet's hands.

the difference is only one of scale from the collections of individually-printed sheets that Cavafy pasted, pinned, and corrected by hand.

If these poems were to reach a wider public after the poet's death in 1933, they would need to be given a form capable of being mass reproduced. Rika Sengopoulou, a close friend of Cavafy's and editor of a periodical to which the poet often contributed, was the first to put together a conventional edition. Sengopoulou's lavish, large-format volume, published in Alexandria in 1935, contained 154 poems (echoing the number of Shakespeare's sonnets): the 138 from his hand-compiled collections; fourteen additional poems from the 1910 volume that Cavafy did not include in later collections, but were already favorites among readers; another early poem which was included in the holograph book he made for Alekos Sengopoulos, Rika's husband and Cavafy's heir; and a final poem that was still in manuscript form when the poet died. The Sengopoulou edition is significant primarily for having brought these 154 poems together as the Cavafy "canon," a grouping and designation that has remained intact ever since. Yet since the expense of the volume made it an unlikely purchase for any but the most affluent admirers, the work of consolidating this "canon" would have to be done by others. The figure who undoubtedly played the greatest role in doing so—and in making public dozens more poems by Cavafy over the years—was George Savidis, whose small, affordable, two-volume edition of 1963, published in Athens, both stabilized the contents of the Cavafy "canon" and radically *de*stabilized the bibliographic forms in which those and many other poems would be presented in the years to follow.[9] While the 1935 edition presents the poems in roughly chronological order of composition, Savidis's edition separates the poems into two volumes, according to his understanding of Cavafy's methods of sharing his work. The first volume brings together the two "thematic" collections in circulation at the time of the poet's death, while the second contains the last chronological collection, plus the final poem that was presumed ready for the printers when Cavafy died.

Not only is this edition still in print (with slight revisions) over a half century later, it remains the most widely available version of Cavafy's main corpus of poems. It also formed the basis for numerous other, sometimes pirated editions that replicate Savidis's texts, usually without acknowledgment. Even the explanatory notes, which Savidis significantly expanded

---

[9] The title of this two-volume edition, published by Ikaros in 1963, is *Ποιήματα (1896–1918) και Ποιήματα (1919–1933)* [*Poems (1896–1918) and Poems (1919–1933)*]. Ikaros had also published three earlier editions in 1948, 1952, and 1958, based on the 1935 Sengopoulou edition. For a history of these early editions of Cavafy, and also a strong critique of Savidis's editions, which he characterizes as an "editorial assault," see Hirst (2009).

in a later printing—notes that provide useful information about little-known historical figures or events, but also make interpretive claims about the poems and often link them to biographical details from Cavafy's life—are now routinely relied upon by scholars and translated as if they were a part of the work itself.[10] In his introduction, Savidis downplays his (significant) editorial interventions by presenting his work as a culmination of Cavafy's own efforts as editor and self-publisher, and presenting his edition as the fullest available embodiment of an editorial fixity toward which Cavafy was headed. "Had he lived longer," Savidis notes, "it is not out of the question that he might have combined these two collections." Thus, Savidis writes, "we could say that the popular edition of his poems was planned and carried out, to a point, by the poet himself" (1963a: 11).

The natural process by which Cavafy would have formed this "canon" was, in other words, cut short only by the poet's death, about which Savidis writes lyrically in the opening paragraphs of his introduction:

> On the 29th of April, 1933 (his birthday), Mr. Kostis Petrou Fotiadis Kavafis, thanks to a surprising consistency of Fate toward the most valuable exiled elder of Greek letters, closed in his birthplace the seventy-year circle of his earthly life, and passed into the circle of eternity: he became, definitively, Cavafy. The day before, the man whose entire conscious life had been a study of death, committed with full lucidity his final duty: he took communion. He had written his will ten years earlier, and his papers were found in exemplary order—a sign that he had been "ready for some time."
>
> Ready doesn't mean certain; probably it indicates tireless consciousness, and steady, if not peaceful, hope. The poet couldn't, for instance, have been sure that twenty years after his death, one of the most renowned bookshops in London would advertise that: "We have all the best books: from Chaucer to Cavafy." (1963a: 9)

Just as the opening sequence of Smaragdis's film juxtaposes a scene of Cavafy in his hospital bed with a scene establishing his importance abroad, Savidis begins by invoking the poet's death, then quickly ushering him into the Greek canon by way of a London bookshop, a metonymy for the canon of world literature. The picture Savidis paints also bears a striking resemblance to a scene

---

[10] The history of these notes demonstrates, once again, how translation can affect the editorial representation of works in their "original" language of composition. The notes for Savidis's 1963 edition are fairly limited; they were expanded at the request of Edmund Keeley and Philip Sherrard, for their 1975 English translation. Savidis then included additionally edited versions of these expanded notes in subsequent reissues of his Ikaros edition of the "canon." I thank Keeley for sharing this information with me.

of *religious* canonization: the poet as "exiled elder"; the emphasis on Cavafy's taking of communion, the miraculous snuffing out of his life by a capitalized "Fate" precisely seventy years to the day after it began—all combine to present Cavafy as a somber, long-suffering martyr to his art, whose death is a passage from the "circle of his earthly life" into the "circle of eternity." Death is thus not only a loss but a gain, of a posthumous literary fame. At the moment of his death, Mr Kostis Petrou Fotiadis Kavafis becomes, simply and definitively, Kavafis—even, in my slight cheat of a translation, Cavafy.

In 1963, when Savidis's edition was published, Cavafy was certainly not an unknown figure among Greek literati. But his distinctive mode of sharing his work, his homosexuality, and his distance from Greece (which he visited only twice in the seventy years of his life) all conspired to keep his work on the fringes of the Greek literary establishment.[11] The opening passage from Savidis's introduction thus acts as a kind of extended speech act: Savidis first willed Cavafy into the canon, and then devoted the greater part of his career to ensuring that "the Alexandrian" did indeed become one of the most valued elders of the Greek literary tribe. For Savidis's role in shaping both Cavafy's reputation and his oeuvre goes far beyond his edition of these 154 poems. In fact, over the next thirty years he produced countless editions on the basis of unpublished material, thanks to his nearly exclusive access to the poet's archive. Savidis first came into contact with Cavafy's archive in 1961, when Sengopoulos, the poet's heir, showed him "a large suitcase full of manuscripts, photographs, and printed matter" (Savidis 1964: 29), and entrusted the 32-year-old aspiring scholar with the task of cataloguing these materials. By the end of 1963, he had organized the collection, prepared microfilms, and published his first major edition, as well as a number of scholarly texts about Cavafy's work. Six years later, Savidis obtained the archive from Sengopoulos's widow. Between then and his death in 1995, he produced an ambitious string of editions that involved the piecemeal release of archival material: unpublished poems in varying states of completion, diaries, notes, miscellaneous prose pieces. As proprietor of the Cavafy Archive, he quite literally shaped both the texts he released and the manner in which those texts were categorized and presented.[12]

---

[11] Even George Seferis, who won the Nobel Prize for Literature the same year this edition was released, and whose respect for Cavafy did much to establish his significance for Greek letters, famously praised him as "one of our three great dead poets who didn't speak Greek" (63). The other two were Dionysios Solomos (1798–1857), now widely considered the national poet of Greece, but whose native language was Italian, and Andreas Kalvos (1792–1869), who likewise grew up speaking Italian, and later spent much of his adult life in Britain, where he died.

[12] Savidis's editions of Cavafy's writings include a quasi-scholarly edition of *Ανέκδοτα Ποιήματα (1882-1923) [Unpublished Poems (1882-1923), 1968], Αποκηρυγμένα*

One Savidis-inspired "truism" about Cavafy's work is the customary division of the poetry into four categories: the 154 "published" or "acknowledged" poems of the "canon"; twenty-seven "repudiated" poems, which Cavafy published in periodicals but never included in his collections; approximately eighty "hidden" or "unpublished" poems, found in fairly finished form among his papers, which he chose not to circulate at all; and about thirty "unfinished" poems also found among his papers, in folders that sometimes contain several drafts and other times a single holograph copy with few corrections. If this all sounds rather confusing, that's because it is. Cavafy's own methods of sharing his work were complex enough; Savidis's tendency to offer multiple editions of the same poems, including initial periodical releases, popular editions, and quasi-scholarly ones, while also changing the names of the categories he had created, and sometimes moving poems from one category to another, makes for a dizzying array of editorial versions of this relatively small body of work. In this sense, Savidis's work as an editor of Cavafy both reflects and contributed to what Jacques Derrida calls (in Eric Prenowitz's translation) an "archive fever," an "irrepressible desire to return to the origin ... the most archaic place of absolute commencement" (57)—a desire always frustrated by the ultimate absence of a stable source, not to mention by the inevitably mediated nature of even the most personal, most private of archives.

When it comes to translation, the trope of a frustrated desire for an original is so common as to verge on banal: even translators themselves often feel compelled to characterize their products as inadequate, mere simulacra (and faulty ones at that) of the "original" works the reader should actually desire. Examples like Cavafy show us, however, that the promise of an "original" body of work can never be fulfilled. The greater our knowledge of the materials Cavafy himself produced, the more unstable this point of origin is shown to be.

Ποιήματα και Μεταφράσεις [*Repudiated Poems and Translations, 1983*], and Κρυμμένα Ποιήματα 1877-1923 [*Hidden Poems 1877-1923, 1993*], a popular edition of the same poems presented in *Unpublished Poems* a few decades earlier, as well as facsimile editions of the notebook Cavafy presented to Sengopulos and of five ornate leaflets of single poems he had printed early in his writing career but likely never distributed. This flurry of editions both makes Cavafy's work available to wider audiences, and makes for a great deal of confusion (see my discussion on the page above). After Savidis's death, the Cavafy Archive was managed by his son, Manolis; it was acquired by the Onassis Foundation in 2013, and has since been opened up to research by a greater number of scholars.

The troubled diplomacy of diplomatic transcription

In 1963, before any of his editions had appeared (and several years before he acquired the archive, when he was still a young scholar desiring greater access), Savidis published an "informative report" that argued in vigorous terms the "pressing need" for these archival materials to be shared with the public "as soon as possible, and in its entirety"—piecemeal if necessary, as time was of the essence.[13] In this report, Savidis explicitly rejected all ethical concerns about sharing writing never intended for public consumption. He also asserted that the methodological problem of *how* to present archival materials had been "solved" fifteen years earlier by Linos Politis, who suggested that the proper editorial form for the unpublished, fragmentary writings of Dionysios Solomos (now widely considered the national poet of Greece) was a "diplomatic" edition, with transcriptions that would register deletions, insertions, unorthodox punctuation and spelling, even mistakes and nonstandard usage. Savidis coopted and generalized Politis's argument: for any writing whose author had not given it a solid, stable state in published form, the only acceptable approach was that of diplomatic transcription.

After acquiring the archive, Savidis did in fact prepare numerous editions on the basis of archival material. Yet he never practiced what he preached in this report. Ironically, the only edition of Cavafy's poetry that uses diplomatic transcriptions is one Savidis did not himself undertake: Renata Lavagnini's 1994 scholarly edition of the *Ατελή ποιήματα* (*Unfinished Poems*). Moreover, as we will see, the idea that a diplomatic transcription would present an objective, interpretation-free account of an unfinished work does not hold up under scrutiny. All editions are interpretive in nature, and diplomatic transcriptions are no exception. Just as Savidis's many editions largely defined the perimeters of this shifting body of work, Lavagnini's volume literally gives shape—interpretive, editorial, partly allographic—to the poems it presents.

The "unfinished" poems, whose textual condition may differ from that of the "unpublished" only by degree, exemplify the issues that mark Cavafy's work as a whole.[14] Cavafy kept the materials for each of what came to be known as the "unfinished" poems together in a folder or packet: loose sheets of paper, at times recycled from printings of earlier poems, bearing crossings-out, corrections, additions, and alternate lines. Sometimes there is only one

---

[13] Savidis (1964: 38). Like his many editions of Cavafy, this text also went through multiple manifestations: first published in periodical form in 1963, it later came out as a stand-alone pamphlet in 1964.

[14] See Emmerich (2011a), as well as Ekdawi and Hirst (1999).

draft; sometimes there are several. Lavagnini rearranges the materials in accordance with what she deems their probable order of composition. She provides transcriptions, detailed descriptions of writing materials, paper size, quality and condition, and a lengthy commentary about each poem that attempts to unpack the stages of the drafting process, in accordance with the methodology of genetic criticism.[8] At the end of each section, in a move she characterizes as "inconsistent" with the theoretical underpinnings of the rest of the edition, Lavagnini also provides what she calls a "last text," which seeks to represent the "last form ... that the poet had given" to each of his poems (Cavafy 1994: 29). These "last texts" take the fairly standard scholarly form of a clear reading text with variants in a textual apparatus below; they usually do not correspond to any extant manuscript, *per se*. At the end of the volume, to top off this mass of materials, she includes color facsimiles of selected manuscripts.

In other words, Lavagnini's volume combines four different editorial treatments of the same texts under a single cover: diplomatic transcription, genetic criticism, best-text editing, and facsimile editing.[15] By offering several ways of exploring the poems and their history of composition, Lavagnini enables an incredibly rich reading experience, though one that can overwhelm the untrained reader. At the same time, however, her volume tries to offer that training: in addition to discussing the specific editorial problems presented by Cavafy's idiosyncratic mode of publishing his poems, her lengthy introduction provides the best Greek-language introduction to textual scholarship to date. In it, Lavagnini warns against separating her "last texts" from the transcriptions that precede them: "From the moment that there is no definitive text, an edition cannot be authoritative that would privilege the last text the poet left, and collect in a critical apparatus [...] all the variants that he rejected in turn," since it would entail our imposing on the work "a hierarchy that is absent from the manuscripts" (25). Yet the form of her edition, the very existence of these "last texts," and the visual prioritization of the clear reading text at the top of the page, with the variants quite literally subordinated below, create a hierarchy so marked as to allow readers to treat the clear reading text as the poem itself, and to downplay the significance of the critical apparatus.[16] And of course only the most dedicated

---

[15] I remind my reader of Shillingsburg's wish that editors choosing a particular orientation "prepare an apparatus that will make the edition useful to persons wishing that another orientation had been employed" (1996: 26). Here Lavagnini pushes this wish to its limit: her apparatus consists, essentially, of three further editions, each created in accordance with another editorial methodology.

[16] As George Bornstein has written, the "disappearance of textual competence among most members of the modern academy" means that this sort of edition "enshrine[s] the latest authorized version of the poem as the authoritative one, with all the information on

readers are likely to study her transcriptions and genetic ordering of texts in any depth. The temptation is indeed great for the reader to skip straight to her "last texts," which are also the easiest to read and enjoy.

The reader who does take the time to compare the edited texts to the transcriptions and notes may be surprised at the extent of Lavagnini's interventions. For instance, of the thirty-four poems in the volume, seven have more than one possible title, and six have titles Cavafy marked (usually in English) as "temporary" or "provisional." In Lavagnini's "last texts," the provisional nature of certain titles is not marked, nor is the existence of alternate titles noted in the list of variants at the bottom of the page. Moreover, while Lavagnini claims in her introduction that there are few true variants ("ones that the poet wrote down without deciding which of all he preferred," Cavafy 1994: 25), a quick glance at the "last texts" reveals that, on the contrary, few of the poems are altogether *without* alternate forms, while some have variants that would, taken together, replace nearly half the poem. "Στην προκυμαία" ("On the jetty"), for instance, has variants for four of its eleven lines, and "Η φωτογραφία" ("The photograph") for six of its ten. Even more extreme is the case of "Του έκτου ή του έβδομου αιώνος" ("Of the sixth or seventh century"), for which Cavafy wrote two separate versions of the first three and last four lines of this twelve-line poem. There are also a number of ambiguities in the manuscripts that Lavagnini does discuss in her notes to the poems, but does not mark in the "last texts," perhaps because scholarly conventions offer her little guidance on how to do so. For the poem Lavagnini presents as "Η διάσωσις του Ιουλιανού" ("The rescue of Julian")—which has *two* alternate titles, "Η διάσωσις του Γάλλου και του Ιουλιανού" ("The rescue of Gallus and Julian") and "Η διάσωσις των Μικρών Παιδίων του Ιουλίου Κωνσταντίου" ("The rescue of the little children of Julian Constantius")—the transcriptions reveal that two separate stanzas are marked with the Roman numeral II, leading Lavagnini to ask in her notes to the poem whether "these two stanzas [are] alternates for one another, or are we to correct the II on 4ᵇB to a III?" She decides only after "a great deal of hesitation" (164) to follow the latter of these two possible interpretations in her "last text." Yet the reader who fails to read the notes will remain unaware of this interpretive move on Lavagnini's part—a move that very easily could have gone the other way, and that makes all the difference to a reader's experience of the poem.

Again, by including transcriptions and facsimiles, Lavagnini makes it possible for an assiduous reader to track her interventions. One could even

variants encoded at the bottom of the page being perceived by most readers as irrelevant debris … . To avoid that, we must either change the way we educate students or else change the way that we construct such editions" (1993: 176).

use the information she provides to create a different "last text," as at least one translator has done (more on this below). Yet the complexity of these poems' textual condition leads me to wonder (as Savidis did in his 1963 report on the archive) whether all editions are equal. Might there be more and less responsible ways of presenting archival materials of this sort, in Greek and in translation? My strongest and perhaps most conservative impulse is to say that an edition in Greek that presents only a clear reading text—as does Sonia Ilinskaya's 2003 Ἅπαντα τα ποιήματα (*Collected Poems*), which appropriates those parts of Lavagnini's editorially constructed "last texts," but presents them without the variants—misrepresents the provisional nature of these unfinished poems, a provisionality that seems central to their mode of meaning. When I think about how one might translate these poems, however, the strength of that conviction begins to waver. If translation is an indication that a work can "survive" even when all of its words are replaced by other words, need we be so concerned about the particularity of the variants? Might the distinction between "unfinished," "unpublished," and even the "published" poems of the "canon" be moot precisely because, as I have been arguing throughout this book, the moment of publication never confers "finishedness," but simply marks a work's entrance into a new realm of potentially infinite iterability? Or, on the contrary, might there be a crucial distinction we want to maintain between the poems Cavafy did circulate in printed forms, however variable, and those he did not? If so, is there a way—perhaps one we haven't yet imagined—of shaping our translations to reflect the lack of fixity that these latter texts exhibit even in their manuscript versions?

To date, there are two English translations of this entire group of thirty-four poems: Daniel Mendelsohn's *C. P. Cavafy: The Unfinished Poems*, a slim book published in 2009 as a companion volume to Mendelsohn's much heftier *C. P. Cavafy: Complete Poems*; and a section titled "Finishing Cavafy's Unfinished" in poet George Economou's recent book *Unfinished and Uncollected* (2015). In 1998, over a decade prior to the publication of Mendelsohn's volume, seven of John Davis's translations appeared in the literary journal *Conjunctions*. Davis had prepared translations of all thirty-four poems, which he circulated among friends, scholars, and fellow translators. I am grateful to him for allowing me to discuss one of his unpublished translations here—an inclusion I find fitting for a chapter on unfinished work. In the next section of this chapter, I show how Mendelsohn and Davis inscribe their respective interpretations of a single poem on the lexical level, while nonetheless delineating the "original" similarly: both texts seem to be based on the clear reading portion of Lavagnini's "last texts." I then turn briefly to Economou's "trans-compositions"—"completed" versions of the poems that "refashion" the elements of any given set of drafts into a "finished poem in English" (11)—and discuss his very different approach to the task of translating works of manifestly indeterminate textual makeup. In looking closely at the various ways these translators approach the instability of their supposed "sources," I invite us to imagine other ways of translating that would respond differently to the challenges posed by such a shape-shifting body of work.

4 + n ways of looking at "The Photograph"

In his nearly fifty-page introduction to the *Complete Poems*, a volume that includes the poems of the "canon" as well as the "unpublished" and "repudiated" (terminology he adopts in his volume), Daniel Mendelsohn notes that a translation of a "significant work of literature" (by which he seems to mean a work that is significant enough already to have been translated) "is to some extent as much a response to other translations of that work as to the work itself" (Cavafy 2009a: xvii). With regard to Cavafy, he writes, other translations have conveyed wonderfully the "unmistakable tone of voice" (in W. H. Auden's oft-quoted words) that we have come to associate with the poet—a tone of voice which, one could argue, is really an *English* tone of voice, the sound of Cavafy in English. Mendelsohn therefore chooses to focus on formal aspects he thinks have been less well accounted for in translation: "the subtleties of language, diction, meter, and rhyme that enrich Cavafy's ostensibly prosaic poetry." His primary preoccupation is with Cavafy's "complex and subtle amalgam of contemporary and archaic forms, one that perfectly mirrored ... the blurring of the ancient and the modern that is the great hallmark of his subject matter." Mendelsohn identifies the mixing of demotic and *katharevousa*—the archaizing Greek used in formal contexts for much of the nineteenth and twentieth centuries—as "perhaps *the* distinctive feature" of Cavafy's poetry, which he gestures toward by using a mix of "high Latinate forms [...] and ordinary, plain Anglo-Saxon derivations"; on occasion, he chooses British over American spellings to give a sense of the "archaic spellings [...] Cavafy often favored."[17]

Mendelsohn can reasonably present this volume as a supplement or even a corrective to existing translations—just as the 2007 bilingual Oxford *Collected Poems*, with translations by Evangelos Sachperoglou and a Greek text newly edited by Anthony Hirst, was conceived in part as a corrective to Savidis's

---

[17] These last three quotations from Cavafy (2009a: xviii, xliii, and xlv). For more on *katharevousa*, see the relevant discussion in Chapter 2.

editorial choices regarding the "canon."[18] Yet the situation of the unfinished poems differs crucially: when it first appeared, Mendelsohn's *Unfinished Poems* was the only published translation of most of these poems in any language. His decisions as a translator therefore have potentially broad repercussions, setting the tone for the presentation and reception of these poems in languages other than Greek. Part of Mendelsohn's goal with the *Unfinished Poems*, he writes in his introduction to that volume, is to show how they "fit into the existing corpus" (Cavafy 2009b: xii), "how fully they partake in Cavafy's special vision" (xi). His stylistic approach to the task of translation is therefore quite similar to the focus on formal elements that he outlines in the introduction to *Collected Poems*. Mendelsohn's version of "Η φωτογραφία" ("The photograph"), for instance, displays his stated interest in Cavafy's rhythms, enjambment, unorthodox syntax, and linguistic heterogeneity:

> Looking at the photograph of a chum of his,
> at his beautiful youthful face
> (lost forever more;—the photograph
> was dated 'Ninety-two),
> the sadness of what passes came upon him.
> But he draws comfort from the fact that at least
> he didn't let—they didn't let any foolish shame
> get in the way of their love, or make it ugly.
> To the "degenerates," "obscene" of the imbeciles
> their sensual sensibility paid no heed.

> (Cavafy 2009b: 18)

The translation is tight and concise, with a single plaintive line of perfect iambs set down in the middle of an otherwise metrically irregular poem. An enjambment in the third line allows "lost forever more" to modify both "youthful face" and "photograph." Mendelsohn's version is also peppered with grammatical and syntactical oddities: the grammatical "mistake" of a dangling participle in the very first line, followed in line 5 by a main verb with a different subject; the inverted word order of the final sentence, which begins with an indirect object and ends with its main verb; the unusual combination in line 3 of a semicolon and an em dash (one of Cavafy's characteristic punctuational quirks). As for mixing registers, the faintly Britishizing yet colloquial "chum" rubs elbows with the Latinate "imbeciles" and "degenerates"; the elegiac "lost forever more" with the contemporary, conversational "get in the way" and "make it ugly"; the contractions in line 7 with the more formal graphical aspect of "'Ninety-two" in line 4.

---

[18] See Hirst's "Note on the Greek Text" (Cavafy 2007: xxxiv–xxxix).

A reader able to access the Greek would certainly be aware that "Η φωτογραφία" is actually composed in fairly standard demotic Greek, and does not display the heterogeneity of register that many scholars consider so characteristic of Cavafy's oeuvre. Yet one could argue that Mendelsohn's approach in "The Photograph" is nonetheless particularly effective, since it complements the poem's themes and structure. By bringing together metered and nonmetered lines, standard and nonstandard syntax, high tone and low, Mendelsohn draws attention to the distinction the lovers try to maintain between the beautiful and the ugly, between their own "sensual sensibility" and the slurs of the "imbeciles"—who, in characterizing the lovers as "degenerates," as "obscene," seem to be expressing their own, very different ideas about the beautiful and the ugly, about proper love and its perversion. Mendelsohn presents the poem as fundamentally about two competing systems of aesthetic valuation—and this heterogeneity in rhythm, tone, and syntax is part and parcel of how he conveys that interpretation.

John Davis's translation of the same poem, while equally effective, exhibits quite different interpretive concerns:

On looking at a photograph of one of his friends
and his handsome young face
(now lost for good—the photograph bore the date
ninety-two), he was seized
by melancholy of the ephemeral.
Yet he is consoled by the fact, at least,
that he—that they—never let any foolish shame
inhibit or degrade their love.
They never let the "Perverts!" and "Debauchees!"
of all those fools disturb their sexual sensibilities.

Despite the presence of a few fairly colloquial phrases, such as "now lost for good" and "all those fools," the poem as a whole exhibits a more elevated tone than Mendelsohn's: "inhibit," "degrade," "melancholy of the ephemeral," "Debauchees!" Davis's translation, written with entirely standard English sentence structure and punctuation, does not share Mendelsohn's fascination with the linguistic unevenness of Cavafy's text (which, again, is not a pronounced element of this particular poem in Greek); instead, it evinces a sustained interest in issues of subjectivity and action. In the first six lines of Davis's poem, which correspond to the present moment, the viewer is the subject of two passive verbs; he does not act but is acted upon. And while Mendelsohn's dangling participle elides the viewer's subjectivity, the strong enjambment of Davis's "he was seized / by melancholy of the ephemeral" actually seizes the reader's attention, highlighting a passivity echoed by the "he is consoled" of the very next line, which shifts the poem abruptly and fleet-ingly into the present tense. Meanwhile, the marked movement from singular to plural in "that he—that they—never let" in line 7 (which seems to track, even visually on the page, the viewer's halting reconstruction of the past), is secured by the unequivocal solidarity of the lovers' action in the phrase "they never let" of line 9, which echoes that earlier line, dispensing only with the hesitation and self-correction. Davis's translation thus emphasizes the rift less between the lovers and their critics than between past and present, by aligning those eras with the initial activity and subsequent passivity of the poem's central character: the lovers' joint action in the past gives way to the passive remembrance of that unity in the present, as the viewer of the photograph is both pained by the loss of that togetherness and consoled by its memory.

Reading these two versions of "The Photograph" in conjunction empha-sizes the fact that any translation of a given "source text" inscribes a particular interpretation on the level of the word, the phrase, the line, the sentence, and the poem as a whole, and the consequent fact that any two translations will differ from one another in the interpretation they put forward. Yet comparing these translations to Lavagnini's Greek demonstrates another, far less widely acknowledged fact: the "source text" is not always—is perhaps never—simply "given." On the contrary, a text only becomes an "original" when another, derivative text comes along to make it so. The trans-lator's choice or construction of a putative original thus constitutes another level of interpretation regarding not what the text means, but what it *is*. This interpretation is not always consciously formed, and is often inscribed even prior to any labor on the level of the word, phrase, sentence, or line. When we choose, in translating, to follow or modify a particular edition of a work, we would thus do well to strive to understand the interpretive labor involved in the construction of *that* edition. Consider Lavagnini's "last text" for this poem, the clear reading portion of which both Davis and Mendelsohn elected to use as their "source":

Βλέποντας την φωτογραφία ενός εταίρου του,[1]
τ' ωραίο νεανικό του πρόσωπο
(χαμένο τώρα πια· —είχε χρονολογία
το ενενήντα δυο η φωτογραφία),[2]
του πρόσκαιρου τον ήλθεν η μελαγχολία.[3]
Μα τον παραμυθεί όπου τουλάχιστον
δεν άφισε—δεν άφισαν καμιά κουτή ντροπή,
τον έρωτά των να εμποδίσει η ν' ασχημίσει.[4]
Των ηλιθίων τα «φαυλόβιοι», «πορνικοί»,[5]
η ερωτική αισθητική των[6] δεν επρόσεξε ποτέ.

¹ ενός εν Καλλονή πλασμένου νέου
² είχ᾽ η φωτογραφία
τριάντα έτη πριν χρονολογία
ή
τριάντα χρόνια πρίν
³ η μελαγχολία τον κατέλαβε
⁴ ή να ρυπάνει
⁵ τα «φαυλόβιοι νέοι»
⁶ η ερωτική καλαισθησία των (Cavafy 1994: 176)

Even a simple visual comparison makes it clear that both English versions differ substantially in form from the Greek text on which they claim to be based: Mendelsohn and Davis have chosen to translate not the "last text" in its entirety but only the clear reading portion. In doing so, they select one set of variants over another, in cases where Cavafy himself made no such decision.

Davis's versions are, of course, unfinished in the same sense as Cavafy's: without a published edition to quote from, it is impossible to say precisely what shape his translations might have taken or what kind of paratextual material would have accompanied them were they to have found their way into print. He may have created a textual apparatus that would translate, discuss, or even quote the variants in Greek, or describe the material condition of the manuscripts. The unpublished version I am working from does not include any such notes, but rather refers the interested reader to Lavagnini's volume, perhaps on the assumption that most readers committed enough to Cavafy's work to want to experience the full chaos of the manuscripts would either already speak Greek or be willing to learn. Mendelsohn, meanwhile, states in his introduction that, "In no case have I chosen to present as part of the translation a variant that has been rejected by Professor Lavagnini" (Cavafy 2009b: xviii). This is a significant misrepresentation of the nature of what Lavagnini has done: she rejects none of the variants presented here, because Cavafy rejected none. The footnoted alternate forms are not old versions Cavafy had decided against but options kept fully in play, between which Lavagnini is adamant that no priority can be established (even as the form of the "last text" visually establishes precisely the prioritization of the clear reading text she decries). In other words, it is no more likely that the clear reading text represents what Cavafy's final choice would have been than any other constellation of variants. Mendelsohn does provide translations of two "noteworthy variants" for this particular poem in the notes at the back of his book:

LINE 1   Looking at the photograph of a youth fashioned in Beauty
LINES 2–3   (lost forever more: —the photograph
                 had a date of thirty years before

(Cavafy 2009b: 71)

Looking at Lavagnini's version, it is unclear why these variants are more "noteworthy" than the others. I suspect Mendelsohn includes them, entirely reasonably, because they diverge most obviously from the lines for which they serve as alternates, and are therefore easier to translate in a way that expresses that difference. Yet even the basic existence of the several variants in Lavagnini's "last text" serves as a reminder of what she describes as the extremely "fluid state of the sketch" (Cavafy 1994: 175)—a reminder to which another translator might have responded differently.

"The Photograph" is actually one of the least complex of Cavafy's unfinished poems, in terms of the amount of manuscript material surviving: its folder contains only a single sheet of paper, handwritten on both sides. One side displays a relatively clean copy of the poem as presented in the clear reading portion of the edited text; about half of its lines are marked with deletions and insertions. At the bottom of the page are three bits of alternate text, two of which are crossed out. The other side of the sheet contains seven more variants. As always in the manuscripts for Cavafy's unfinished poems, there is no indication of where each might belong. Lavagnini's task in this case might seem to be relatively simple: she merely has to copy out any words left standing, in order to come up with her "last text"—and then, as an optional next step, peg variants to what they might be intended to replace. Yet the diplomatic transcription of the materials complicates our image of the poem. One of the phrases Cavafy crosses out is not rejected but rather incorporated into the text above, while other words reappear in the variants on the back of the page. All of these possibilities remained open—not to mention those infinite possibilities afforded by potential revisions that had yet to be drafted when Cavafy died. If Savidis saw the stabilization of a "canon" as a process cut short by the poet's death, one could just as easily make precisely the opposite supposition: on the contrary, Cavafy's death cut short a process of continual recycling and revision that otherwise would have altered the poems in ways we can only imagine.

The inclusion of the diplomatic transcriptions in the volume also allows us to check Lavagnini's work. Here, if we compare her last text with the notes and transcriptions, we see that she has changed the grammatically incorrect "το πρόσκαιρου" to "του πρόσκαιρου." She likewise adds quotation marks around the phrase in variant 5, presumably to make it accord more closely to the reported speech in line 9 that she wagers it would replace. There is also one additional variant, "πράγματα τελειωμένα" ("finished things"), which Lavagnini is unable to place; she identifies it in her notes as a "variant of uncertain position" (Cavafy 1994: 176) and leaves it out of the last text altogether. There is an irony to this particular elision: unable to find a fixed location for these "finished things," Lavagnini excludes the phrase from her "last text," which becomes a shade *more* fixed or finished for that absence. Taken together, these examples make clear the substantial interpretive work Lavagnini is doing in assigning variants to particular lines, even in a poem as relatively straightforward as this one. The final example also shows us the shortcomings of a system that leaves no space for variants whose meaning cannot easily be accommodated to the text above.

In choosing to translate only the clear reading text, Davis and Mendelsohn fix a particular interpretation not of what the "original" *means* but of what it *is*, even before they embark on the work of translation "proper." It is thus worth considering how even slight differences in word choice or order can invite significantly different interpretations, particularly when dealing with texts so dense and painstakingly composed. Here is a provisional translation of these variants, to help us imagine how our interpretation of the poem might be affected were we to encounter a version that made another set of decisions in fixing on a text to translate:

[1] of a youth fashioned in Beauty
[2] the photograph had
a date thirty years [έτη] before
or
thirty years [χρόνια] before
[3] melancholy overcame him
[4] or to pollute
[5] the "degenerate youths"
[6] their sexual/erotic elegance/taste

Greek is an inflected language with flexible word order; English is not. The syntactic difference, then, between such lines as "του πρόσκαιρου τον ήλθεν η μελαγχολία" and "του πρόσκαιρου η μελαγχολία τον κατέλαβε" (in line 3 and footnote 3, respectively) might not register in a translation that strove to maintain standard English syntax (a decision we need not take for granted). In terms of word choice, however, "τον κατέλαβε" ("overcame him") in footnote 3 is far more forceful than "τον ήλθεν" ("came to him"), while "να ρυπάνει" ("to pollute") in footnote 4 bears a stronger sense of moral wrong-doing than "ν' ασχημίσει" ("to make ugly")—on the part not of the homosexual lovers but of those who condemn them. Likewise, the tricky phrase "ερωτική αισθητική" ("sexual/erotic aesthetic/sensibility") has a less positive valence than "ερωτική καλαισθησία" ("sexual/erotic elegance/taste") in footnote 6: not only does the prefix "καλ-" suggest something good or beautiful, but "καλαισθησία" connotes the capacity to judge the good from the bad, the ugly from the beautiful, as opposed to the more neutral, less value-laden "αισθητική." If Lavagnini had chosen to include one or more of these variants—again, possibilities never foreclosed by Cavafy, yet relegated by the format of the edition to the secondary status of a textual apparatus—in the text at the top of the page, the "original" (and, perhaps, the translations as well) might have emerged with a stronger sense of the lovers' aesthetic purity, and of the threat posed by the others' potentially polluting verbal violence.

The substitution of the relevant lines in the clear reading text with the two variants Mendelsohn judges noteworthy would likewise affect our interpretation of the poem in significant ways. The replacement of "ενός εταίρου του" ("a chum of his," in Mendelsohn's rendering; "one of his friends" in Davis's) with "ενός εν Καλλονή πλασμένου νέου" (which Mendelsohn renders as "a youth fashioned in Beauty") could alter dramatically our sense of the relationship between the two men: the equality, similarity, and camaraderie suggested by "chum" or "friend" would give way to a potentially less balanced relationship between the beautiful youth and his beholder. This variant also seems to color the past through the present moment, as the viewer beholds the static photographic image of the youth (and conjures an accompanying mental image of his own youth) from a distance of many years. In fact, while the dating of the photograph to the year "ninety-two" (or "'Ninety-two") says nothing about how much time has passed between then and the moment of viewing, the alternate versions in footnote 2 inform us that thirty years have gone by, giving us a better sense both of the degree of nostalgia involved and of at least the approximate age of the viewer. The enumeration of these years—"χρόνια" in the second of these variants, and the more formal "έτη" in the first—further emphasizes the passage of time by echoing the root "χρόνος" ("time") in "χρονολογία" ("date"), and, obliquely, the "καιρός" ("time") in "πρόσκαιρο" ("transient"). The variants in footnotes 1, 4, and 6 highlight the beauty of the beloved as well as the sequestered goodness of the lovers' encounters, with the "καλ-" in both "καλαισθησία" ("elegance" or "taste") and "Καλλονή" ("Beauty") counterbalancing the negativity—the threatened pollution—of the slurs uttered by the depraved, degenerate, or obscene individuals in line 9. Drawing on the available materials, one could thus envision an "original" of this poem that would focus more insistently on the passage of time and on the positive nature of the relationship described. Such a version might be more dramatically steeped in the melancholy or nostalgia the viewer feels in looking at this photograph, the trace of not just a face but a time, a relationship, an age forever in the past. I certainly don't wish to privilege such an alternate version, but simply to note the subtle differences in interpretation we might have were we to encounter a clear reading text based on a different understanding of the variants.

We could also imagine a translation that would take the entire "last text" as the object of translation, combining rather than choosing among variants. This is precisely what George Economou has done in his recent versions of these poems. In a brief prefatory note, the poet, scholar, and translator calls his approach one of "trans-composition," which "combines the work of translator and poet in a collaborative process with Cavafy."[19] Economou's translations look very similar to Davis's and Mendelsohn's: they, too, display no variants, and have the appearance of finished poems. In fact, Economou explicitly states that his primary goal is to create "finished poems in English" on the basis of the available drafts, including not only the variants from Lavagnini's "last texts," but sometimes even information from prior drafts, taking an accretive approach to the task of translating these highly unstable materials. Consider his version of "The Photograph":

> Looking at the photograph of one of his partners,
> his handsome—no, beautiful face
> (lost for good now—dating back to
> 'Ninety-two, the thirty-year old picture),
> the sadness of how brief it is overcame him.
> But there is some consolation at least
> in that he didn't—they didn't allow a single bit of stupid shame
> to obstruct, to taint or distort their love.
> To the idiots' jeers, 'degenerates,' 'queers,'
> their sense of eros paid no mind ever. (27)

This translation is more idiomatic and current in its lexical choices than either of the two we have already seen: "stupid shame," "idiots," "queers," even a rather twenty-first-century-sounding "partner." The conversational tone is strengthened by the easy flow of Economou's strings of iambs, the in-line rhyme of "jeers" and "queers," the ungrammatical participle in the opening line, and the dashes in lines 2 and 7, marking self-correcting stutters that sound almost like moments of free indirect discourse. The shift from "handsome" to "beautiful" in Economou's second line doesn't

---

[19] In his prefatory note, Economou upends what we might consider the natural relationship between the number of drafts and the role of authorial intent. While we might think a more finished draft might correspond to a greater clarity of intention, Economou suggests that the more "drafts, variants, and marginal comments and corrections in the condition of an original, the greater the possibilities the poet's work will play a major role in the refashioning of its elements into a finished poem in English" (11).

have an obvious precedent in the Greek—yet this additional moment of self-correction brings a wonderful sense of immediacy to the very opening lines of the poem. This sense of being invited straightaway into the viewer's perspective is underscored by Economou's insistent focus on the present: "now," "it is," "there is." Economou's translation offers a solid, cohesive version of the poem that differs substantially from Mendelsohn's and Davis's, focusing closely not on the events of the past but on the present inner state of the reminiscing lover.

But what interests me most is how Economou incorporates material from the variants, not replacing but supplementing the material of Lavagnini's clear reading text. In lines 3 and 4, where Mendelsohn and Davis give only a date, Economou gives both that date *and* a sense of how much time has elapsed, thus incorporating information from the two variants for this phrase. This indication of a thirty years' lapse arguably allows him to bypass the "young" or "youthful" that appears in the other translators' versions of line 2, opening up space for the doubling of "handsome" and "beautiful" I noted above. In line 8, meanwhile, Economou offers three verbs, "obstruct," "taint," and "distort," rather than the two of Lavagnini's edited text, thus treating the verb in the footnote at the bottom of the page as a potential addition rather than alternate. At times, Economou's accretive approach to the materials in these manuscripts may weigh his poems down with more information than seems suited to the concise, laconic tone for which Cavafy is so well known. Yet his project is important precisely because of his quite different—and daring, given critics' tendency to quibble with translators' word-level choices, particularly with figures as canonical as Cavafy—approach to the full range of materials Lavagnini's edition makes available. Economou's translations evince a thorough consideration not only of the complete last texts, variants and all, but also of the drafts and notes in Lavagnini's genetic unpacking of the process of composition. He relies upon her analyses, yet often diverges from her in his decisions about how to constitute his text on the basis of the information she provides. In this, he makes implicit claims for both his right and his responsibility as a translator to create an edition in translation of his own, consulting the available materials and creating a translation that presents them as he sees fit.

In offering the foregoing analysis of these three versions of a single poem, I modelled a way of engaging with translations that takes them at their word. I read all three translations closely and with respect for their interpretive differences, examining the various approaches these skilled, knowledgeable translators have taken to the available materials. I also took care to discuss the Greek-language texts without replicating the all-too-familiar demand for an ill-conceived "fidelity" to a presumed source, or painting a translator's interpretation as a "mistake" merely because I as a critic prefer another. At the same time, there is one aspect of Cavafy's drafts that I wonder whether these three versions do enough to address: their unfinishedness. How significant is the unfinished nature of these poems to our encounter with the materials? And is it possible to imagine new ways of accounting for that unfinishedness in translation?

"Finished things"?

In a 2009 review of Mendelsohn's translations in the *New Criterion*, Eric Ormsby wrote that it wasn't "always obvious why Cavafy considered these poems unfinished" (4). Indeed, the texts in Mendelsohn's *Unfinished Poems* give little indication that the Greek versions are in manuscript form, in texts riddled with variants. Each poem in his volume stands cleanly on a page of its own, no different in appearance from those in his *Complete Poems*; the only gesture toward the unfinishedness of these texts comes in the poem "Zenobia," which ends with two crosses indicating missing text. Davis's and Economou's translations look no less finished than Mendelsohn's. In fact, the explicit goal of Economou's project is precisely to finish these poems, in a "collaborative" exchange with the long-dead Cavafy.[20] In theory, I am not opposed to this approach. At the end of Chapter 3, I quoted R. W. Franklin's contention that we always encounter poems in "hybrid" versions created by editors and others, and what truly matters is the poetry, which transcends any particular material form. Dickinson's poetry, Franklin suggested, lies elsewhere than in its manuscript manifestations. In keeping with the larger argument of the book, I suggest that the poetry of Cavafy's unfinished poems, too, can be located elsewhere than in the manuscripts, and even otherwise than in Greek—that these unfinished works can be, if not "finished" or "completed," at least continued by others, in languages other than the one in which Cavafy composed. The poetry, in other words, might not inhere in any particular material form, or even in any set of words. In fact, translation makes the wager that it doesn't.

And yet, largely for reasons of historical responsibility and transparency, the scholar in me wishes we could find ways of making the textual instability of these works manifest in translation, could devise new tools and models for translators who want to engage this aspect of a work in their interpretation. Davis's, Mendelsohn's, and Economou's approaches all treat the textual

---

[20] In this, Economou's project is reminiscent of Jack Spicer's translations of Federico García Lorca, to which I turn in Chapter 5.

condition of the manuscripts as secondary to this vague, metaphysical, abstract entity, the "poetry" itself—as did Lavagnini, for that matter, in including a "last text," without which, she argued, no reader would be interested in the manuscripts to begin with. Yet is unfinishedness incompatible with good poetry? I would like to think that readers' experience of these poems is not compromised but on the contrary rendered far richer by the sense of the provisionality of Cavafy's texts offered by Lavagnini's transcriptions. In fact, Lavagnini's edition might give us a few ideas of how, precisely, we might go about creating translations that approach the issue of textual instability head-on, in inventive and exciting ways. After all, as I noted above, she follows four separate approaches in editing these poems: she offers facsimiles, transcriptions, genetic unpackings, and best-text versions. We might, then, imagine a translation that would use any one of these four as a starting point. A translator might choose to translate Lavagnini's entire "last text," variants and all. Or she might tackle the diplomatic transcriptions, as my own translation does in the first epigraph above. Or she might choose Lavagnini's genetic edition, with its notes and unpacking of the stages of composition. In any of these cases, selected facsimiles might also be provided, to give the reader a more immediate sense of the material condition of the texts being rendered.

Each of these options would offer a different view onto the works in question. Translations of the entire last text would seem to balance an interest in the poem's unfinishedness with an investment in the poem being recognizable as a poem in English. Yet to translate these last texts would also be to accept a compromise Lavagnini herself only reluctantly makes in constructing them in the first place. Translations of the transcriptions, meanwhile, might give us less a poem per se than an account of a poem's formation, halted midway: we would see particular phrases being written and crossed out, returning again later on, coming to rest in a state of suspended potentiality. While it might be difficult to grasp the "meaning" of the poem as conventionally understood, we would more easily develop a sense of Cavafy's process, and also of the provisionality of meaning, made obvious by the provisionality of the text itself. We might be invited to enter into a more engaged *readerly* process, one that would encourage us to become editors of sorts. In other words, a translation of the diplomatic transcriptions might allow a reader with no knowledge of Greek to create a "last text" of her own, on the basis of variants and prior drafts, or even to undertake the level of creative completion Economou favors.

In one sense, any one of these options would seem to represent more adequately the textual condition of these materials. Yet I don't want to be proscriptive about the particular form an engagement with these texts should take. To do so would, first of all, put me in the same position as those editors of Dickinson who claim that the most essential meaning of her poems resides in their manuscript forms. In addition, the sorts of translation I just described open the door to potential misrepresentations of a different order. One could in fact argue that, properly speaking, there can be no such thing as a diplomatic transcription in translation. I do not mean this literally, of course—the first epigraph to this chapter presents my translation of one small fragment of such a transcription, so I know it can be done. At the same time, there is a tension worth unpacking as regards the usefulness of such an endeavor and the validity of its conceptual underpinnings. A diplomatic transcription attempts to reproduce (in altered form) all linguistic markers in a document. Translation, meanwhile, *replaces* all the words on a page with other words. A translation that seeks to present variants where they appear in a translated "source" inevitably has to proceed as if word-level equivalence exists, as if "να ρυπάνει" really *meant* "to pollute" and "ν' ασχημίσει" *meant* "to make ugly"—which, of course, we know is not the case. Indeed, one of the most difficult quandaries I have faced in this chapter has been deciding how to discuss textual variants in a language I presume my audience does not know, without recourse to translations on the level of the word that feel disingenuous in their simplicity. While a careful reader might note those instances that break this impression of one-to-one correspondence—"χρόνια" ("years") and "έτη" ("years"), or "χρόνος" ("time") and "καιρός" ("time"), or my doubling-up of definitions for "καλαισθησία" ("elegance"/"taste") and "φαυλόβιοι" ("depraved"/"degenerate")—I remain uncomfortable with this conventional format of "foreign" word and bracketed translation, a format that both rests on and further promotes an understanding of word-level equivalence that I unequivocally reject.

One could, of course, imagine translations in other media that would gesture quite differently to the unfinishedness of these poems. Imagine a digital version designed such that a single clear-text version appeared on the screen—yet every few seconds, a word or phrase would fade into an alternate form, in a continual loop of algorithmic textual variance. In some sense, this is similar to what happens with the textual and bibliographic forms of Cavafy's oeuvre as a whole, though in media most tend to think of as more resistant to this sort of continual reconfiguration. Think, for instance, of those 2,200 packets and pamphlets created in Cavafy's home on rue Lepsius, or the baffling array of volumes, chapbooks, and provisional publications Savidis produced during his thirty-year career as editor of Cavafy's work. The desire to present Cavafy's slippery oeuvre as a coherent, cohesive canon has plagued scholars and editors for decades—precisely because, one might argue, the instability of the texts feels so threatening to our conventional notions of authorship and literary meaning alike. As I demonstrated above, even the "canon" of 154 "acknowledged" poems is a posthumous construction open to continual renegotiation. The many divergent forms in which Cavafy's work has been circulated reflects a need for fixity while also presenting, in aggregate, an ironic challenge to any particular editorial attempt to give these poems a stable bibliographic form. My examination of the editorial challenges involved in making these unfinished poems public, in Greek or in translation, may invite us to ask searching questions about the status of poems and even volumes that we may previously have considered more finished, more stable, than they really are. In fact, given the many variant forms listed in the notes to Savidis's scholarly edition of Cavafy's "unpublished" poems, diplomatic transcriptions might reveal a similar degree of instability in some of those poems as well.[21] We could see Lavagnini's treatment of the unfinished poems as a model for the kind of edition that could be pursued, at least in Greek, for other material in the Cavafy Archive—the kind of edition that Savidis himself originally proposed in 1963, at the very beginning of his career as a scholar and editor of Cavafy. At the same time, rather than fetishize the manuscripts in this way, I urge us also to recognize the unavoidably mediated nature of any encounter we have with Cavafy's work—mediated not only by editors and translators, but by the knowledge of his stature, and by the sheer fact that nearly a dozen major translations of his work have been published in English alone in the last fifteen years (including, most recently, Economou's ironically titled *Complete Plus*).

As with all the chapters in this book, the issues I have been addressing are not limited to the particular texts at hand. This is not just about Cavafy's unfinished poems, or even just about unfinished texts as a category, but about all texts and all translation. Textual scholars have demonstrated that there can never be a single "definitive" text for a work; *all* texts, in that sense, are unfinished texts. Translation is a process that destabilizes the text of a work even further, while also turning a particular text into an "original" in the first place, imbuing it with value *as* an original—which becomes, in turn,

---

[21] I have written elsewhere on Savidis's scholarly and popular editions of the "unpublished" poems, suggesting that, while the introduction to his 1968 *Unpublished Poems* claims that the manuscripts on which Savidis's texts are based are "more or less complete" (x), the staggering number of poems for which variants and alternate forms are recorded in the notes undercuts the supposed finality of the texts Savidis offers. Moreover, a number of those texts are quite unmistakably fragments rather than finished poems: Savidis even gives one the quasi-title "Σπάραγμα από άτιτλου ποιήματος" ("Fragment of untitled poem"). It remains unclear, then, precisely what the dividing line between "unpublished" and "unfinished" poems is.

the stick against which translations are so often measured. Likewise, editing, and particularly the modes of recuperative editing I have been discussing in the last two chapters, is beset by this tension between the urge to fix a text, to arrive at some point of origin that precedes editorial intervention, and the inescapable fact that this new editorial product itself comprises yet another mediated image of the work in question. In Cavafy's case, the incessant need to reinforce, worry, or contest the editorial forms that have shaped our understanding of his work reveals nothing so much as the work's insistent resistance to those attempts at editorial fixity.

5

"The Bone-Yard, Babel Recombined": Jack Spicer and the Poetics of Citational Correspondence

Dear Sir:
My mouth has meanings
It had not wanted to argue.

—Jack Spicer[1]

There would be no cause for concern
if one were rigorously assured
of being able to distinguish with rigor
between a citation and a non-citation.

—Jacques Derrida (tr. Ronell)[2]

Previous chapters of this book have been concerned with works that are strikingly unstable in their textual makeup, including ancient works in unknown languages for which only fragmentary texts exist; works arising from an oral tradition; and unfinished works riddled with variants, whose visual and material aspect many consider crucial to their modes of meaning. I have explored how translators, like editors, configure texts for the works they are presenting: a translator not only creates a new textual iteration of a work in a different language, but often helps choose or construct an "original" on which to model her own embodied interpretation. Throughout, I have championed an understanding of translation as iteration, as repetition-with-a-difference, a mode of textual proliferation rather than a mode by which semantic content is transferred.

This final chapter moves in a different direction. It, too, presents translation as a mode of iterative proliferation. Yet while earlier chapters treat the quasi-editorial ways in which translators intervene in the unstable textual histories of

---

[1] Spicer (2008: 193).
[2] Derrida (1980: 58).

particular works, this chapter folds that discussion into a broader treatment of literary derivation and citationality, reminding us that writers, like translators, receive, engage, and build upon preexisting literary traditions. Translations have been disparaged on the basis of countless metaphorical models: for being unfaithful lovers, ill-fitting clothes, blurry mirrors, or fogged-over windows, weak links in a translingual game of telephone. This chapter seeks to break the chain of these metaphors by insisting that, like writing, translation does not convey but creates meaning and messages, if always in relation to a specific prior text or texts. Conversely, like translation, writing is fundamentally citational in nature, though a writer's "sources" may be more diffuse than a translator's. I make these arguments by engaging the work of poet and translator Jack Spicer (1925–65), who saw poetry, not translation, as a matter of taking "dictation," of transmitting messages from an undefined "outside."

Spicer is perhaps most famous for precisely this idea, for his refusal of copyright, his belief that no poet's work is really his or her own. Poets, he claimed, are only mediums or radio sets picking up signals from elsewhere— from ghosts or Martians who rearrange the furniture or alphabet blocks of the poet's memories and language. In recent years, Spicer's reputation has spread, thanks in large part to two important editions that made his work widely available for the first time, Peter Gizzi's *The House That Jack Built: The Collected Lectures of Jack Spicer* (1998) and Gizzi and Kevin Killian's *My Vocabulary Did This To Me: The Collected Poetry of Jack Spicer* (2008). Spicer has received excellent treatment from scholars and writers interested in his theories about poetry; his commitment to an emphatically local community of Bay Area writers and artists; and the way his work prefigures the socially engaged writing of subsequent generations of California poets. While I hope to contribute meaningfully to these discussions, my primary aim is to situate Spicer's 1957 *After Lorca*—which contains translations of poems by Federico García Lorca, as well as pseudotranslations and letters (or pseudoletters) to the deceased Spanish poet—in the context of his broader habits of citation. Spicer's work, I argue, comprises a web of intertextual borrowings by means of which he connected his local poetic milieu to a translingual, transnational, transhistorical, imagined literary community. Translation became, for him, a way of queering literary production, while also creating links between queer poets across space and time. Translation also became a way of coming to grips with the fundamentally citational nature of all writing.

If Spicer sees poetry not as a form of self-expression but as a means of channeling messages from "outside," this process entails the reworking of previously existing materials: the products of Spicer's dictation are saturated with citations for which sources—some among many, at any rate—can in fact be identified. Taken together, Spicer's poems and translations seem to attempt a recombination, stone on stone, of the ruins of the fallen tower he describes in a striking unpublished fragment:

> If I could hear some whisperings among
> The ruins in that Babylonish tongue
> Which shattered with the tower. If that tower fell
> Less wholly or less cunningly what well
> Of words and meaning could a differ find
> Replacing stone on stone; the bone-yard, Babel
> Recombined
> Would make the angels moan[3]

Like so much in Spicer's oeuvre, this stanza resonates with Walter Benjamin's writings on language and translation, and anticipates Jacques Derrida's reading of Benjamin's work in his 1985 "Des Tours de Babel." In true precursor-to-Derrida fashion, Spicer likens writing to translation not because writing "translates" experience into language, but because writing, too, is deeply citational in nature. Throughout this chapter, I use Spicer's insistent denial of authorial originality to present translating and writing as related modes of citational "correspondence" (a key term for Spicer that I will unpack below).[4] In doing so, I take Spicer at his word: rather than holding him up as an exemplary poet-translator whose status as such frees him from the ideological strictures usually placed on translators, I draw on his rhetoric and work to present *all* translators and writers as figures who, if they create, do so only by recombining the stones and bones of already written, or already rewritten, texts.

---

[3] Box 23, folder 2 in the Jack Spicer Papers (1939–82), at the Bancroft Library of the University of California, Berkeley. For the remainder of this chapter, when I cite box and folder numbers, it is from this same archival collection. I am grateful to the Bancroft Library and to Peter Gizzi and Kevin Killian for permission to cite unpublished material from the Spicer archive in this chapter.

[4] In her thoughtful response to a work-in-progress version of this chapter that I presented at Princeton in 2015, Cate Reilly rightly noted that Spicer's idea of correspondence could fruitfully be put in conversation with Baudelaire's "Correspondences." Benjamin's "Die Aufgabe des Übersetzers" offers a link between Spicer and Baudelaire, since that text served as an introduction to a volume of Benjamin's translations of Baudelaire (though not of the poem in question). I am unable to do justice here to the virtues of such a direction, which would undoubtedly also draw on Paul de Man's fascinating analysis of Baudelaire's poem in "Anthropomorphism and Trope in the Lyric" (1983). I'll simply note that, to my view, Spicer's idea of correspondence is at odds with (though it certainly engages) Baudelaire's: "Correspondences" establishes a link between nature and language, a mystical relation beyond or outside mediation. For Spicer, on the contrary, "*correspondence*" creates a relationship between texts and between languages that dissolves any direct, unmediated connection between language and objects in nature. See also my commentary on Spicer's letter on correspondence below.

The resting place of writing

Late in 1956, after a miserable year in New York and Boston—where, he wrote to friends back in Berkeley, "Nobody loves anybody" and "Nobody speaks Martian"[5]—the thirty-one-year-old, barely-published poet Jack Spicer returned to the Bay Area, where his friend Robert Duncan finagled him a teaching job at the Poetry Center of San Francisco State College. Writing to Robin Blaser, the third in this triumvirate of queer poets, Spicer solicited help with the upcoming workshop: "How about sending me some ideas. My main one so far is that Houdini is the figure of the poet and that translation is cheating at poker."[6] Spicer titled the course "Poetry as Magic" and advertised it in the course bulletin as a "group exploration of the practices of the new magical school of poetry," naming Lorca as a central figure in that school.

Admittance to Spicer's "pro-seminar in the West Martian dialect"[7] was determined on the basis of a long, rather cheeky questionnaire: roughly fifty applicants angling for a spot responded to such prompts as "What insect do you most resemble?" and "What is your favorite political song?" and "Write the funniest joke that you know." At the end were three poems with words excised; for each, applicants were asked to create "a complete and satisfactory poem" by filling in the blanks. One of the poems looked like this:

In … … … . endlessness
Snow, … … … . . salt
He lost his … … …

The color white. He walks
Over a … … … . . carpet made
… … … . .

Without eyes or thumbs
He suffers … … … .
But the … … … quiver

In the … … … endlessness
How … … … . a wound
His … … … . left.

---

5   I quote here from a letter to John Allen Ryan, sent from New York in 1955, now held in Box 3, folder 26 of the Jack Spicer Papers. Similar statements pepper the letters he sent during this period.

6   Quoted in Ellingham and Killian (1998: 81).

7   I quote here from a contributor's note to the *Evergreen Review* dating to 1957.

Snow, ... salt ... .
In the ... ... endlessness.

(Spicer 2008: 103)

Readers familiar with Spicer's work might recognize the text behind the gaps as the opening poem of his 1957 *After Lorca*, first published several months after the workshop concluded. "When I'm through," Spicer wrote to Blaser while feverishly at work on this project, "I'd like someone as good as I am to translate these translations into French (or Pushtu) adding more."[8] Hence, perhaps, his inclusion in this questionnaire of an effaced version of his translation of Lorca's "Juan Ramón Jiménez," whose title invokes a distant community of writers in its implicit dedication to Lorca's friend, another of Spain's great twentieth-century poets. This fill-in-the-blank poem is, moreover, only one moment in the form's extended exercise in guided citation: throughout, participants are invited not to express their thoughts or views but to identify themselves with insects and songs, to categorize, judge, quote, rearrange, or embellish the works and views of others. This, then, is the entrance exam for Spicer's "magical school of poetry": an invitation to see poetry not as self-expression but as the art of escape, and translation as an essential trick of the trade.

Many scholars point to *After Lorca* as the beginning of Spicer's elaboration of a poetics of dictation. In doing so, they echo Spicer's explicit statement to this effect, in the first of three lectures he gave in Vancouver just a few months before his death of alcoholism in 1965 at age forty: "It happened about halfway through when I was writing *After Lorca* when the letters to Lorca started coming and being dictated and the poems, instead of being translations, were dictated" (1998: 135). *After Lorca* presents Spicer's translations of twenty-two poems and one short play by Lorca, interspersed with another ten poems and play that, while presented as translations, do not represent any known text by Lorca. Both translations and pseudotranslations bear dedications, mostly to members of Spicer's circle of friends. The intimate yet public correspondence implied by these dedications is echoed in the more generically conventional (though one-sided) correspondence of six letters to the dead Lorca—all signed "Love, Jack"—that treat questions of poetics and translation. In keeping with the closing phrase of one of these letters, which describes the poetic tradition as "how we dead men write to each other" (2008: 134), Lorca does in fact write back: in an introduction

---

[8]   Spicer (1987: 47). The questionnaire was recently included in Gizzi and Killian's volume of Spicer's collected poetry (Spicer 2008: 103), making it possible for a number of contemporary poets to offer less directly solicited responses to Spicer's original invitation. Versions by Christian Hawkey, Lisa Jarnot, and Matthew Rohrer appear in *Jubilat* 16 (2009).

signed "Federico García Lorca, Outside Granada, October 1957," this poet two decades in the grave chides Spicer for "inserting or substituting one or two words" that change a poem's mood or meaning, or "tak[ing] one of my poems and adjoin[ing] to half of it another half of his own, giving rather the effect of an unwilling centaur." As for the apocryphal texts, Lorca admits to having sent Spicer a few posthumously written poems—"with malice afore-thought, I must admit," in order to "further complicat[e] the problem." "Even the most faithful student of my work," Lorca declares, "will be hard put to decide what is and what is not García Lorca as, indeed, he would if he were to look into my present resting place" (107).

Lorca's present resting place remains famously undiscovered to this day, somewhere outside Granada. Anyone who looked into it would find not only the bones of the poet, who was executed for his socialist leanings and open homosexuality, but those of a schoolteacher and two bullfighters who were shot alongside him by Franco's forces in July 1936. Fifteen years later, Spicer's refusal to sign a loyalty oath led to his expulsion from a doctoral program at Berkeley, while his homosexuality during the McCarthyite 1950s put him on the fringes of American society writ large. In *After Lorca*, Spicer positions himself as Lorca's peer in death ("we dead men"), rhetorically placing his own bones in a metaphorical mass grave that symbolizes Lorca's transhistorical, transcultural, translingual, poetic, political, and homosocial community. Despite the book's sometimes lighthearted tone, in the course of his correspondence with Lorca—including the intimate work of selecting, translating, and ordering the poems that will comprise this limited view into Lorca's oeuvre—Spicer assumes the weight of Lorca's tragic tradition as his own. The poems and letters in *After Lorca* evince an understanding of the ethical responsibility involved in shouldering this weight, one that has much to do with Spicer's concept of tradition. In one letter to Lorca, Spicer glosses tradition as "generations of different poets in different countries patiently telling the same story, writing the same poem, gaining and losing something with each transformation—but, of course, never really losing anything" (110–11). Each "new" poem is merely a resting place in a never-ending stream of tradition, an instantiation of a single, timeless, languageless story or poem. In contrast to prevalent figurations of translation as loss, Spicer's concept of tradition folds translation into a vast circuit of translingual, diachronic poetic homeostasis whose losses are counterbalanced by gains elsewhere—or, better, into a mechanism of constant accretion and continual gain in which losses are never real, only ever *apparent*.

Spicer, in other words, treats translation as iteration rather than transfer. In doing so, he implicitly challenges normative paradigms of equivalence and places translation at the heart of a poetics of citational correspondence, shifting the translator's responsibility from repetition to continuation by other means. The translator's underlying task becomes strikingly similar to the poet's: to keep the chain of correspondence alive even in death. *After Lorca* accordingly invites us not to attempt to "decide what is and what is not García Lorca," as Lorca's introduction would have it, but rather to explore the consequences of the very impossibility of deciding.

Translation's "peramblant bones"

Jack Spicer's fascination with languages and linguistics is well documented. His graduate studies in medieval English literature at Berkeley afforded him formal training in Anglo-Saxon, Old Norse, Latin, and German, while his voracious reading gained him some Spanish and a bit of French. His only scholarly publication was a co-authored piece about California idiolects that appeared in the linguistics journal *Language*, whose cover he repurposed for his 1965 book of poetry of the same name, a poetic sequence invested in issues of morphology, etymology, phonology, and graphemics. Spicer, a great lover of myths, legends, folklore, and folk song—all modes of cultural production for which authorship is a moot category—also experimented with forms of appropriative writing that may strike us as belonging more to our moment than to his. Kevin Killian describes Spicer's unpublished "The Slaying of the Jabberwock, by W. B. Yeats" as an example of an early mashup, while a poem he sent to Robin Blaser in 1956 replaces all but the last word in each line of Shakespeare's Sonnet 76—a "Sonnet Exercise" that gestures forward not only to his workshop questionnaire, but also to contemporary erasures of Shakespeare, including Jen Bervin's *Nets* and Gregory Betts' *The Others Raisd in Me*, whose treatments of these eminently canonical English-language poems challenge notions of textual stability and authorial originality alike.[9]

As do Spicer's translations. While Spicer's only published translations are contained in *After Lorca*, his archive at the Bancroft Library holds several others, most of which were completed during his graduate studies at Berkeley with medievalists Ernst Kantorowicz and Arthur Brodeur. A series of notebooks contain a nearly complete translation of *Beowulf*. There are also fragments from the Old Norse *Poetic Edda*, as well as a thick sheaf of pages bearing translations of selected passages from the Gothic Bible, itself a translation of portions of the Old and New Testaments into fourth-century

---

[9]   The quote from Killian can be found at http://jacketmagazine.com/37/killian-spicer. shtml (last accessed 7 May 2017).

Gothic. David Hadbawnik and Sean Reynolds, coeditors of a recent edition of Spicer's *Beowulf*, suggest that his fascination with the medieval helped shape his subsequent poetics; certainly his interest in literary periods and traditions that do not emphasize the trope of the solitary, self-expressive author is of a piece with his later rejection of authorial originality. His engagement with *Beowulf*, for instance—including the contention of one character in his unfinished novel *The Tower of Babel* that *Beowulf*, like James Macpherson's Ossian, was a scholarly invention—reflects a view of medieval texts as ones in which "origins are inherently unstable and the very idea of cohesive authorship is a hoax" (Hadbawnik 2011: 2).

Most of these translations, recorded in interlinear format, seem to have served as language-learning tools, and focus largely on assigning equivalents at the level of the word. Yet the archive also contains his version of Stefan George's German version of Charles Baudelaire's "Spleen (Je suis comme le roi)"—which, though completed around the same time, evinces a very different understanding of what translation can do and be. I present it here, with a text of George's translation (Spicer's "source") below:

A Translation of George's Translation of "Spleen"
from "Le Fleur [*sic*] de Mal" ("Die Blumen Des Bösen")

I am a prince in lands gloomy and cold
Passive in riches and aging in youth
Blinded to beauty and deafened to truth
And only with horses and falcons consoled
Who plays without pleasure and dares without fear
And dulled by the seed of the poppy who tries
The sleep of no dream on the couch where he lies,
So richly bedecked it resembles a bier
And courtly ladies with seductive tones
Seeking to lighten their sad monarch's reign
Perfumed and sweet to sight, await in vain
A ragged smile from these peramblant bones.
No bath of blood as sorcerers propose,
To translate life and youth from other men
Can make a vital current pulse again
In vessels where the oozing Lethe flows.

Trübsinn

Ich bin ein fürst in landen trüb und kalt
Reich aber machtlos· jung und doch schon alt·

Der seiner lehrer bücklinge verachtet·
Bei seinem hund und andren tieren schmachtet.

Nicht spiel nicht jagd das leben ihm verschönt
Und nicht sein volk das unterm fenster stöhnt.
Des lieblingsnarren possenhafte lieder
Erwecken seine heiterkeit nicht wieder.
Sein reichgesticktes bett wird ihm zum sarg.

Der damenkreis an lockungen nicht karg
Erhofft umsonst mit schamloser toilette
Ein lächeln von dem wandelnden skelette.
Und nicht gelangs dem arzt der gold doch schafft
Aus ihm zu bannen den verderbten saft·

Kein bad im blut wie es die Römer lehren
Wie altersschwach despoten es begehren
Erneute kraft dem stumpfen leib gewinnt
Wo blutes statt der schlamm der Lethe rinnt.[10]

In translating from George's German rather than Baudelaire's French, Spicer both honors George's importance to his own poetic development and pulls both poets into an improvised *Kreis*, continuing the poem's perambulation from language to language and gay male poet to gay male poet.[11] Even a mere glance shows us that Spicer's is a pared-down version, shorter by two lines and collapsed into a single stanza, tighter and more compact. It is, to be sure, a translation. Yet it does not concern itself with word-level equivalence, or even with what some would consider the facts of George's version. Unlike George's "fürst" (or Baudelaire's "roi" before him), who takes pleasure in nothing, neither falcons nor doves nor dogs, Spicer's prince *is* consoled by his horses and falcons, as by an opium habit nowhere to be found in the German or the French. Spicer's "courtly ladies," meanwhile, are the only other people in the poem: there are no starving crowds, no tutors or jester or royal alchemist.

There is translation, however, and "peramblant bones": while George's "skelette" is "wandelnden" ("changed") (and Baudelaire's "squelette" is

[10] The translation is contained in Box 6, folder 67 of the Jack Spicer Papers. The archive does not contain a text of George's translation, so I cannot be sure what specific text Spicer may have based his own translation on; I quote here from Baudelaire (2014: 53–4).
[11] The *Georg-Kreis* was a mystical literary group centered around George, including Kantorowicz, who went on to create a similar circle with students at Berkeley. For more on Kantorowicz's role in Spicer's education, see Ellingham and Killian (1998: 19–21), as well as Holt (2011).

"jeune" ["young"]), Spicer's translation makes the bones move. His collapsed quatrains display vibrant rhythm and rhyme, as well as the dynamic parataxis of his opening lines. The iambic rush toward the first period, which comes three-quarters of the way through the poem, offers a marked contrast to the thickly punctuated, lugubrious couplets of George's German. Even as the "bath of blood" is declared unable to "translate" other men's vitality to this young prince, Spicer's version does in fact liven things up, replacing George's focus on decrepitude and ennui with words such as "plays," "dares," "lighten," "life," and "youth." And by employing the verb "translate" in the poem's closing sentence, Spicer turns translation into the mechanism of that enlivening. Spicer's arguably "unfaithful" translation does precisely what his poem says it can't; it performs its own lie. In doing so, it both addresses and embodies a mode of translation that breaks the constricting norms of equivalence, privileging instead a "vital current" of "life and youth from other men" that lets the poem "pulse again." In the context of the interlinear translations of medieval texts he was producing around the same time, this very different exercise shows us Spicer questioning the notion of translation as a transfer of word-level semantic content, and exploring different ways in which literary works can be made to mean in other languages, contexts, and times.

The quivering bones of correspondence

In its flexible treatment of word-level meaning, Spicer's translation of George's translation of Baudelaire anticipates the texts he would produce for *After Lorca*, including his discussions of poetry and translation in the letters addressed to Lorca from Jack. Consider the following sweeping rejection of the conventional understanding of equivalence, trumped by the discovery of a correspondence between (linguistic) objects that need not obey our expectations of likeness or similarity:

> But things decay, reason argues. Real things become garbage. The piece of lemon you shellac to the canvas begins to develop a mold, the newspaper tells of incredibly ancient events in forgotten slang, the boy becomes a grandfather. Yes, but the garbage of the real still reaches out into the current world making *its* objects, in turn, visible—lemon calls to lemon, newspaper to newspaper, boy to boy. As things decay they bring their equivalents into being.
> Things do not connect; they correspond. That is what makes it possible for a poet to translate real objects, to bring them across

language as easily as he can bring them across time. That tree you saw in Spain is a tree I could never have seen in California, that lemon has a different smell and a different taste, BUT the answer is this—every place and every time has a real object to *correspond* with your real object— that lemon may become this lemon, or it may even become this piece of seaweed, or this particular color of gray in this ocean. One does not need to imagine that lemon; one needs to discover it.

Even these letters. They *correspond* with something (I don't know what) that you have written (perhaps as unapparently as that lemon *corresponds* to this piece of seaweed) and, in turn, some future poet will write something which *corresponds* to them. That is how we dead men write to each other.[12]

Spicer's discussion of the decay of the real refers back to an earlier letter, which figures words as what we use "to push the real, to drag the real into the poem." Words themselves, however, are fated to "shrivel and decay"; even the word "shit" will inevitably lose its immediacy, until it is "as dead as 'Alas'" (2008: 122). It is difficult not to hear echoes in these passages of "Die Aufgabe des Übersetzers" ("The Translator's Task," in Stephen Rendall's translation), a text by Walter Benjamin published as a foreword to his translations of Baudelaire's *Tableaux Parisiens*. (Throughout this chapter, when I quote from this work by Benjamin, I do so from Rendall's translation.) "What once sounded fresh," Benjamin writes, "may come to sound stale, and what once sounded idiomatic may later sound arcane." Given these "constant transformations both in language and in the sense" of even a fixed text, Benjamin flatly declares that the translator's task cannot be to "strive for similarity to the original" or to convey "the form and the sense of the original as accurately as possible," since form and sense are eternally in flux, and therefore impossible to replicate or even imitate in another language. Moreover, Benjamin doesn't seem entirely convinced that even *texts* are ever wholly fixed. "Even if one were to consider the last stroke of the author's pen the work's *coup de grâce*," we read in Rendall's translation (with the implicit

---

[12] Spicer (2008: 133–4). I have modified Gizzi and Kllian's edition here in order to bring the word "correspond," which they italicize, closer to its first published appearance, in the 1957 White Rabbit Press edition of *After Lorca*, which printed the word as *"corre-spond*," with all letters italicized apart from the first "r." A few years later, when Donald Allen wanted to include this letter to Lorca as Spicer's statement on poetics in his *The New American Poetry* (1960), Spicer asked that it again be printed "correspond,"—or, if that wasn't feasible, as *"correspond"* or "co-respond"—to reflect the "pun" of correspondence as a dual or split response. "[T]he word itself," Kelly Holt writes in her fine article on Spicer, thus "illustrates the 'unwilling centaur' of Spicer's quasi-collaborative poetic transformations" of Lorca's poetry (59).

suggestion that we should *not* consider it such), "that would not be enough to save this dead theory of translation" (2012: 77–8).

Benjamin's text famously ends with a passage championing the interlinear translation of the Bible as the "prototype or ideal of all translation" (83), a statement that would seem to favor a model of word-for-word equivalence. Yet scholars who cite this passage in defense of neoliteralist modes of translating seem to be reading it out of context, and failing to consider that Benjamin is not praising interlinear translation *in general*, but of a very particular set of texts: the Holy Scripture, from which all "sense" has been evacuated due to the revelatory rather than communicative nature of its language. The "prototype or ideal" is not interlinear translation per se. It is, rather, a mode of translation that rejects communication in favor of something we might well call correspondence. Throughout, Benjamin continually refutes the notion that the translator's task is to seek equivalence on the level of the word. "Accuracy" and "similarity" are both rejected as unhelpful concepts; the latter is characterized as "indefinable," "sterile," and "vague" (77–8). In perhaps his best known metaphor for translation, Benjamin offers instead an image based on contiguity, a metonymic rather than metaphoric model:

> Just as fragments of a vessel, in order to be fitted together, must correspond to each other in the minutest details but need not resemble each other, so translation, instead of making itself resemble the sense of the original, must fashion in its own language, carefully and in detail, a counterpart to the original's mode of meaning, in order to make both of them recognizable as fragments of a vessel, as fragments of a greater language. For that very reason translation must, in large measure, turn its attention away from trying to communicate something, away from the sense; the original is essential to translation only insofar as it has already relieved the translator and his work of the burden and organization of what is communicated. (81)

No work of art, Benjamin states in the opening lines of his piece, has communication as its aim, nor should any translation. The communication of "sense" is null and void. What we need instead is the iterative growth of the work, the creation of a "counterpart to the original's mode of meaning" that will expand our sense of the "greater language" to which *all* languages, *all* works belong.

Correspondence rather than resemblance: this is at the heart of Spicer's presentation of both poem and translation as fragments of a greater vessel called poetry. And writers are themselves only vessels of another sort, radio sets tuning in to Benjamin's "pure language"—or at least the "alien word," those "whisperings [...] in that Babylonish tongue" that Spicer mentions in the unpublished fragment above. For Spicer as for Benjamin, the supposed problem of equivalence is less to be solved than circumvented: "One does not need to imagine that lemon; one needs to discover it." Like Benjamin, Spicer jettisons the dead theory that translation is invested in similarity or likeness. In its place, he encourages the formation of a tradition through a series of additive translations, texts that both exceed their supposed originals and invite subsequent excesses from others. If Benjamin conceptualizes translation as an operation not of seeking equivalents but of producing counterparts, not of transferring sense but of fashioning another iteration of a work, a counterpart to its mode of meaning, Spicer's *After Lorca* pushes this claim even further. For Benjamin, the work seems to remain a recognizable entity across its transformations. Spicer, however, undoes even that assumption: the lines of correspondence, he suggests, can be *there* without being *traceable*. That lemon might become this lemon, but it might also become this seaweed, or a particular shade of gray. A reader can never truly know how (or whether) a translation corresponds to some supposed original—or, conversely, whether a text she takes to be an original might be a translation of some other text whose very existence is unknown to her. This claim becomes central when we consider the interplay of translation, pseudotranslation, and supposedly original writing that comprises *After Lorca*. In fact, Spicer's volume seems intentionally to contest our ability to separate these categories.

While we can only assume that Spicer authored the introductory note attributed to the dead Lorca, the last paragraph of the letter about correspondence I quoted above insists that even the letters from "Jack" might be no more Spicer's than the introduction is Lorca's. The letters bearing his signature could, rather, be translations of sorts, with "originals" even Spicer himself could never hope to locate: "Even these letters. They *correspond* with something (I don't know what) that you have written (perhaps as unapparently as that lemon corresponds to this piece of seaweed) and, in turn, some future poet will write something which *corresponds* to them." Many scholars cite the letters in *After Lorca* as Spicer's most cogent statements on poetics. I, too, have turned to them for interpretive guidance in reading the rest of the volume in which they appear. Yet in the first Vancouver lecture I quoted above, Spicer explicitly claims that the letters were dictated—that they came from elsewhere, and are therefore not properly his, not texts that can bear his authorial signature. If these texts we take as "originals"—and what more authentic, more personal, more self-expressive than a letter, particularly one signed "Love"?—may in fact not be, we must also entertain the possibility that the pseudotranslations in *After Lorca* might in fact correspond to something in Lorca's oeuvre (or, perhaps, in someone else's). In disabusing us of the notion that we can ever really determine whether or not a text is a translation, and whether or not two texts, two phrases, two words, actually correspond, Spicer preemptively challenges attempts to judge his translations on that basis.

That doesn't, of course, stop others from making those judgments. Take, for instance, Clayton Eshleman's piece in the 1977 *boundary 2* special issue on Spicer. Eshleman has done future scholarship a great service by identifying the sources of those poems that *have* clear sources in Lorca. Yet his analyses are heavily invested in word-level comparisons that find fault with Spicer's choices on the basis of dictionary definitions of words in Spanish. Take Eshleman's response to the very first poem in *After Lorca*, the one Spicer included in his workshop questionnaire, which (at the risk of inviting the very lexical comparisons I have been calling into question) I present alongside Lorca's Spanish:

Juan Ramón Jimencz   Juan Ramón Jiménez

A Translation for John Ryan

In the white endlessness   En el blanco infinito,
Snow, seaweed, and salt   nieve, nardo y salina
He lost his imagination.   perdió su fantasía.

The color white. He walks   El color blanco, anda,
Upon a soundless carpet made   sobre una muda alfombra
Of pigeon feathers.   de plumas de paloma.

Without eyes or thumbs   Sin ojos ni ademán

He suffers a dream not moving   immóvil sufre un sueño.
But the bones quiver.   Pero tiembla por dentro.

In the white endlessness   En el blanco infinito,
How pure and big a wound   ¡qué pura y larga herida
His imagination left.   dejó su fantasía!

Snow, seaweed, and salt. Now   En el blanco infinito.
In the white endlessness. (109)   Nieve. Nardo. Salina.[13]

[13] Lorca: 84. "Lorca's Spanish" is, of course, a complicated phrase: see the opening page of this book, where I contest scholars' reliance on phrases such as this. As with the text by George above, I cannot be sure what edition of Lorca Spicer consulted in preparing

In his brief analysis, Eshleman calls this poem a "typical Spicer translation," relatively "accurate" though marred by "patches of mistranslation, some of which appear to be meaningful, some of which appear to be arbitrary." He questions, in particular, Spicer's rendering of "nardo" as "seaweed" rather than "spikenard," as well as his choice of "thumbs" for "ademán." "Surely," Eshleman writes in a tone of baffled exasperation, "Spicer knew what the words actually meant" (33)—and of course definitions would be easy to track down even for someone with limited Spanish. Yet precisely for this reason, Lori Chamberlain argues that Eshleman's analysis only serves to expose "the problem of attempting to distinguish 'meaningful' from 'arbitrary' mistranslation—or, for that matter, translation from mistranslation. To do either is to assume that Spicer's purpose in translating Lorca is to render an equivalent poem, judged in terms of Lorca's intentions, a project that the introduction to these poems undercuts" (429).

In dismissing "seaweed" and "thumbs" as arbitrary mistranslations, Eshleman locates meaning at the level of the word, and declines Spicer's implicit invitation to imagine how these words might operate *as* translations, or as part of a larger translational project or approach. This classification of mistranslation ignores Spicer's claim that a Spanish lemon might become not just a California lemon, but a bit of seaweed or the ocean's gray—and thus that "nardo," too, might become "seaweed," or that Spicer might feel his translation needed quivering bones where Lorca's poem needed the more abstract "dentro." It also ignores the far more sweeping claim that even the letters and pseudotranslations may correspond with or to something Lorca wrote, though the terms of that correspondence—not to mention the "originals" themselves—may be impossible to trace. In his introductory note, "Lorca" declares that the poems in this volume "are not translations"; Eshleman seeks to demonstrate the truth of this disavowal. Ron Silliman, on the contrary, argues that "in a larger and more important sense," the poems *are* translations, "even where we might begin to say the work is entirely Spicer's own creation. For Spicer's poetics are fundamentally a poetics of translation. One need merely substitute that word and its cognates for *dictation* wherever it occurs in his writing. All that is missing are the authors, the Martians, and their original texts" (1987: 69). Silliman resists the impulse, so common when dealing with translations produced by poets, to treat the translations as "original" poems; instead, he argues convincingly that even Spicer's poems, not just in *After Lorca* but throughout his career, are in fact translations that pass for originals.

I myself am not quite willing to collapse the categories of translation and writing so fully. Yet I recognize that in *After Lorca* Spicer elaborates a

his translations; I quote here from Gareth Walters' 2007 Oxford edition. The accent in "Jiménez" is missing from Spicer's translation.

model of translation and writing as twin forms of correspondence across divides of language and time: "this is how we dead men write to each other." Translation becomes Spicer's point of access to the idea that writing comes from elsewhere, is an act of self-incorporation into a broader tradition via an engagement with the work of others. That process entails the reciprocal incorporation of a tradition into one's "own" poetic corpus. The first poem, quoted above, begins with a blind "he" losing his imagination. A later stanza takes Lorca's "Pero tiembla por dentro," a trembling on the inside, and concretizes it into a quivering with a subject, "But the bones quiver," which recalls the "peramblant bones" in Spicer's version of Baudelaire's "Spleen" as well as the "bone-yard" of the unpublished poem I quoted early in this chapter—a parade of bones that gestures toward the endlessly recombinatory capacities of a literary tradition. In "Juan Ramón Jimenez," as in the rest of this volume, it remains crucially impossible to tell which bones belong to whom, to distinguish "what is and what is not García Lorca" (or, for that matter, anyone else) in the "present resting place" of this translation, or in the grand bone-yard of this book. Any translated text has as mixed a lineage as Spicer's Lorca's "unwilling centaurs," with sources as intermingled as the bones in Spicer's post-Babelian charnel house. The reader is indeed "hard put" to know what belongs to which. This is the condition of translation. It is also, in Spicer's terms, the condition of writing. Lorca, like Spicer, becomes less a source than a resting place in the stream of tradition, a node through which tradition—an outside—flows.

Ditching equivalence: The stream, the river, the ocean of tradition

My choice of the word "flows" is not arbitrary. The selection and ordering of the poems that make up this volume, I argue, stage a turning away from the idea of translation as replication toward the idea of translation as correspondence—a turning whose pivot is the trope of tradition as a flowing stream. If the (perhaps apocryphal) moment when dictation enters Spicer's conception of his work comes halfway through the writing of *After Lorca*, that does not mean the book is split between translations in the first half and pseudotranslations in the second; on the contrary, translations, pseudotranslations, and letters are dispersed fairly evenly throughout. We can, however, draw a different dividing line: the letter about correspondence comes about halfway through, separating the poems into an initial group of fairly conventional translations of poems full of shadows, mirrorings, elusive meanings, and failed attempts at replication, and later poems that evince a less rigid translation practice (adding or reordering stanzas, for instance) and are thematically preoccupied with movement, transformation, and flow. This arc describes a subtle yet clear progression in the volume's attitude toward translation, an embodied argument about how poems might correspond in and between languages differently than we are used to thinking.

The poems in the volume also correspond, in a sense, with one another: taken from a few different volumes of Lorca's poetry, they are bound together by common images, themes, and vocabulary. Once the first poem brings us into a space void of imagination, its "white endlessness" is echoed by the "infinite sidewalk" in the following poem, "Ballad of the Little Girl Who Invented the Universe," a translation of Lorca's "Gacela del sueño al aire libre." Spicer's title confuses Eshleman, as does his rendering of Lorca's last line, "y en el toro el esqueleto de la niña," as "The skeleton of a little girl turning": "There appears to be no reason," Eshleman writes, "for taking the bull out and making the little girl turn" (34). Like many critics of texts in translation, Eshleman looks for reasons only by comparing the words of a translation to the words of an assumed original, and judging on the basis of a desire for a particular kind of semantic transfer. If we look instead at how the fabric of Spicer's volume unfolds, we see that the questions of imagination and invention posed in these first two poems (including Spicer's rather inventive title for the second) initiate a meta-discursive thread about poetry and translation that will remain central to the book. Spicer doesn't so much take the bull out as free the girl from inside it—and in letting her turn *away* from Lorca's text, Spicer prefigures the preoccupation with motion that runs through the book's latter half. If these opening poems treat the construction of a world through writing, Spicer is careful to keep us from seeing that construction as tied to authorial *or* translatorial expression. On the contrary, these two poems are followed by the first letter, which describes tradition as "generations of poets in different countries patiently telling the same story," and therefore rejects the notion that a story is ever really new, or ever ours to claim.

Translation is of course one mode by which poets in different times and places tell the same story. It is also an activity that forms the practical and conceptual backbone of *After Lorca*: not only do the letters from Jack to Lorca offer explicit meditations on translation and poetry both, but several of the poems can also be read as implicit commentaries on the act of translation. Take the following poem, which appears early in the volume:

Debussy   Debussy

A Translation for the University of Redlands

My shadow moves silently	Mi sombra va silenciosa
Upon the water in the ditch.	por el agua de la acecia.
Upon my shadow are the frogs	Por mi sombra están las ranas
Blocked off from the stars.	privadas de las estrellas.
The shadow demands from my body	La sombra manda a mi cuerpo
Unmoving images.	reflejos de cosas quietas.
My shadow skims the water like a huge	Mi sombra va como immenso
Violet-colored mosquito.	cínife color violta.
A hundred crickets try to mine gold	Cien grillos quieren dorar
From the light in the rushes.	la luz de la cañavera.
A light born in my heart	Una luz nace en mi pecho,
Upon the ditch, reflected. (112)	reflejado, de la acequia.[14]

In contrast to the expanses of moving water that will enter the second half of *After Lorca*, this poem is confined to a ditch populated by tiny creatures. A body blocks off the stars, casting a shadow that makes demands on it, requiring "unmoving images" (in a line that, ironically, also seems to turn sharply from Lorca's "reflejos de cosas quietas"). The light is reflected light; the stars are unattainable; the shadow is silent yet unable to cease its motion. It is difficult in context not to read this poem as an allegory for the limitations and frustrations of translation as conventionally understood, suggesting that the translator's (failed) task is to stay still, to fit one's self to the poet's self in hopes of matching shadow to shadow—an allegory that, of course, is actualized in the poem only *as* a translation, *in* translation, stalked by Lorca's unseen Spanish.

Shadows abound in *After Lorca*, or at least in its opening half. In a volume with an extreme economy of language, the word "shadow" appears no fewer than seventeen times, mostly in the first handful of poems. As the volume progresses, this overdetermined metaphor for translation is supplanted. The poems increasingly rebel against the demand for stillness and reflections, until in "Suicide," the young man in the poem, "conscious that there is nothing left / In his mouth but one word," "shatters the mirror with an ax," and the mirror "submerges everything / in a great spurt of shadow" (118). One could read the poem as a rejection of this metaphor: the mirror as equivalence, the shadow a failed attempt to achieve it, the violent shattering a defiance of the demand to do so. After the shadow escapes its confines through "Suicide," it slowly slips from the volume as a whole, as the

---

[14] Lorca 2009: 86–8.

shattered, spurting mirror begets a torrent of activity that gushes through a series of rivers: "At the dim heart of the river" (134); "I want a river lost from its bed" (136); "Child / How you keep falling into rivers" (139); "Every afternoon the river sits itself down" (140); "The fountain and a river and an old song" (142). At the end of this stream of rivers we finally reach the ocean itself: "I have become lost many times along the ocean / Along the vastness of water I wander searching / An end to the lives that have tried to complete me" (146). The last poem in the book, "Radar," dedicated to Marianne Moore and identified as a "postscript" rather than a "translation," bids farewell to Lorca—"I crawled into bed with sorrow that night / Couldn't touch his fingers"—while also celebrating the continued movement of something that sounds, in context, like poetry going on its way: "They are going on a journey / Those deep blue creatures / Passing us as if they were sunshine / Look / Those fins, those closed eyes / Admiring the last drop of the ocean" (154).

The second half of the book, in other words, is full of poems propelled by the forward motion of the stream of poetic tradition, until that stream meets the ocean that surrounds us all. Folded among these poems are others that seem to address and reject the concept of equivalence. If "Debussy" and "Suicide" demonstrate an anxiety over the demand that a translation replicate its source, the pseudotranslation "A Diamond" contains an implicit challenge to that demand—one staged first and foremost in its lack of a "source" to replicate, but also in the poem's blending of Lorcan and non-Lorcan materials.[15] In this poem—which draws on tropes and images that recur throughout the volume while also channeling other voices (including that of Allen Ginsburg, whom Spicer reportedly despised)[16]—the universe "falls apart and discloses a diamond / Two words called seagull are peacefully floating out where the waves are. […] And there is nothing in the universe like diamond / Nothing in the whole mind" (120). If "the poem is a seagull" early in "A Diamond," by the end of the poem there are in fact not one but two "words called seagull," a doubling that destabilizes the notion of linguistic *or* literary self-sameness. There is, the poem seems to suggest, no such thing as equivalence, in the universe or in the mind; correspondences are not given but made. The following text, "The Little Halfwit," a translation of "El Niño Loco," destabilizes still further the tenuous connection between words and things, and between words and words, as the word "afternoon"

---

[15] Gideon Toury suggests that pseudotranslations operate by incorporating, even exaggerating, textual elements from the category of work being imitated. This is certainly the case with this poem, with its rhetorical ties to many other poems in the volume. See Toury (2011: 40–51).

[16] Spicer's distaste for Ginsberg and the Beats is well documented. For more on this see Katz, as well as Davidson (1989: 170–1).

fails to find its match: "I said 'Afternoon' / But it wasn't there. / The afternoon was another thing / Which had gone someplace. [...] 'Afternoon' But this is useless, / This is untrue, this has to it / Half a moon of lead. The other / Will never get here" (120–1).

The volume's strongest allegorical account of how translation works may come in "He Died at Sunrise," a translation of "Murió al amanacer":

Night of four moons	Noche de cuatro lunas
And a single tree,	y un solo árbol,
With a single shadow	con una sola sombra
And a single bird.	y un solo pájaro.
I look into my body for	Busco en mi carne las
The tracks of your lips.	huellas de tus labios.
A stream kisses into the wind	El manantial besa al viento
Without touch.	sin tocarlo.
I carry the No you gave me	Llevo el No que me diste,
Clenched in my palm	en la palma de la mano,
Like something made of wax	como un limón de cera
An almost-white lemon.	casi blanco.
Night of four moons	Noche de cuatro lunas
And a single tree	y un solo árbol.
At the point of a needle	En la punta de una aguja
Is my love, spinning. (135)	está mi amor ¡girando![17]

Coming as it does just two pages after the letter about correspondence, whose talk of lemons foreshadows the "almost-white lemon" of the third stanza, it is difficult not to read this poem as a commentary on the creation of the very work we are reading. Daniel Katz is one scholar who has read this translation as a reflection on translation itself. Comparing Spicer's English and Lorca's Spanish, Katz points to the (seeming) cross-lingual identicality of a single word, which therefore "need not be rendered—precisely this 'No', the object of transit within each poem, which happens to be identical in English and Spanish and can be simply carried over from one poem to the next." Katz sees this word as an exception that unmasks the unfortunate rule of what translation is: it "permits of a transit entirely different from everything else Spicer must undertake, and of course raises the spectre of the most faithful translation of all—one in which Lorca's actual Spanish words could all simply be retained" (2004: 91). Yet the identicality between an English "No" and a

---

[17] Lorca 2009: 90–2.

Spanish "No" is, I submit, only visual, not semantic or even really aural. And what Katz (who refers twice in this passage to translation as "transit") praises as "the most faithful translation" is in fact no translation at all; it is, rather, the parodic *non*translation of Jorge Luis Borges's Pierre Menard's translation of *Don Quixote*, which simply rewrites Cervantes' Spanish text without altering a single word.

In my reading, *After Lorca* rejects this model of translation as repetition or replication in favor of another set of tropes that figure translation as a mode of iterative flow. We could, then, look to the second stanza of "He Died at Sunrise" for a competing vision of what translation is—of how, carrying that "No," we might write translation differently: "I look into my body for / The tracks of your lips / A stream kisses into the wind / without touch." If we see these as the tracks of Lorca's "original," they are to be sought in "*my* body" (emphasis added), the body of the poem in translation, in a text speaking of and for itself while also in place of another. This, then, may be the correspondence of which "Jack" writes in his letter to Lorca: not likeness or similarity but contiguity, a stream kissing into the wind without touch. This final image of course recalls another moment in Benjamin's "Die Aufgabe des Übersetzers" (which I quote again in Rendall's translation): "Just as a tangent touches a circle fleetingly and at only a single point [...] in the same way a translation touches the original fleetingly and only at an infinitely small point of sense, in order to follow its own path in accord with the law of fidelity in the freedom of linguistic development" (82). Likewise, in Spicer's translation, when that stream passes, it leaves the poem changed: the "shadow" of the first stanza has disappeared, leaving instead "my love, spinning." Like the turning girl in "Ballad of the Girl Who Invented the Universe," here too we have a kind of movement in place. Only that movement is faster, spinning rather than turning, and seeks the traces of the other in the self in order to propel poetry forward in place, with that unchanging "No," that refusal of equivalence, carried always in hand.

The sausage-machine of tradition

In moving away from the idea of translation as equivalence-seeking toward the idea of translation as correspondence, *After Lorca* does not jettison translation altogether in favor of pseudotranslation, or in favor of Spicer's "own" poems. Spicer is not trying to replace so-called strict translation with a looser kind of versioning, but rather to contest the terms according to which distinctions between translation and writing are usually drawn. *After Lorca* thus keeps translation and pseudotranslation in productive tension throughout its deepening exploration of the terms by which a tradition shapes and is shaped by writing and translation alike. The last letter to Lorca, which marks the end of the "intimate communion" of this particular form of correspondence, explicitly invokes a tradition of other moments of poetic channeling: "It was a game, I shout to myself. There are no angels, ghosts, or even shadows. [...] It was a game like Yeats' spooks or Blake's sexless seraphim." Only the game was serious, predicated on a pressing "need for a poetry that would be more than the expression of my hatreds and desires." And while Lorca returns to "the printed page [...] a disembodied but contagious spirit," Spicer's poetry is changed by this experience of hosting "an undramatic ghost who occasionally looked through my eyes and whispered to me" (2008: 153). Lorca's ghost may "never reappear" in Spicer's poetry, but the ghost of this game certainly does. It is present, first of all, in Spicer's conceptual elaboration of a poetics of dictation that empties out all claims to authorial control or responsibility. It is also present in the recombinatory channeling of other voices that becomes so central to Spicer's way of writing.

In the lectures he gave in Vancouver only months before his death, Spicer repeatedly speaks of his poems as being dictated by something outside himself. And he doesn't consider his work peculiar in this sense; for Spicer, this is simply what poetry is. Poets do not create texts. Rather, they are radio sets, or mediums, or rooms full of furniture or alphabet blocks (memories, words, accrued knowledge) that visiting Martians arrange into poems. He is consistently cagy about the sources of the "messages" he transmits. "I would guess that there are a number of sources," he responds at one point during the discussion after the first talk, "but I have no idea what they are, and frankly I don't think it's profitable to try to find out" (1998: 17). To a more targeted question after the third lecture about whether the work of earlier poets belongs to the "outside" he claims to channel, Spicer replies that the conscious attempt to structure a composition around particular poets has, for him, only ended in failure—except for Lorca, whose presence was "a direct connection like on the telephone" (137–8). And yet two decades earlier, as an undergraduate at the University of California Redlands, he was already recognizing others' work, if not his own, as deeply citational in nature. In a paper about Aristotle and James Joyce, two writers often admired for the originality of their thinking, Spicer flippantly likens them to mere combinative machines: "Aristotle was at the same end of Greek culture that Joyce was for the European. He acted—again like Joyce—as a sort of a philosophical sausage-machine into which the mixed meats of Greek culture were shoved."[18] The metaphor of the sausage-machine seems

---

[18] Box 26, folder 17 in the Jack Spicer Papers.

oddly suited to Spicer's own practice, which produced poem after poem thick with references and citations. Peter Gizzi suggests that Spicer's "view of poetry as a tradition based in copying" results in a constant "mirroring of other texts [that] occurs as a narrative gesture throughout his books." "Spicer writes from his reading," Gizzi continues, "as a way of engaging in discourse with what is otherwise isolated, keeping poetry in play by simultaneously borrowing, copying, critiquing, and adoring the living, the dead, peers, and legends" (1998: 219).

Indeed, though *After Lorca* contests the idea that we can ever truly trace the lines of correspondence between translation and source, Spicer's later work is full of sources that are in fact traceable: "Homer, Ovid, Dante, William Dunbar, Malory, Donne, Blake, Matthew Arnold, Lewis Carroll, Edward Lear, Yeats, Hawthorne, Poe, Dickinson, Whitman, Rimbaud, Baudelaire, Lorca, Rilke, Cocteau, Jeffers, Stevens, Pound, Eliot, Marianne Moore, W. C. Williams, Stein, Hart Crane, L. Frank Baum, Jessie Weston, Creeley, Blaser, Olson, Duncan, Kantorowicz, the King James Bible, Plato, Josephine Miles, and Johnny Mercer, to name a few" (Gizzi 1998: 174). Spicer's poetry is also full of "sources" one can see but not trace, apparent references that may in fact be mere apparitions, the ghosts of one's own reading rather than his. Take this passage from his "Textbook of Poetry," the last long sequence in *The Heads of the Town*:

> It does not have to fit together. Like the pieces of a totally unfinished jigsaw puzzle my grandmother left in the bedroom when she died in the living room. The pieces of poetry or of this love.
>
> Surrealism is a poem more than this. The intention that things do not fit together. As if my grandmother had chewed on her jigsaw puzzle before she died.
>
> Not as a gesture of contempt for the scattered nature of reality. Not because the pieces would not fit in time. But because this would be the only way to cause an alliance between the dead and the living. To magic the whole thing toward what they called God.
>
> To mess around. To totally destroy the pieces. To build around them.
>
> (2008: 302)

This passage, like many in *After Lorca*, offers a striking refraction of Benjamin's thinking on language and translation. The puzzle pieces recall the shards of Benjamin's vessel—only the matching of intention becomes, here, an intention *not* to fit. The "alliance between the dead and the living" conjures not only Spicer's many discussions of ghosts, tradition, and poetry as a conversation between dead men, but Benjamin's notion that a translation constitutes the "afterlife," "continuing life," or "survival" of a work (depending on which translation of "Die Aufgabe des Übersetzers" you read).[19] The phrase "magic the whole thing toward what they called God," meanwhile, recalls the notion that translation is a privileged form or mode able to gesture to "pure language," which Benjamin identifies with the language of God in "Über Sprache überhaupt und über die Sprache des Menschen" (translated by Edmund Jephcott as "On Language as Such and the Language of Man," 1979). At the same time, like Spicer's dodging of questions after his lectures, the passage above seems to resist the attempt to match literary creations to specific sources, proposing instead a metonymic model that "destroy[s] the pieces" and "build[s] around them," trusting that they will "fit in time" into an accretive whole made possible by the magic of an ultimately authorless poetry.

In the conversation following his first Vancouver lecture, one audience member asked how he would respond if a poet claimed to be writing her own poems. "I just have never met a poet who's gone beyond just, you know, the first couple of years of poetry, who would say that," Spicer answered. "I don't think that anyone who's a practicing poet, even a practicing bad poet, who's done it for a long enough time, would disagree with the fact that there *is* something from the outside" (1998: 10). For Spicer, dictation was not just his mode of writing; it was how all writing happened, or at least all good writing. Spicer's "sources"—the names I cited above, among others—are therefore not points of origin but rather resting spots in the continual flow of tradition, who themselves took dictation from countless prior outsides and engaged in similar processes of recombinatory citation. Spicer's dictation could be seen as an umbrella term, a poetics that treats translation, pseudotranslation, and poetic composition as intertwined modes of writing that correspond both to and with other texts, which correspond to and with yet other texts, and so on and so forth. This is Spicer's tradition; this is the bone-yard of the fallen tower of Babel. By placing translation in a broader array of citational practices (citation being, in a sense, the flip side of dictation, where only the agent is changed), and by un-pairing citation from intention (the Martians cite, while we as poets simply define the limits of their library), Spicer's work turns translation into a particular subset of writing, a kind of writing with constraint. It does so not by positing translation as "original" creation, but by figuring all writing as rewriting, all authorship as multiple and at least partly anonymous, and all claims to authorial originality wishful thinking at best, damaging ideology at worst.

[19] See Benjamin (1968; 2004; 2012).

De-frauding translation

Spicer's insistence that all good poets are merely conduits for outside forces was not always well received; the transcriptions of the discussions after his lectures show how strongly some audience members resisted his attempt to undermine the prevailing rhetoric of authorial intention and poetic originality. His rather freewheeling treatment of Lorca, meanwhile, has raised few objections over the years. I suspect that, notwithstanding his outspoken rejection of the role of creative originator, this lack of unease with his Lorca project has everything to do with his status (at least in the eyes of others) as poet-translator, which frees him from the expectations and even contractual obligations—to give back the whole text, and nothing but the text—placed on translators who don't also happen to be poets. Jonathan Mayhew is one of few scholars who expresses conflicted feelings toward Spicer's project: while he wants to protect the particular complexity of Lorca in Spanish, he also celebrates the "inventiveness" of the Lorcas created not only by Spicer but by Robert Creeley, Kenneth Koch, Frank O'Hara, and Jerome Rothenberg. In his monograph on these "apocryphal Lorcas," Mayhew declares that a "standard practice of translation, which aims for a satisfactory compromise between fidelity to the source text and acceptability by the target audience, remains necessary," but also concludes that "the ways in which U.S. poets have reinvented Lorca, while problematic in many respects, are felicitous, generative of new poetic possibilities" (xiii).

In distinguishing between "standard" translation and the generative work of poetic reinvention, Mayhew champions Spicer by implicitly assigning him a poet's prerogative of authorship over his translations, despite Spicer's consistent rejection of this model of authorial control. My choice to discuss the translations of a widely influential American poet could likewise be interpreted as privileging the presumed creative license of the poet-translator over the assumed responsibilities of the unhyphenated translator. I hope, however, that in focusing on a figure who explicitly denounced the very notions of authorial intention and originality, this chapter will help deflate rather than exceptionalize the category of poet-translator. Spicer's collapsing of the line between writing and translation is not as an exception to the rule of what translation really is, an exception available only to poets, but rather a different model for what translation can be, whose possibilities are open to all who translate, regardless of what we call them. If all "originals" are products of recombinatory methods, if all translations draw on multiple, usually unnamed "sources" in their construction of generically recognizable textual forms in other languages, and if the lines of correspondence between a translation and an "original" can never be drawn with confidence or accuracy, the field seems open for forms of translation that, like Spicer's, reject models of transfer and equivalence in favor of iterative proliferation and openly acknowledge the existence of many sources, rather than just one.

I do not mean, here, to suggest that Spicer's translations and pseudotranslations are categorically the same, any more than I would suggest that Christian Hawkey's incorporation of translations of Georg Trakl in his Spicer-inspired *Ventrakl* (2010) is the same kind of work as Robert Firmage's or James Riedel's translations of Trakl, or that Kent Johnson's likewise Spicer-inspired pseudotranslations of Araki Yasusada, fictional poet and Hiroshima survivor, are in fact translations whose sources have simply been sublated, just because they draw so heavily on Spicer's own citational practices. Translation and writing are both citational, recombinatory modes; that does not mean they are the same, though the difference may be one of degree rather than kind. Spicer's use of pseudotranslation is so interesting to me precisely because of the way it is woven so seamlessly not into a larger poetic work, as with Hawkey's, but into a project of *actual* translation, such that readers are effectively unable to distinguish between the two. As Douglas Robinson notes, pseudotranslation "calls into question some of our most cherished beliefs, especially the belief in the absolute difference between a translation and an original work" (2001a: 185)—a belief Spicer's entire oeuvre challenges from start to finish. It is a challenge that many may find threatening. In *The Translation Zone* (2006), Emily Apter presents pseudotranslation as a mode that reveals our desire or expectation that translation "transmit," while also revealing the conceptual confusion caused by its unavoidable "failure" to do so. "[I]f a translation is not," Apter writes, "a form of textual predicate, indexically pointing to a primary text, then what is it? Can a literary technology of reproduction that has sublated its origin still be considered a translation? Or should it be considered the premier illustration of deconstructed ontology insofar as it reveals the extent to which all translations are unreliable transmitters of the original, purveyors, that is, of a regime of extreme untruth?" (212).

The second and third of these questions offer opposed understandings of both pseudotranslation and translation itself. A "yes" to the second question aligns with a Spicerean view: a translation can still be a translation even if its "original" cannot be located. If we remember back to Eshleman's identification of what he termed "mistranslations" within Spicer's translations, we might argue instead that these are merely translations whose relationship to their "originals" is not legible to Eshleman, because he is looking in the wrong places for their points of "origin." A "yes" to Apter's third question, on the contrary, presents pseudotranslation as a limit case of the fraud that translation supposedly always is. Apter comes down solidly in support of this latter understanding. Pseudotranslation becomes, for her, an illustration of the fact that *all* translations fail to represent their sources adequately:

> The revelation of translational false coin leaves the reader aware of the dimension of epistemological scam or faked-up alterity inherent in all translation. The translation business is geared to keeping this scam from view, for it wants to convince readers that when it markets an author in translation, the translated text will be a truly serviceable stand-in for the original; affording a genuine translinguistic encounter with a foreign literature in the language of selfsame. But cases of pseudotranslation reveal the fundamental unreliability of a translation's claim to approximating the original in another tongue. (220)

"False coin," "epistemological scam," "faked-up alterity": the language is remarkable in its imputation to translation of the guilt of false premises, false promises, and betrayal. But who, precisely, is making these promises of reliability, approximation, and genuine experience for which Apter criticizes the "translation business"?

I am a translator who would never think to use the words "genuine" or "serviceable" in talking about my work. I am also a scholar of translation who hopes to encourage suspicion not of translation but of the very idea that stable originals exist. I am therefore far more likely to charge readers—even the professional readers of the academy—with ignorance about what translation is than I am to convict a depersonalized "translation business" of trying to convince readers to buy into its supposed epistemological scam. As someone who has been part of the translating community in the United States for the past fifteen years, I am frankly baffled at who might comprise this "translation business"; in fact, to most of us involved in producing, publishing, and promoting literary translations on a would-be professional basis, these activities seem just about as far from a business as you can get. Might, then, the impossible promise of translation be made less by the community of those who produce translations than by readers, reviewers, and even literary scholars who perpetuate this conventional understanding of translation as (failed) transfer that many translators and scholars of translation have tried so hard to counteract? Translation as a mode—like specific translations—will only disappoint if we ask it to do things we should already know it can't; translation can only be an "unreliable transmitter" if transmission is what we expect of it. The trope of untranslatability, to whose popularity Apter has greatly contributed, sets up a kind of conceptual straw man, a false demand that translation provide a "genuine translinguistic encounter with a foreign literature"—a demand which translation can, of course, never meet. If these are the terms of engagement, whatever a translation provides will always be judged wanting, because the doctrine of untranslatability in fact demands recall and equivalence, rather than a Spicerean correspondence that builds a tradition from the recombined bones of others' work, within and among languages. The double bind of Derrida's "necessary impossibility" has bound us to an expectation that forces translation to fail time and again to be something it manifestly never was.[20]

Spicer's work as a writer, translator, and theorist of writing and translation shows us one way out of this double bind. But we may have to learn to read him differently. Eshleman reads the translations like a detective looking for a crime, or a judge convicting Spicer's texts of failing to make good on promises Spicer steadfastly refuses to make. Katz, who has written brilliantly on so many aspects of Spicer's work, still sees the perfect translation as *no* translation, as a linguistic replication that would erase the very need for translation. In Apter's work, the trope of pseudotranslation serves to reinstate and police the boundary between translation and writing. Spicer, on the contrary, erodes that boundary by evacuating writing of the very authorial authenticity and control that keeps us wedded to an ideal of translation as accurate representation, adequate conveyor of a stable content. Anxieties about what translation is and is not may betray, in the end, equally deeply-rooted anxieties over what writing is and is not; the cultural hostility toward translation we find even in academic circles may stem from our lingering hesitation to explore the full consequences of poststructuralist challenges to the notion of writing as individual expression.

Spicer, who renounced copyright and opposed its ideological grounds, offers another way of approaching the divide between writing and translation: by denying authorship its privileged status and recognizing that translation and writing are both citational, derivative endeavors, for which lines of correspondence can never be precisely drawn. This is not to say that translation and writing are one and the same thing. At the very most, translation could be considered a particular form of writing with constraint. The recent surge in interest in other modes of citational composition should, meanwhile, show us that "original writing" is a misnomer with deep, and deeply problematic, ideological underpinnings.[21] One goal of this chapter

---

[20] For Derrida's much-cited passages on the "necessary and impossible" nature of translation, see Derrida (1985).

[21] See, for instance, many of the projects discussed in Kenneth Goldsmith's 2011 *Uncreative Writing*, such as Simon Morris's *Getting Inside Jack Kerouac's Head*, a page-by-page blog rewriting of *On the Road*, or Goldsmith's own 840-page *Day*, in which he copies out every word of the September 11, 2001 print edition of the *New York Times*. Other projects that manipulate works in the public domain include Jen Bervin's *Nets* or Gregory Betts' *The Others Raisd in Me*, both reworkings of Shakespeare's sonnets, or M. NourbeSe Philip's *Zong!*, which performs multiple erasures of a seventeenth-century

has been to argue that the relation between translation and writing need not be quite so heavily policed, and certainly should not be policed in a way that reinforces statements about each that we already know are false. We should, instead, let figures such as Spicer shine a light on our continuing unwillingness to let go of certain dearly-held yet problematic preconceptions, and let projects such as *After Lorca* push us toward new conceptions of what both translation and writing can be. What might it look like if we, as translators, gave ourselves the freedom to engage in forms of citational correspondence whose goal was not to reflect or represent but to grow, to mess around, to destroy the pieces, to magic poetry forward in excitingly non-original ways?

court decision concerning the murder of 300 slaves for insurance money. Projects such as these are reminders that, as Bervin writes in a short note at the end of her volume, "When we write poems, the history of poetry is with us, pre-inscribed in the white of the page; when we read or write poems, we do so with or against this palimsest" (2004, n.p.).

Coda: Toward a Pedagogy of Iterability

I close this book with a third and final origin story concerning the intellectual preoccupations that gave rise to its writing. During my last two years of graduate school at Columbia University, I was one of a few dozen instructors of Literature Humanities, a required course for first-year students that has been a part of the undergraduate Core Curriculum since 1937. The course is taught in seminar style but with a shared syllabus and final exam. The Core Curriculum uses the term "great books" in its description of the course, and its reading list introduces students to canonical texts drawn exclusively from the Western literary tradition. The first semester covered works by Homer, Herodotus, Aeschylus, Sophocles, Euripides, Aristophanes, Thucydides, and Plato, as well as *Gilgamesh* and selections from the Bible, while the second semester flew at breakneck speed through the next two millennia: Virgil, Ovid, Augustine, Dante, Boccaccio, Montaigne, Shakespeare, Cervantes, Austen, Dostoevsky, and Woolf.[1]

As great a challenge as the course poses for first-year undergraduates, who end the year having worked their way across a solid three feet of bookshelf space, it is arguably even more difficult for instructors. Who among us feels qualified to teach such a vast—though, in the far vaster world of possibilities, also extraordinarily limited—swath of material, particularly to first-year undergraduates who invariably expect instructors to provide historical and cultural contextualization for the weighty books they hold in their hands? In response to this difficulty, program administrators had instituted a series of lunchtime pedagogy workshops: each week or so, a guest speaker would come to lecture on the next book on the syllabus, offering contextual information on the work, its time period, and its later reception, drawing parallels or inviting contrasts with other works we had read, and identifying passages on which we might encourage our students to focus. The speed with which we had to barrel through the long list of works, and our own unfamiliarity with many or all of the historical moments and literary traditions from which they arose, made the close reading of selected passages our default

---

[1] The most recent syllabus at the time of writing adds Anne Carson's translations of Sappho and moves Virgil and Ovid to the fall term, to make room for Milton and Toni Morrison in the spring. A detailed account of the authors and works that have been taught in the course since its inception can be found at https://www.college.columbia.edu/core/1937.php (last accessed 7 May 2017).

pedagogical methodology. The primacy of close reading was enshrined even in the format of the final exam, on which the identification and analysis of short passages featured prominently.

While close reading need not exclude consideration of the processes of rewriting that shape the passages it treats, in practice it often does. Certainly at our lunchtime pedagogy sessions, the history of the translations we were reading, and of the "sources" on which they were based, rarely entered our discussions. If the topic of translation arose at all, it usually did so as a problem: the speaker might express a preference for a translation other than the one we were reading; identify "mistakes" on the level of the word or phrase; offer a reading of a passage that also served as a corrective, because the translator had failed to preemptively share the speaker's interpretation; or mark the inadequacy not only of a translator's choices but of the English language itself to account for qualities the speaker valued in the work's "original" form. And it wasn't just the invited speakers who made comments of this sort—instructors who were able to read the works in their language of composition would occasionally offer commentary that likewise subjected the assigned translations to a similar rhetoric of failure, shortcoming, or inadequacy. Rather than treating translation as a series of interpretive decisions based on scholarly knowledge and research, our discussions usually framed the texts before us as flawed (if valiant) representations of what we were *really* supposed to be interested in: the works *behind* the translations, whose ultimate inaccessibility was signaled by the occasional disappointing blotches on a translation's otherwise un-noteworthy façade. Our pedagogy sessions, whose explicit purpose was to set the tone for instructors' encounters with students in the classroom, thus perpetuated the idea that translations are poor substitutes for "originals"—though these works were, of course, made accessible to us and our students by the very editions-in-translation we were being told both to honor (for what they gestured toward) and to distrust (for their inability to do so adequately).

As someone who had been working as a literary translator for several years, and was frankly quite grateful for the opportunity to encounter so many works in what struck me as rich and fascinating translations, I was surprised and dismayed by the consistently dismissive attitude to translation displayed by those around the table. Most of these individuals seemed to have thought very little about translation itself, even though they were experts in humanistic disciplines that rely heavily on the products of translation. In my own classroom, at least, I felt capable of raising issues of translation, to whatever limited degree our tight schedule allowed. I could, for instance, remind students of the boundedness of the claims we could make about Montaigne's language if we were reading in J. M. Cohen's 1958 translation. I could even allow them to read translations other than the ones assigned (at the risk of imperiling their grades, of course, given the structure of the final exam), and let our classroom discussions reflect this multiplicity of texts. Students arrived at our first session having read over the summer the first several books of the *Iliad* (according to the organization of the epic undertaken by scholars in third-century B.C.E. Alexandria, a fact I did not then know) in Richmond Lattimore's translation. I would pass out a sheet with ten or twelve versions of the opening invocation to the muse, including George Chapman's seventeenth-century version in rhyming couplets, an illustrated prose translation from 1950, and a number of twentieth- and twenty-first-century verse translations. A crucial inclusion was a passage from David Melnick's 1983 *Men in Aida*, a homophonic translation that conveys little of the story, but focuses instead on its (hypothesized) sound, and presents itself in the opening lines as "a hideous debt to lay at a bully"—the bully being the idea of Homer, as imagined, constructed, and maintained over the centuries by processes of canon formation that call for a unity of work and text and promote what Lawrence Venuti calls an "instrumental model of translation" (2013: 178). While the pace of the course rarely allowed us to repeat such exercises, our discussion during this first session would set the tone for the year, both in its focus on practices of rewriting and in its insistence on treating translations as rich, historically situated objects of interpretation that need not focus solely on semantic meaning.

Translation comparison is a basic tool in the pedagogy of translated literature, at least for texts that have been sufficiently canonized to boast multiple translations. It is wonderfully effective in sensitizing students to the thoroughly interpretive nature of the act of translating, and thus in encouraging the kind of "double focus" that Venuti suggests a discussion of any literary text in translation requires (1996: 332). In my classroom, once we were all attuned to the basic fact that Aeschylus or Thucydides didn't write in English, we were able to keep that fact and its consequences always in mind, regardless of the translator's approach.[2] Encouraging this understanding of the mediated nature of the products of translation can, of course, have undesired effects: it risks strengthening even further students' desire for an unmediated "original". Indeed, continually reminding students that we are reading not Dante's words but Alan Mandelbaum's, not Dostoyevsky's but Richard Pevear and Larissa Volokhonsky's, runs the risk of turning them

---

[2] In this I differ from those who favor either "foreignizing" (Venuti) or "radically domesticating" (Douglas Robinson) approaches as more likely to raise awareness about the fact and consequences of translation: I prefer to treat this as a challenge to be met by a change in our broader cultural discourse, including academic conversations, rather than a change in how we translate.

away from translated literature altogether—though in my experience, the richness of their engagement generally persuades them of the value of even these "inauthentic" encounters.

One way of responding to dismissive attitudes toward translation in the classroom is to question students' beliefs, first, in the paradigm of translation as transfer, and second, in the "authenticity" or unmediated nature of so-called originals. While I felt capable of tackling this first issue, I was unprepared to manage the second on any but vague theoretical grounds students found unconvincing. Over the course of my two years teaching Literature Humanities I became increasingly frustrated by my inability—shared by most of my colleagues—to provide students with reliable, detailed information about the highly mediated textual histories of the "original" works these translations were taken to represent. Where on earth did the *Iliad* come from, anyhow? Issues of a text-critical nature arose only occasionally during our lunchtime pedagogy sessions, and the editions from which we taught rarely included explicit information about the "source(s)" for the translations they presented. One noteworthy exception was Andrew George's edition of *The Epic of Gilgamesh*, which registers lacunae and editorial interpolations in the body of the translation, and includes an extensive introduction that discusses the history of the text's circulation in ancient Mesopotamia, as well as an appendix that gives an account of the textual (re)construction of the "sources" he and other Assyriologists treat. Yet the other books on our syllabus would include, at most, only a brief note from the translator, listing the editions he (almost always he) had consulted in the creation of his own edition-in-translation. I therefore found myself at a loss when trying to convince students that, for instance, Mandelbaum's translation of *La Divina Comedia* wasn't of some easily defined "original" but of a work with a complicated textual history whose particular construction had been elided by the Bantam edition they had been assigned.

My own "teachable moment" came halfway through the second semester of my first year in the program, when my students and I were unpacking the language of King Lear's monologue mourning Cordelia. Midway through our discussion, a student raised her hand to tell us that her text said something different: she was reading another edition, based on the quarto rather than the folio, and her version didn't support the analyses the rest of us had been busily producing. A similar dilemma arose a few weeks later in our session on *To the Lighthouse*, when students came with both British and American editions, and the minor differences in the texts again took on a heightened significance under the scrutinizing gaze of the close reading exercise. Each of these was what John Bryant calls a "fluid text moment."[3] Each was also a

[3]   Quoted in Keleman (2012: 121).

moment that made me sorely aware of my ignorance of textual scholarship. My graduate education in literary studies, which had trained me to be both researcher and educator, had not encouraged an awareness either of the textual instability of literary works or of its consequences, including the theoretical challenges this instability poses to many of our most common methodologies of literary criticism and teaching alike.

Frustration can be generative. It was in fact my frustration with scenarios like these that spurred me to reconceive of syllabus design as an opportunity to pose certain challenges to how both I and my students customarily thought about works and texts. Teaching Literature Humanities led me to explore ways of putting issues of textual instability and translation at the center of my courses rather than at the periphery, in asides quickly uttered and just as quickly forgotten. I began by auditing a graduate seminar required for doctoral candidates in comparative literature at another institution, which included several sessions on textual bibliography. This course gave me a sense of the stakes of these discussions, and encouraged me to consider how graduate students in the humanities might benefit from a similar education in translation literacy.[4] In this, I was unwittingly joining the ranks of many who came before me. Scholars of textual criticism and translation have been arguing vociferously for years about the need to make students at all levels aware of the interpretive nature of those activities, and to encourage what David Greetham calls a "suspicion of texts" inside and outside of the academic setting.[5] As André Lefevere wrote in 1992, "Rewriting manipulates, and it is effective. All the more reason, then, to study it. In fact, the study of rewriting might even be of some relevance beyond the charmed circle of the educational institution, a way to restore to a certain study of literature some of the more immediate social relevance the study of literature as a whole has lost" (9). This study of rewriting need not be limited to undergraduate or even graduate students; arguments in support of pedagogical modes that incorporate a consideration of textual scholarship and translation could be fruitfully applied even to faculty pedagogy sessions of the kind I described above.

---

[4] While on faculty at the University of Oregon from 2011–13, I was given the opportunity to teach just such a course. The Department of Comparative Literature at UO is the first such department in the country to require a graduate course in the pedagogy of translated literature of all incoming PhD candidates. For an account of my version of this course, see Emmerich (2016).

[5] David Greetham (1998: 204). Greetham was also the instructor of the course to which I refer, at the CUNY Graduate Center. I am grateful to him for allowing me to sit in on his course, and for his help in putting together a syllabus of self-study on the history of textual criticism.

I particularly want to stress the importance of teaching about editing and translating *together*, so as to avoid reifying yet again an "original" we hope to destabilize, or unwittingly leading students to (continue to) dismiss the very processes and products of translation we hope to validate. It is imperative that we and our students come to understand that translation does not transfer content but rather puts forward an embodied interpretation of a literary work. Yet that in itself is not sufficient: if we fail to consider the fact that each edition of a work in its language of composition is also an embodied interpretation, we may unintentionally reinforce the widespread belief that an "original" is a stable, unchanging whole—a belief goes hand in hand with the notion that a translation can only ever be a partial, inadequate representation. By the same token, encouraging students to consider the instability of so-called originals without giving them the tools to think about translation as a legitimate interpretive process that offers a new iteration of a work in another language also runs the risk of encouraging a heightened distrust of translation. If instability is a condition of textuality itself, if there's simply no *there* there to begin with, how can we ever translate anything at all? Teaching textual scholarship and translation together, as mutually implicated processes of textual iteration, in a Derridean sense that resists fixity or closure, can help us avoid this incessant return to the idea of a stable point of origin. While Derrida's work on iteration focuses on an instability of meaning, throughout this book I have stressed the textual instability of works themselves, both "within" and "across" languages (terms around which Derrida has, of course, taught us to put scare quotes). All textual iterations of a work ultimately point to a *there* that is elsewhere, to a work that is only ever a hypothetical sum of its continually proliferating parts. By helping students understand the distinction between work and text, we can encourage them to treat editions *and* translations as textual iterations rather than transparent representations of a given work.

This book has treated literary works exclusively—yet my argument is of relevance to disciplines across the humanities and even social sciences that depend on texts in translation for teaching and research alike: history, philosophy, sociology, anthropology, political science. Though many in these fields employ translation in the course of research and writing—think, for instance, of the many anthropologists who work in translingual situations, and must present their research to readers unfamiliar with the language in which that research was conducted—discussions *about* translation remain rare. In the early days of comparative literature, when scholars felt strongly that a work could only be properly read in its language of composition, the field was actively hostile to translation. This hostility has not disappeared: we now see it in the newfound popularity of the term "untranslatability," which, as I have argued elsewhere in this book, simply has no place in discussions of translation per se. The notion of untranslatability is fundamentally based on a mistaken paradigm that sees translation as the transfer of invariant content. While the term has been employed by scholars engaged in admirable efforts to resist the worst versions of "world literature" and the commodification of literary objects from elsewhere, I see it as yet another incarnation of a problematic ideology we would do well to avoid, particularly as it currently overshadows far more pressing considerations of what translation actually does. As comparative literature broadens its scope to incorporate "new cultures, languages, and texts" (Bermann: 83)—new, that is, to an "us" newly able to encounter them—it urgently needs to grapple in more constructive ways with the practical and theoretical consequences of reading and teaching in translation. As David Damrosch has said, there is simply too much world and too little time to restrict ourselves only to those texts from the relatively few languages any of us could expect to learn.[6] And if we teach *in* translation we must also—as scholars including Damrosch, Venuti, Sandra Bermann, Gayatri Spivak, and Emily Apter contend[7]—teach *about* translation, so as to help students be "both self-critical and critical of exclusionary cultural ideologies by drawing attention to the situatedness of texts and interpretations," including the interpretations put forward in the translations we assign (Venuti 1996: 331).

This last claim could just as easily be reframed to apply to the situatedness of editorial interpretations. Many textual scholars are insistent that students of all levels, including senior literary scholars, need to cultivate basic knowledge about textual criticism and textual bibliography in order to become more adept readers not just of literary texts but of the editions that give them shape. As George Bornstein writes, "the texts we study and teach never come to us unmediated, but are always the product of individual and social forces" (1996: 148). While editors themselves are certainly attuned to the conceptual underpinnings and practical consequences of various editorial methodologies, David Holdeman suggests that most readers have scarcely "begun to confront the fact that such ontological assumptions underlie any attempt to read a literary work" (1996: 162). For students of literature particularly, learning about textual scholarship and translation is also one of the most direct routes to acquiring the interpretive tools of our discipline. "To concern our students with the textual matters raised by manuscript studies," Erick Keleman writes, "is to introduce them to the most

---

[6] See the last chapter of Damrosch (2003).

[7] See Venuti (1996), Bermann (2009; 2010), Apter (2015), Spivak (2005), and Damrosch (2003; 2009), indicatively.

fundamental questions of the field, such as 'What is an author?' or 'What is a work?' and 'How do we form canons?' and, perhaps most problematically [...] 'What is literary value?'" (125–6). Such considerations can, of course, present "a potentially destabilizing force for the discipline as a whole" (125), as they invite students to reflect critically on the disciplinary mechanisms of our fields—a disturbing prospect for some educators.

In an environment where the norm is a willingness to put aside reflections on translation and textual instability in order to privilege coverage of a certain kind of content, it is important for at least some of us to open our pedagogy to precisely that disruptive capacity, so that students can return to other contexts better able to challenge (internally or externally, as thought or as speech) this prevailing, unreflective reliance on mediated texts. In my own pedagogical practice, I have come to feel the need to incorporate discussions of textual criticism and translation into almost every course I teach, such that students will be equipped to distinguish between a work of literature and its specific textual incarnations, and therefore to recognize the fact of textual iteration both within and across languages. Students in my courses are encouraged to consider the paratext, peritext, and history of production and circulation of the texts they encounter, regardless of whether they are "originals" or translations. This might mean devoting an entire section of a poetry course to the editorial history of Emily Dickinson's work, or taking students into the library stacks in search of an "original" *Iliad*, or teaching two translations of *Gilgamesh* back to back. There is a cost, of course: paying attention to issues of rewriting takes time. Reading two complete versions of a single work cuts down on the total number of works a course can cover. Yet since these are issues many of my colleagues are *not* addressing, it seems worth spending the time to cultivate modes and habits of encountering texts that I hope will continue to be of use to students long after a particular course draws to a close.

Scholarship on the pedagogy of translation and on the pedagogy of textual criticism abounds with anecdotal examples of the successful incorporation in the classroom, even on a small scale, of assignments involving translation or editorial practice. Having students engage practically with the activities of translating and editing can sharpen close-reading skills while also inviting historical contextualization and research into the prior stages of a work's production and reception. Even the most basic exercises can cultivate a sense of "how many decisions—and therefore how many interpretations—are silently made for [us] by editors" or translators of the texts we read (Rebecca Barnhouse, quoted in Keleman 2012: 122). I now routinely offer students in my undergraduate and graduate courses the option of undertaking a final project that involves translating, editing, or rewriting of some other kind, always accompanied by critical reflections on those activities. These projects tend to be far more time-consuming than a traditional term paper; they also have the potential to be more intellectually challenging. While some of the results are less polished than a conventional paper might have been, students report having learned far more from the process of editing or translating than they do from other genres of academic writing. This is not because those other genres are ineffectual, but rather because students have usually already developed the skills necessary to produce at least a passable term paper; the learning curve associated with translating or editing is steep, and these first steps have much to offer. And unlike term papers, which are a genre unto themselves with no obvious equivalent in the world outside the university, student editions and translations resemble the genres of many of the texts we assign. These final projects thus allow students to feel that they belong to an intellectual community whose engagements with literary texts can be shared in meaningful ways. Some of them even go on to make their work public, in blogs, literary journals, podcasts, or performance videos that they share online.

Textual scholars and scholars of translation have long advocated the recognition of editing and translating as legitimate forms of doctoral research, as well. As early as 1998, Susan Bassnett argued that the growth of a field depended on the vitality of the work of its graduate students, and that the relatively young field of translation studies would do well to recognize translation as a mode of scholarly investigation. Noting her own institution's encouragement of PhD dissertations that take the form of "original translation work […] along with a detailed commentary and notes," Bassnett declared that, "As an academic exercise, this is both respectable and demanding, and I refute any suggestion that research in Translation Studies that may involve a practical element is any less rigorous than any other kind of research in the humanities" (112). Hans Walter Gabler, best known for his genetic edition of James Joyce's *Ulysses*, likewise noted in 1996 the need for the professional training of scholarly editors, and suggested that doctoral programs in literary fields encourage dissertations comprising an edition or commentary (169).

The promotion of these activities at all levels benefits our entire community in myriad ways. When we incorporate them into our pedagogy, we validate the intellectual efforts of our students by choosing to evaluate them on the basis of forms of work that are themselves already valued, in however limited a way, by the nonacademic world to which we also all belong. At the same time, raising student (and colleague) awareness of the intellectual challenges of editing and translating has the capacity not merely to destabilize the notion of literary value but also to confer value on those forms of intellectual labor that are currently most *under*valued in the university setting, even for faculty. In its 2007 report, the Modern Language Association's Task Force on Evaluating Scholarship for Tenure and Promotion called for a reevaluation of tenure and promotion policies at institutions of higher education. The task force suggested that, across the board, colleges and universities should give greater recognition to certain forms of scholarship, including critical editing and the translation of "important primary texts," both of which "may contribute to a body of scholarly and professional work that can meet the highest standards of scholarship in the tenure-review process" (39–40). Referring explicitly to the MLA Task Force report, Keleman suggests that one way of combatting the narrow definition of scholarship at the faculty level would be to expand that definition in practice, at *all* levels, beginning with our undergraduate pedagogy: "Broadening our minds about what kind of writing we should ask of our students might go a long way toward making our profession's definition of scholarship more 'capacious' [...] If we wish to change the way we value scholarship, we must do more than pay lip service to other forms of scholarship in faculty handbooks and committee rooms; we would do well to begin by changing the genres of writing we require" (135).

In helping the next generation of scholars see what they have to learn from the activities of editing and translating, we may slowly begin to shift our institutional cultures in this direction. We have much to gain, as an academic community, from valuing those modes and products of intellectual labor that are most valued beyond our campuses. We have much to gain, too, as a community that stretches far beyond the academy, from encouraging readers of all sorts—ourselves first and foremost—to treat texts of all sorts with healthy doses of suspicion, when needed, and respect, when earned.

Bibliography

Abrahams, Roger D. (1993), "Phantoms of Romantic Nationalism in Folkloristics," *The Journal of American Folklore* 106 (419): 3–37.

Adams, Robert and Erica Reiner (2002), "An Adventure of Great Dimension: The Launching of the Chicago Assyrian Dictionary," *Transactions of the American Philosophical Society* 92 (3) New Series: i–140.

Adkins, Lesley (2003), *Empires of the Plain: Henry Rawlinson and the Lost Languages of Babylon*, New York: St. Martin's Press.

Alexiou, Margret (1984), "Folklore: An Obituary?" *Byzantine and Modern Greek Studies* 9 (1): 1–28.

Allan, Michael (2016), *In the Shadow of World Literature: Sites of Reading in Colonial Egypt*, Princeton: Princeton University Press.

Allen, Esther (2013), "Footnotes *sans Frontiéres*: Translation and Textual Scholarship," in Brian Nelson and Brigid Maher (eds), *Perspectives on Literature and Translation: Creation, Circulation, Reception*, 210 –20, London: Routledge.

Anonymous (1836), review of G. L. Maurer, *Das Griechische Volk in öffentlicher, kirchlicher und privatrechtlicher Beziehung, vor undnach dem Freiheitskampfe bis zum* [*The Greek folk in public, ecclesiastical, and private relations, before and after the struggle for freedom*], James Emerson, *History of Modern Greece*, and Jacovaky Rizo Néroulos, *Cours de Littérature Grecque Moderne, donnée à Genève* [*Courses in modern Greek literature, given in Geneva*], *The North American Review* 43 (93): 337–56.

Apostolakis, Giannis (1929), *Τα δημοτικά τραγούδια, Μέρος Α΄, οι συλλογές* [*Folk Songs, Part A, The Collections*]. Athens: Kontomaris.

Apter, Emily (2006), *The Translation Zone*, Princeton: Princeton University Press.

Apter, Emily (2015), *Against World Literature: On the Politics of Untranslatability*, Princeton: Princeton University Press.

Armistead, Samuel G. and Joseph H. Silverman (1963), "A Judeo-Spanish Derivative of the Ballad of *The Bridge of Arta*," *The Journal of American Folklore* 76 (299): 16–20.

Barthes, Roland (1986), "From Work to Text," *The Rustle of Language*, trans. Richard Howard, 56–68, New York: Hill and Wang.

Bassnett, Susan (1998), "Researching Translation Studies: The Case for Doctoral Research," in Peter Bush and Kirsten Malmkjaer (eds), *Rimbaud's Rainbow: Literary Translation in Higher Education*, 105–18, Amsterdam: John Benjamins.

Bassnett, Susan (2012), "Translation Studies at a Cross-Roads," *Target* 24 (1): 15–25.

Bassnett, Susan (2014), *Translation*, Oxon and New York: Routledge.

Baudelaire, Charles (2014), *Die Blumen des Bösen* [*Flowers of Evil*], trans. Stefan George, Berlin: Hoffenberg.

Bauman, Richard (1993), "The Nationalization and Internationalization of Folklore: The Case of Schoolcraft's 'Gitshee Gauzinee'," *Western Folklore, Theorizing Folklore: Toward New Perspectives on the Politics of Culture* 52 (2/3): 247–69.

Beals, Kurt (2014), "Alternatives to Impossibility: Translation as Dialogue in the Works of Paul Celan," *Translation Studies* 7 (3): 284–99.

Beaton, Roderick (1980), *Folk Poetry of Modern Greece*, Cambridge: Cambridge University Press.

Bellos, David (2011), *Is That a Fish in Your Ear?: Translation and the Meaning of Everything*, New York: Farrar, Strauss, and Giroux.

Benjamin, Walter (1968), "The Task of the Translator," trans. James Hynd and E. M. Valk, *Delos* 2: 76–99.

Benjamin, Walter (1979), "On Language as Such and on the Language of Man," trans. Edmund Jephcott, in *One-Way Street, and Other Writings*, 107–23, London: New Left Books.

Benjamin, Walter (2004), "The Task of the Translator," trans. Harry Zohn, in Lawrence Venuti (ed.), *The Translation Studies Reader*, 2nd edn, 72–82, New York: Routledge.

Benjamin, Walter (2012), "The Translator's Task," trans. Stephen Rendall, in Lawrence Venuti (ed.), *The Translation Studies Reader*, 3rd edn, 75–83, London: Routledge.

Bermann, Sandra (2009), "Working in the *And* Zone: Comparative Literature and Translation," *Comparative Literature* 61 (4): 432–46.

Bermann, Sandra (2010), "Teaching in—and about—Translation," *Profession 2010*, Modern Language Association of America: 82–90.

Bermann, Sandra and Michael Wood (eds) (2005), *Nation, Lanugage and the Ethics of Translation*, Princeton: Princeton University Press.

Bervin, Jen (2004), *Nets,* Brooklyn: Ugly Duckling Presse.

Bervin, Jen (2010), *The Dickinson Composites*, New York: Granary Books.

Betts, Gregory (2009), *The Others Raisd in Me*, Toronto: Pedlar Press.

Bielsa, Esperança and Susan Bassnett (2009), *Translation in Global News*, London and New York: Routledge.

Black, Jeremy (1998), *Reading Sumerian Poetry*, Ithaca: Cornell University Press.

Black, Jeremy, Andrew George and Nicholas Postgate (eds) (2000), *A Concise Dictionary of Akkadian*, 2nd (corrected) printing, Weisbaden: Harrassowitz Verlag.

Bohrer, Frederick N. (2003), *Orientalism and Visual Culture: Imagining Mesopotamia in Nineteenth-Century Europe*, Cambridge: Cambridge University Press.

Booth, Marilyn (2008), "Translator vs. Author," *Translation Studies* 1 (2): 197–211.

Bornstein, George (1991), "Introduction: Why Editing Matters," in George Bornstein (ed.), *Representing Modernist Texts: Editing as Interpretation*, 1–17, Ann Arbor: University of Michigan Press.

Bornstein, George (1993), "What is the Text of a Poem by Yeats?," in George Bornstein and Ralph G. Williams (eds), *Palimpsest: Editorial Theory in the Humanities*, 167–93, Ann Arbor: University of Michigan Press.

Bornstein, George (1996), "Teaching Editorial Theory to Non-Editors: What? Why? How?" *Text* 9: 144–60.

Bornstein, George (2001), *Material Modernism: The Politics of the Page*, Cambridge: Cambridge University Press.

Bowers, Fredson (1959), *Textual and Literary Criticism*, Cambridge: Cambridge University Press.

Bradford, Lisa Rose (2013), "Generative Translation in Spicer, Gelman, and Hawkey," *CLCWeb: Comparative Literature and Culture* 15 (6). Available online: http://dx.doi.org/10.7771/1481-4374.2365

Budge, E. A. Wallis (1925), *The Rise & Progress of Assyriology*, London: Richard Clay & Sons.

Calotychos, Evangelos (2005), "From Arta to NATO: Building and Bombing Bridges in the Balkans," in Panagiotis Roilos and Dimitris Yatromanolakis (eds), *Ritual Poetics in Greek Culture*, 227–44, Cambridge: Harvard University Press.

Calotychos, Evangelos (2013), *The Balkan Prospect: Identity, Culture, and Politics in Greece after 1989*, New York: Palgrave Macmillan.

Cavafy, C. P. (1935), *Ποιήματα* [*Poems*], ed. Rika Sengopoulou, Alexandria.

Cavafy, C. P. (1951), *Poems*, trans. John Mavrogordato, London: Hogarth.

Cavafy, C. P. (1963), *Τα Ποιήματα, Α΄ (1897–1918), Β΄ (1919–1933)* [*Poems, I (1897–1918) and II (1919–1933)*], ed. G. P. Savidis, Athens: Ikaros.

Cavafy, C. P. (1968), *Ανέκδοτα Ποιήματα (1882–1923)* [*Unpublished Poems (1882–1923)*], ed. G. P. Savidis, Athens: Ikaros.

Cavafy, C. P. (1975), *Collected Poems*, trans. Edmund Keeley and Philip Sherrard, ed. George Savidis, Princeton: Princeton University Press.

Cavafy, C. P. (1993), *Κρυμμένα Ποιήματα 1877–1923* [*Hidden Poems 1877–1923*], ed. G. P. Savidi, Athens: Ikaros.

Cavafy, C. P. (1994), *Ατελή ποιήματα 1918–1932* [*Unfinished Poems 1918–1932*], ed. Renata Lavagnini, Athens: Ikaros.

Cavafy, C. P. (1998), "Seven Unfinished Poems," trans. John Davis, *Conjunctions* 31: *Radical Shadows*: 81–7.

Cavafy, C. P. (2002 [1968]), *Αυτόγραφα Ποιήματα (1896–1910), Το Τετράδιο Σεγκοπούλου σε πανομοιότυπη έκδοση* [*Autograph Poems (1896–1910), the Sengopoulos Notebook in Facsimile Edition*], ed. G. P. Savidis, Athens: Ermis/

Cavafy, C. P. (2003a), *Άπαντα τα ποιήματα* [*Complete Poems*], ed. Sonia Ilinskaya, Athens: Narkissos.

Cavafy, C. P. (2003b [1983]), *Πανομοιότυπα των πέντε πρώτων φυλλαδίων* του *(1891–1904)* [*Facsimile of the First Five Leaflets (1891?-1904)*], ed. G. P. Savidis, Athens: Hellenic Literary and Historical Archive.

Cavafy, C. P. (2007), *The Collected Poems*, trans. Evangelos Sachperoglou, Greek text ed. Anthony Hirst, Oxford: Oxford University Press.

Cavafy, C. P. (2009a), *Collected Poems*, trans. Daniel Mendelsohn, New York: Knopf.

Cavafy, C. P. (2009b), *Unfinished Poems*, trans. Daniel Mendelsohn, New York: Knopf.

Cavafy, C. P. (2013), *Complete Plus: The Poems of C.P. Cavafy in English*, trans. George Economou, Bristol: Shearsman Books.

Chamberlain, Lori (1985), "Ghostwriting the Text: Translation and the Poetics of Jack Spicer," *Contemporary Literature*, 26 (4): 426–42.

Chamberlain, Lori (2004), "Gender and the Metaphorics of Translation," in Lawrence Venuti (ed.), *The Translation Studies Reader*, 2nd edn, 306–21, London: Routledge.

Chesnokova, Anna (2009), "Dickinson in Ukraine: Slavic Traditions and New Perspectives," in Domhnall Mitchell and Maria Scott (eds), *The International Reception of Emily Dickinson*, 189–203, London and New York: Continuum.

Cohen, Philip (ed.) (1991), *Devils and Angels: Textual Editing and Literary Theory*, Charlottesville: University Press of Virginia.

Cohen, Philip (1996), "Introduction: Textual Scholarship in the Classroom," *Text* 9: 135–43.

Cohen, Philip and David H. Jackson (1991), "Notes on Emerging Paradigms in Editorial Theory," in Philip Cohen (ed.), *Devils and Angels: Textual Editing and Literary Theory*, 103–23, Charlottesville: University Press of Virginia.

Constantine, Mary-Ann (1996), *Breton Ballads*, Aberystwyth, Wales: CMCS Publications.

Constantine, Peter, Rachel Hadas, Edmund Keeley and Karen Van Dyck (eds) (2010), *The Greek Poets: Homer to the Present*, New York: W. W. Norton & Co.

Cregan-Reid, Vybarr (2013), *Discovering Gilgamesh: Geology, Narrative & the Historical Sublime in Victorian Culture*, Manchester: Manchester University Press.

Crumbley, Paul (1997), *Inflections of the Pen: Dash and Voice in Emily Dickinson*, Lexington: University Press of Kentucky.

Damrosch, David (2003), *What is World Literature?*, Princeton: Princeton University Press.

Damrosch, David (2007), *The Buried Book: The Loss and Rediscovery of the Great Epic of Gilgamesh*, New York: Holt.

Damrosch, David (2009), *How to Read World Literature*, Oxford: Wiley-Blackwell.

Davidson, Michael (1989), *The San Francisco Renaissance: Poetics and Community at Mid-Century*, Cambridge: Cambridge University Press.

Davis, Kathleen (2001), *Deconstruction and Translation*, Manchester and Northampton, MA: St. Jerome.

Derrida, Jacques (1980), "The Law of Genre," trans. Avital Ronell, *Critical inquiry* 7 (1): 55–81.

Derrida, Jacques (1985), "Des Tours de Babel," trans. Joseph F. Graham, in Joseph F. Graham (ed.), *Difference in Translation*, 165–248, Ithaca, NY: Cornell University Press.

Derrida, Jacques (1995), "Archive Fever: A Freudian Impression," trans. Eric Prenowitz, *Diacritics* 25 (2): 9–63.

Dickie, Margaret (1995), "Dickinson in Context," *American Literary History* 7 (2): 320–33.

Dickinson, Emily (1890), *Poems of Emily Dickinson,* ed. Mabel Loomis Todd and Thomas Wentworth Higginson, Boston: Roberts Brothers.

Dickinson, Emily (1891), *Poems of Emily Dickinson, Second Series,* ed. Mabel Loomis Todd and Thomas Wentworth Higginson, Boston: Roberts Brothers.

Dickinson, Emily (1894), *Letters of Emily Dickinson,* ed. Mabel Loomis Todd, Boston: Roberts Brothers, 2 vols.

Dickinson, Emily (1914), *The Single Hound: Poems of a Lifetime,* ed. Martha Dickinson Bianchi, Boston: Little, Brown.

Dickinson, Emily (1929), *Further Poems of Emily Dickinson: Withheld by her Sister Lavinia*, ed. Martha Dickinson Bianchi and Alfred Lee Hampton, Boston: Little, Brown.

Dickinson, Emily (1945), *Bolts of Melody: New Poems of Emily Dickinson*, ed. Millicent Todd Bingham, New York: Harper & Brothers.

Dickinson, Emily (1955), *The Poems of Emily Dickinson: Including Variant Readings Critically Compared with All Known Manuscripts*, ed. Thomas H. Johnson, Cambridge: Belknap Press of Harvard University Press, 3 vols.

Dickinson, Emily (1958), *The Letters of Emily Dickinson*, ed. Thomas H. Johnson, Cambridge: Belknap Press of Harvard University Press, 3 vols.

Dickinson, Emily (1981), *The Manuscript Books of Emily Dickinson*, ed. R. W. Franklin, Cambridge: Belknap Press of Harvard University Press, 2 vols.

Dickinson, Emily (1998), *The Poems of Emily Dickinson: Variorum Edition*, ed. R. W. Franklin, Cambridge: Belknap Press of Harvard University Press.

Dickinson, Emily (2013), *The Gorgeous Nothings*, ed. Jen Bervin and Marta Werner, New York: New Directions.

Dizdar, Dilek (2007), "Translational Transitions: 'Translation Proper' and Translation Studies in the Humanities," *Translation Studies* 2 (1): 89–102.

Economou, George (2015), *Unfinished & Uncollected,* Bristol: Shearsman.

Ekdawi, Sara and Anthony Hirst (1999), "Left Out, Crossed Out and Pasted Over: The Editorial Implications of Cavafy's Own Evaluation of his Uncollected and Unpublished Poems," *Modern Greek Studies (Australia and New Zealand)* 5–7: 79–132.

Ellingham, Lewis and Kevin Killian (1998), *Poet Be Like God: Jack Spicer and the San Francisco Renaissance,* Hanover and London: Wesleyan University Press.

Emmerich, Karen (2011a), " 'Impossible Things': Editing and Translating the Unfinished Poems of C. P. Cavafy," *Arion* 17 (3): 111–32.

Emmerich, Karen (2011b), "The Afterlives of C. P. Cavafy's Unfinished Poems," *Translation Studies* 4 (2): 197–212.

Emmerich, Karen (2013), "The Ordering of Things: Visual Syntax in the Poetry of Eleni Vakalo," *Word & Image* 29 (4): 384–408.

Emmerich, Karen (2016), "'A message from the antediluvian age': The Modern Construction of the Ancient *Epic of Gilgamesh*," *Comparative Literature* 68 (3): 251–73.

Emmerich, Karen (2017), "Teaching Literature in Translation," in Lawrence Venuti (ed.), *Teaching Translation: Programs, Courses, Pedagogies,* 149–55, New York: Routledge.

Emmerich, Michael (2013), "Beyond Between: Translation, Ghosts, Metaphors," in Esther Allen and Susan Bernofsky (eds), *In Translation: Translators on Their Work and What it Means,* 44–57, New York: Columbia University Press.

Eshleman, Clayton (1977), "The Lorca Working," *boundary 2* 6 (1): 31–50.

Fahy, Conor (2004), "Old and New in Italian Textual Criticism," in Raimonda Modiano, Leroy F. Searle, and Peter Shillingsburg (eds), *Voice, Text, Hypertext: Emerging Practices in Textual Studies,* 401–41, Seattle: University of Washington Press.

Fallmerayer, Jakob Philipp (1830), *Geschichte der Halbinsel Morea während des Mittelalters* [*History of the Morea Peninsula during the Middle Ages*], Stuttgart.

Fauriel, Claude (1824), *Chants populaires de la Grèce moderne, recueillis et publiés, avec une traduction Française, des éclaircissements et des notes par C. Fauriel* [*Folk songs of modern Greece, collected and published, with a French translation, clarifications and notes by C. Fauriel*], Paris: Firmin Didot Père et fils, 2 vols.

Fauriel, Claude (1999), *Ελληνικά δημοτικά τραγούδια, Α' η έκδοση του 1824–1825, Β'Ανέκδοτα κείμενα* [*Greek Folk Songs, I The Edition of 1824–1825, II Unpublished Texts*], trans. and ed. Alexis Politis, Irakleio: Crete University Press.

Ferry, David (1992), *Gilgamesh: A New Rendering in English Verse,* New York: Farrar, Strauss, and Giroux.

Foster, Benjamin (2001), *The Epic of Gilgamesh: A New Translation, Analogues, Criticism,* New York: Norton.

Franklin, R. W. (1967), *The Editing of Emily Dickinson: A Reconsideration,* Madison, Milwaukee, and London: University of Wisconsin Press.

Gabler, Hans Walter (1996), "Training Textual Critics in Textual Criticism," *Text* 9: 168–74.

Gambier, Yves and Luc van Doorslaer (eds) (2009), *The Metalanguage of Translation,* Amsterdam: John Benjamins.

Gardner, John and John Maier (1984), *Gilgamesh: Translated from the Sin-leqi-unninni Version*, New York: Knopf.

Garnett, Lucy M. J. (1885), *Greek Folk-Songs from the Turkish Provinces of Greece, Η δούλη ἑλλας [Enslaved Greece]: Albania, Thessaly, (Not yet Wholly Free), and Macedonia: Literal and Metrical Translations*, London: Elliot Stock.

Gelb, Ignace J., Benno Landsberger, A. Leo Oppenheim, and Erica Reiner (eds) (1998), *The Assyrian Dictionary of the Oriental Institute of the University of Chicago*, vol. 1, Chicago: Oriental Institute.

George, Andrew R. (1999/2003a), *The Epic of Gilgamesh: The Babylonian Epic and Other Texts in Akkadian and Sumerian*, London: Penguin Classics.

George, Andrew R. (2003b), *The Babylonian Gilgamesh Epic: Introduction, Critical Edition and Cuneiform Texts*, Oxford: Oxford University Press, 2 vols.

George, Andrew R. (2008), "Shattered Tablets and Tangled Threads: Editing Gilgamesh, Then and Now," *Aramazd: Armenian Journal of Near Eastern Studies* 3 (1) 7–30. Available at: https://eprints.soas.ac.uk/7497/2/Editing_Gilgamesh.pdf, 1–19.

Ghazoul, Ferial J. (2014), "*Majnun Layla*: Translation as Transposition," in Sandra Bermann and Catherine Porter (eds), *A Companion to Translation Studies*, 375–87, West Sussex: John Wiley & Sons.

Gizzi, Peter (1998), "Jack Spicer and the Practice of Reading," in Jack Spicer, *The House That Jack Built: The Collected Lectures of Jack Spicer*, ed. Peter Gizzi, 173–225, Middletown, CT: Wesleyan University Press.

Goldsmith, Kenneth (2011), *Uncreative Writing*, New York: Columbia University Press.

Gordon, Cyrus H. (1968), *Forgotten Scripts: How They were Deciphered and Their Impact on Contemporary Culture*, New York: Basic Books.

Gourgouris, Stathis (1996), *Dream Nation: Enlightenment, Colonization and the Institution of Modern Greece*, Stanford: Stanford University Press.

Greetham, D. C. (1996), "Foreword," in Peter L. Shillingsburg, *Scholarly Editing in the Computer Age: Theory and Practice*, 3rd edn, Ann Arbor: University of Michigan Press.

Greetham, D. C. (1998), "A Suspicion of Texts," in D. C. Greetham, *Textual Transgressions: Essays Toward the Construction of a Biobibliography*, 204–18, New York: Garland.

Groden, Michael (1991), "Contemporary Textual and Literary Theory," in George Bornstein (ed.), *Representing Modernist Texts: Editing as Interpretation*, 259–86, Ann Arbor: University of Michigan Press.

Guthenke, Constanze (2008), *Placing Modern Greece: The Dynamics of Romantic Hellenism, 1770–1840*, Oxford: Oxford University Press.

Hadbawnik, David (2011), "'*Beowulf* is a hoax': Jack Spicer's Medievalism," in Jack Spicer, *Beowulf*, ed. David Hadbawnik and Sean Reynolds, Lost &

208   *Bibliography*

Found: The CUNY Poetics Document Initiative, Series 2, Number 5, Parts I and II.

Hafstein, Valdimar Tr. (2004), "The Politics of Origins: Collective Creation Revisited," *The Journal of American Folklore* 117 (465): 300–15.

Halverson, Sandra L. (2008), "Translations as institutional facts: An ontology for 'assumed translation'," in Anthony Pym, Miriam Shlesinger, and Daniel Simeoni (eds), *Beyond Descriptive Translation Studies: Investigations in Homage to Gideon Toury*, 343–61, Amsterdam: John Benjamins.

Hart, Ellen Louise and Martha Nell Smith (eds) (1998), *Open Me Carefully: Emily Dickinson's Intimate Letters to Susan Huntington Dickinson*, Ashfield, MA: Paris Press.

Hartmann, R. R. K. (1987), "Translation Equivalence and Bilingual Lexicography: A Personal View," *Revista canaria de estudios ingleses* 13–14: 55–66.

Haupt, Paul (1884–91), *Das babylonische Nimrodepos. Keilschrifttext der Bruchstücke der sogenannten Izdubarlegenden mit dem keilinschriftlichen Sintfluthberichte* [*The Babylonian Nimrodepos. Cuneiform text of the fragments of the so-called Izdubar legends with the cuneiform account of the flood*], Leipzig: J. C. Hinrichs.

Hawkey, Christian (2010), *Ventrakl*, Brooklyn: Ugly Duckling Presse.

Helgason, Jón Karl (1999), *The Rewriting of Njáls Saga, Translation, Ideology and Icelandic Sagas*, Clevedon, England: Multilingual Matters.

Helgesson, Stefan (2016), "How Writing Becomes (World), Literature: Singularity, The Universalizable, and the Implied Writer," in Stefan Helgesson and Pieter Vermeulen (eds), *Institutions of World Literature. Writing, Translation, Markets*, 22–38, Oxon and New York: Routledge.

Henitiuk, Valerie (2008), " 'Easyfree Translation?' How the Modern West Knows Sei Shonagon's Pillow Book," *Translation Studies* 1 (1): 2–17.

Henitiuk, Valerie (2010), "Clarice Lispector, J. M. Coetzee and the Seriality of Translation," *Translation Studies* 3 (3): 318–33.

Hermans, Theo (ed.) (1985), *The Manipulation of Literature: Studies in Literary Translation*, London and Sydney: Croom Helm.

Hermans, Theo (1999), *Translation in Systems. Descriptive and System-Oriented Approaches Explained*, Manchester: St. Jerome.

Hernández Guerrero, María José (2009), *Traducción y periodismo* [*Translation and Journalism*], Berna: Peter Lang.

Hincks, Edward (1866), *Specimen Chapters of an Assyrian Grammar*, London: Trübner & Co.

Hirst, Anthony (2002), "Cavafy's Cavafy versus Savidis's Cavafy: The Need to De-Edit the 'Acknowledged' Poems." Available at: http://www.greekworks.com/content/index.php/weblog/extended/cavafys_cavafy_versus_savadiss_cavafy_the_need_to_de_edit_the_acknowledged/ (last accessed 7 May 2017).

Hirst, Anthony (2009), "Correcting the Courtroom Cat: Editorial Assaults on Cavafy's Poetry," in Alexandra Georgakopoulou and Michael Silk (eds),

Standard Languages and Language Standards—Greek, Past and Present, 149–66, Farnham, England; Burlington, VT: Ashgate.

Hofmeyr, Isabel (2004), *The Portable Bunayn: A Transnational History of* The Pilgrim's Progress, Princeton: Princeton University Press.

Holdeman, David (1996), "Beyond Editing: Textual Studies, Literary Interpretation, and Pedagogy," *Text* 9: 160–67.

Holland, Jeanne (1994), "Scraps, Stamps, and Cutouts: Emily Dickinson's Domestic Technologies of Publication," in Margaret J. M. Ezell and Katherine O'Brien O'Keefe (eds), *Cultural Artifacts and the Production of Meaning: The Page, the Image, and the Body,* 139–81, Ann Arbor: University of Michigan Press.

Holmes, James S. (1988), *Translated! Papers on Literary Translation and Translation Studies,* Amsterdam: Rodopi.

Holt, Kelly (2011), "Spicer's Poetic Correspondence: 'A Pun the Letter Reflects,'" in John Emil Vincent (ed.), *After Spicer,* 36–68, Middletown, CT: Wesleyan University Press.

Howe, Susan (1985), *My Emily Dickinson,* Berkeley, CA: North Atlantic Books.

Howe, Susan (1993), *The Birth-Mark: Unsettling the Wilderness in American Literary History,* Middletown, CT: Wesleyan University Press.

Jackson, Virginia (1996), "Dickinson's Figure of Address," in Martin Orzeck and Robert Weisbuch (eds), *Dickinson and Audience,* 77–103, Ann Arbor: University of Michigan Press.

Johnson, Kent (1997), *Double Flowering: From the Notebooks of Araki Yasusada,* New York: Roof Books.

Katz, Daniel (2004), "Jack Spicer's *After Lorca*: Translation as Decomposition," *Textual Practice* 18 (1): 83–103.

Katz, Daniel (2013), *The Poetry of Jack Spicer,* Edinburgh: Edinburgh University Press.

Kelemen, Erick (2012), "Critical Editing and Close Reading in the Undergraduate Classroom," *Pedagogy* 12 (1): 121–38.

Kothari, Rita (2005), "The Fiction of Translation," in Eva Hung and Judy Wakabayashi (eds), *Asian Translation Traditions,* 262–73, Manchester and Northampton, MA: St. Jerome.

Kovacs, Maureen Gallery (1989), *The Epic of Gilgamesh,* Stanford: Stanford University Press.

Landsberger, Benno (1976), "The Conceptual Autonomy of the Babylonian World," trans. T. Jacobsen, B. Foster, and H. von Siebenthal, *Monographs on the Ancient Near East,* Vol. 1, fascicle 4, 355–72, Malibu: Undena Publications. [Translation of "*Die Eigenbegrifflichkeit der Babylonischen Welt,*" *Islamica* 2: 1926.]

Larsen, Mogens Trolle (1994), *The Conquest of Assyria: Excavations in an Antique Land, 1840–1860,* London: Routledge.

Layard, Austen Henry (1849), *Nineveh and its Remains: With an Account of a Visit to the Chaldean Christians of Kurdistan, and the Yezidis, or*

Devil-Worshippers; and an Enquiry into the Manners and Arts of the Ancient Assyrians, London: Spottiswoode and Shaw.

Lefevere, André (1992), *Translation, Rewriting and the Manipulation of Literary Fame*, London and New York: Routledge.

Lefevere, André (1998), "The Gates of Analogy: The Kalevala in English," in Susan Bassett and André Lefevere (eds), *Constructing Cultures, Essays on Literary Translation*, 76–90, Clevedon: Multilingual Matters.

Lemercier, Nepomucène (1824), *Chants Héroiques des Montagnards et Matelots Grecs [Heroic Songs of the Greek highlanders and Sailors]*, Paris: Urbain Canel.

Levine, Madeline G. (2013), "*In Red* by Magdalena Tulli," *Translation Review* 85 (1): 81–4.

Littau, Karin (1997), "Translation in the Age of Postmodern Production: From Text to Intertext to Hypertext," *Forum for Modern Languge Studies* 33 (1): 81–96.

Liu, Lydia H. (1995), *Translingual Practice. Literature, National Culture, and Translated Modernity, China 1900-1937*, Stanford: Stanford University Press.

Lorca, Federico García (2007), *Selected Poems: With Parallel Spanish Text*, trans. D. Gareth Walters, Oxford: Oxford University Press.

Lorca, Federico García (2009), *Selected Poems, with parallel Spanish text*, eds. Martin Sorrell and D. Gareth Walters. Oxford: Oxford University Press.

Mackridge, Peter (2009), *Language and National Identity in Greece, 1766–1976*, Oxford: Oxford University Press.

Malley, Shawn (2012), *From Archaeology to Spectacle in Victorian Britain: The Case of Assyria 1845-1854*, London: Ashgate.

Man, Paul de (1984), "Anthropomorphosim and Trope in the Lyric," *The Rhetorics of Romanticism*, New York: Columbia University Press.

Manousos, Antonios (1933 [1850]), Τραγούδια εθνικά συναγμένα και διασαφηνισμένα υπό Αντωνίου Μανούσου [*National Songs Collected and Explained by Antonios Manousos*], Athens: Karavia.

Mayhew, Jonathan (2009), *Apocryphal Lorca: Translation, Parody, Kitsch*, Chicago: University of Chicago Press.

McGann, Jerome (1983), *A Critique of Modern Textual Studies*, Chicago: University of Chicago Press.

McGann, Jerome (1993), *Black Riders: The Visible Language of Modernism*, Princeton: Princeton University Press.

McGann, Jerome (1998), "Rossetti's Iconic Page," in George Bornstein and Theresa Tinkle (eds), *The Iconic Page in Manuscript, Print, and Digital Culture*, 123–40, Ann Arbor: University of Michigan Press.

McKenzie, D. F. (1999), *Bibliography and the Sociology of Texts*, Cambridge: Cambridge University Press.

Miller, Cristanne (2000), "Whose Dickinson?," *American Literary History* 12: 230–54.

Miller, Cristanne (2004), "The Sound of Shifting Paradigms, or Hearing

Dickinson in the Twenty-First Century," in Vivian R. Pollack (ed.), *A Historical Guide to Emily Dickinson*, 201–34, Oxford: Oxford University Press.

Miller, Cristanne (2008), "Dickinson's Structured Rhythms," in Martha Nell Smith and Mary Loeffelholz (eds), *A Companion to Emily Dickinson*, 391–414, London: Blackwell.

Mitchell, Domhnall (1999), "Emily Dickinson, Ralph Franklin, and the Diplomacy of Translation," *Emily Dickinson Journal* 8 (2): 39–54.

Mitchell, Domhnall and Maria Scott (eds) (2009), *The International Reception of Emily Dickinson*, London and New York: Continuum.

Morris, Simon (2010), *Getting Inside Jack Kerouac's Head*, Information as Material.

Morris, Tim (2008), "Aunie Gus Felled It New," in Martha Nell Smith and Mary Loeffelholz (eds), *A Companion to Emily Dickinson*, 281–7, London: Blackwell.

Moullas, Panayiotis (1994), "Ο Ν. Γ. Πολίτης, ο Αλ. Πολίτης και η έκδοση των δημοτικών τραγουδιών" [*N. G. Politis, Alexis Politis, and the Publication of Folk Songs*], in *Ζητήματα ιστορίας των νεοελληνικών γραμμάτων. Αφιέρωμα στον Κ.Θ. Δημαρά* [*Issues in the History of Modern Greek Letters. Tribute to K. Th. Dimaras*], 315–31. Thessaloniki: Paratiritis.

Müller, Wilhelm (1825), *Τραγούδια Ρωμαϊκα, σταλεχθέντα και εκδοθέντα υπό του κ. Φωριέλου. Μεταφρασθέντα εις τα γερμανικά και εξηγηθέντα δια των του εκδότου Φραντζέζου και των εδικών του σημειωμάτων υπο του Βιλέλμου Μύλλερου, Neugriechische Volkslieder, Gesammelt und Herausgegeben von C. Fauriel. Übersetzet und mit des Französischen Herausgebers und Eigenen Erläuterungen Versehen* [*Romaic Songs, Collected and Published by C. Fauriel, Translated into German by Wilhelm Müller*], Leipzig: Leopold Voss.

Nappi, Carla (2015), "Full. Empty. Stop. Go.: Translating Miscellany in Early Modern China," in Karen Newman and Jane Tylus (eds), *Early Modern Cultures of Translation*, 206–20, Philadelphia: University of Pennsylvania Press.

Newman, Karen and Jane Tylus (2015), *Early Modern Cultures of Translation*, Philadelphia: University of Pennsylvania Press.

O'Brien, Bruce R. (2011), *Reversing Babel: Translation among the English during an Age of Conquests, c. 800 to c. 1200*, Lantham, MA: University of Delaware Press.

O'Neill, Patrick (2005), *Polyglot Joyce*, Toronto: University of Toronto Press.

O'Neill, Patrick (2014), *Transforming Kafka: Translation Effects*, Toronto: University of Toronto Press.

Oppenheim, A. Leo (1960), "Assyriology—Why and How?," *Current Anthropology* 1 (5/6): 409–23.

Ormsby, Eric (2009), "Waiting for the Grammarians," *The New Criterion* 27 (8): 4–8.

Parpola, Simo (ed.) (1997), *The Standard Babylonian Epic of Gilgamesh: Cuneiform Text, Transliteration, Glossary, Indices and Sign List*, Helsinki: Neo-Assyrian Text Corpus Project.

Passow, Arnold (2007 [1860]), *Ρωμαίικα τραγούδια, επιλογή δημοτικών τραγουδιών* [*Romaic Songs, Selection of Follk Songs*], Athens: Elliniki Paideia. [Reprint of *Popularia Carmina Graeciae Recentioris*, 1860, Leipzig.]

Philip, M. NourbeSe (2008), *Zong!*, Middletown: Wesleyan University Press.

Pinches, T. G. (1889–90), "Exit Gistubar!," *Babylonian and Oriental Record* 4: 264.

Politis, Alexis (1984), *Η Ανακάλυψη των ελληνικών δημοτικών τραγουδιών* [*The Discovery of the Greek Folk Songs*], Athens: Themelio.

Politis, Alexis (2010), *Το δημοτικό τραγούδι: Εποπτικές Προσεγγίσεις, Περνώντας από την προφορική στη γραπτή παράδοση* [*The Folk Song: Supervisory Approaches, Moving from the Oral to the Written Tradition*], Heraklion: University Press of Crete.

Politis, Nikolaos (1914/2009), *Δημοτικά τραγούδια. Εκλογαί από τα τραγούδια του ελληνικού λαού* [*Folk Songs. Selection of the Songs of the Greek Folk*], Athens: Pelekanos.

Politis, Nikolaos (1920 [1903]), "*Λαογραφία*" [*Folklore*] *Λαογραφικά σύμμεικτα* [*Various Pieces on Folklore*], vol. 1, 1–13, Athens: Typografeio Paraskeva Leoni.

Portela, Manuel (2000), "Typographic Translation: The Portuguese Edition of *Tristram Shandy*," in Joe Bray, Miriam Handley, and Anne C. Henry (eds), *Ma(r)king the Text: The Presentation of Meaning on the Literary Page*, 291–308, Aldershot: Ashgate.

Prousis, Theophilus C. (1994), *Russian Society and the Greek Revolution*, Dekalb, IL: Northern Illinois University Press.

Proust, Marcel (1992), *In Search of Lost Time*, vol. 1, *Swann's Way*, trans. C. K. Scott Montcrieff and Terence Kilmartin, rev. D. J. Enright, London: Chatto and Windus.

Pym, Anthony (2009), "Natural and Directional Equivalence in Theories of Translation," in Yves Gambier and Luc van Doorslaer (eds), *The Metalanguage of Translation*, 81–104, Amsterdam: John Benjamins.

Pym, Anthony (2010), "Translation Theory Today and Tomorrow – Responses to Equivalence," in Lew N. Zybatow (ed.), *Translationswissenschaft - Stand und Perspektiven* [*Translation Science - Stance and Perspective*], 1–14, Frankfurt: Peter Lang.

Rendall, Steven (1997), "Translation, Quotation, Iterability," *TTR: traduction, terminologie, rédaction* 10 (2): 167–89.

Report of the MLA Task Force on Evaluating Scholarship for Tenure and Promotion (2007), *Profession*: 9–71.

Ricci, Ronit (2010), "On the Untranslatability of 'Translation': Considerations from Java, Indonesia," *Translation Studies* 3 (3): 287–301.

Robinson, Douglas (1991), *The Translator's Turn*, Baltimore: Johns Hopkins University Press.

Robinson, Douglas (1997), *What is Translation? Centrifugal Theories, Critical Interventions*, Kent, OH: Kent State University Press.

Robinson, Douglas (2001a), "Pseudotranslation," in Mona Baker (ed.), *Routledge Encyclopedia of Translation Studies*, 183–5, New York: Routledge.

Robinson, Douglas (2001b), *Who Translates? Translator Subjectivities Beyond Reason*, Albany: State University of New York Press.

Rundle, Christopher (2012), "Translation as an Approach to History," *Translation Studies* 5 (2): 232–40.

Ruthven, K. K. (2001), *Faking Literature*, Cambridge: Cambridge University Press.

Said, Edward (1994 [1974]), *Orientalism*, New York: Vintage Books.

Sakai, Naoki (2007), "How Do we Count a Language? Translation and Discontinuity," *Translation Studiesi* 2 (1): 71–88.

Sandars, N. K. (1960), *The Epic of Gilgamesh*, New York: Penguin Books.

Savidis, G. P. (1964), *Το αρχείο Κ.Π. Καβάφη: πρώτη ενημερωτική έκθεση [The C. P. Cavafy Archive: Initial Informative Report]*, Athens: n.p.

Savidis, G. P. (1966), *Οι Καβαφικές εκδόσεις (1891–1932), περιγραφή και σχόλιο [Cavafy's Editions (1891–1932), Description and Commentary]*, Athens: Ikaros.

Sayce, Rev. A. H. (1877), *Lectures upon the Assyrian Language, and Syllabary; Delivered to the Students of the Archaic Classes*, London: Samuel Bagster and Sons.

Schacker, Jennifer (2003), *National Dreams: The Remaking of Fairy Tales in Nineteenth-Century England*, Philadelphia: University of Pennsylvania Press.

Schäffner, Christina (2012), "Rethinking Transediting," *Meta: journal des traducteurs / Meta: Translators' Journal* 57 (4): 866–83.

Schalkwyk, David (2014), "Shakespeare's Untranslatability," in Robert Henke and Eric Nicholson (eds), *Studies in Performance and Early Modern Drama: Transnational Mobilities in Early Modern Theater*, 229–45, Surrey: Ashgate.

Seferis, George (1999 [1944]), *Δοκιμές, Α' (1936–1947) [Essays, vol. 1 (1936–1947)]*, Athens: Ikaros.

Sheridan, Charles Brinsley (1822), *Thoughts on the Greek Revolution*, London: John Murray.

Sheridan, Charles Brinsley (1825), *The Songs of Greece, from the Romaic Text, ed. M.C. Fauriel, with Additions, Translated into English Verse, by Charles Brinsley Sheridan*, London: Longman, Hurst, Rees, Orme, Brown, and Green.

Shillingsburg, Peter (1993), "Polymorphic, Polysemic, Protean, Reliable, Electronic Texts," in George Bornstein and Ralph G. Williams (eds), *Palimpsest: Editorial Theory in the Humanities*, 29–44, Ann Arbor: University of Michigan Press.

Shillingsburg, Peter (1996 [1984]), *Scholarly Editing in the Computer Age: Theory and Practice*, Ann Arbor: University of Michigan Press.

Shillingsburg, Peter (1997), *Resisting Texts: Authority and Submission in Constructions of Meaning*, Ann Arbor: University of Michigan Press.

Shillingsburg, Peter (2006), *From Gutenberg to Google: Electronic Representations of Literary Texts*, New York: Cambridge University Press.

Smaragdis, Yannis (1997), *Καβάφης [Cavafy]*, Athens: Livanis.

Smith, George (1876), *The Chaldean Account of Genesis. Containing the Description of the Creation, the Fall of Man, the Deluge, the Tower of Babel, the Times of the Patriarchs, and Nimrod. Babylonian Fables, and Legends of the Gods; From the Cuneiform Inscriptions*, London: Sampson Low, Marston, Searle, and Rivington.

Smith, Martha Nell (1992), *Rowing in Eden: Rereading Emily Dickinson*, Austin: University of Texas Press.

Snell-Hornby, Mary (1986), "The Bilingual Dictionary—Victim of its Own Tradition?," in R. R. K. Hartmann (ed.), *The History of Lexicography, Papers from the Dictionary Research Centre Seminar at Exeter*, 207–18, Amsterdam: John Benjamins.

Snell-Hornby, Mary (1988), *Translation Studies: An Integrated Approach*, Amsterdam: John Benjamins.

Spicer, Jack (1957), *After Lorca*, San Francisco: White Rabbit Press.

Spicer, Jack (1987), "Letters to Robin Blaser," transcribed by Lori Chamberlain, *Line* 9: 26–55.

Spicer, Jack (1998), *The House That Jack Built: The Collected Lectures of Jack Spicer*, ed. Peter Gizzi, Middletown, CT: Wesleyan University Press.

Spicer, Jack (2008), *My Vocabulary Did This to Me: The Collected Poetry of Jack Spicer*, ed. Peter Gizzi and Kevin Killian, Middletown, CT: Wesleyan University Press.

Spicer, Jack (2011), *Beowulf*, ed. David Hadbawnik and Sean Reynolds, Lost & Found: The CUNY Poetics Document Initiative, Series 2, Number 5, Parts I and II.

Spivak, Gayatri (2005), "Translating into English," in Sandra Bermann and Michael Wood (eds), *Nation, Language, and the Ethics of Translation*, 98–110, Princeton: Princeton University Press.

St. Andre, James (ed.) (2010), *Thinking through Translation with Metaphors*, Manchester: St. Jerome.

Sterne, Laurence (1997–8), *A Vida e Opiniões de Tristram Shandy [The Life and Opinions of Tristram Shandy]*, trans. Manuel Portela, Lisbon: Antígona, 2 vols.

Stetting, Karen (1989), "Transediting—A New Term for Coping with the Grey Area between Editing and Translating," in *Proceedings from the Fourth Nordic Conference for English Studies*, 371–82, Copenhagen: University of Copenhagen, Department of English.

Stillinger, Jack (1994), *Coleridge and Textual Instability: The Multiple Versions of the Major Poems*, New York: Oxford University Press.

Sturrock, John (2010), "The Language of Translation," in Mona Baker (ed.), *Critical Readigns in Translation Studies*, 49–64, New York: Routledge, 2010.

Tanselle, G. Thomas (1989), *A Rationale of Textual Criticism*, Philadelphia: University of Pennsylvania Press.

Taylor, Gary (2009), "From Jerome through Greg to Jerome (McGann)," *Textual Cultures* 4 (2): 88–101.

Thompson, R. Campbell (1930), *The Epic of Gilgamesh: Text, Transliteration, and Notes*, Oxford: The Clarendon Press.

Tigay, Jeffrey H. (1982), *The Evolution of the Gilgamesh Epic*, Philadelphia: University of Pennsylvania Press.

Tiglath-Pileser I (1857), *Inscription of Tiglath Pileser I, King of Assyria, B.C. 1150, as translated by Sir Henry Rawlinson, Fox Talbot, Esq., Dr. Hincks, and Dr. Oppert*, London: J. W. Parker and Son.

Todd, Mabel Loomis (1945), *Ancestors' Brocades: The Literary Debut of Emily Dickinson*, New York and London: Harper Brothers.

Tommaseo, Niccolò (1843), *Canti Popolari toscani, corsi, illirici e greci* [*Tuscan, Corsican, Illyrian, and Greek Folk Songs*], Vol. 3, Venice.

Topol, Jáchym (2000), *City, Sister, Silver*, trans. Alex Zucker, New York: Catbird Press.

Toury, Gideon (2011), *Descriptive Translation Studies—and Beyond: Revised Edition*, Amsterdam: John Benjamins Publishing.

Tymoczko, Maria (1990), "Translation in Oral Tradition as a Touchstone for Translation Theory and Practice," in Susan Basnett and André Lefevere (eds), *Translation, History and Culture*, 46–55, New York: Bloomsbury.

Tymoczko, Maria (2010), "Western Metaphorical Discourses Implicit in Translation Studies," in James St. André (ed.), *Thinking through Translation with Metaphors*, 109–43, Manchester: St. Jerome.

Tymoczko, Maria (2014), "Cultural Hegemony and the Erosion of Translation Communities," in Sandra Bermann and Catherine Porter (eds), *A Companion to Translation Studies*, 165–78, West Sussex: John Wiley & Sons.

Vakalo, Eleni (2017), *Before Lyricism*, trans. Karen Emmerich, Brooklyn: Ugly Duckling Presse.

Valdeón, Roberto A. (2015), "(Un)stable Sources, Translation and News Production," *Target* 27 (3): 440–53.

Vassilikos, Vassilis (1974), Γλαύκος Θρασάκης, μυθιστόρημα [*Glafkos Thrassakis, Novel*], Athens: Pleias.

Vassilikos, Vassilis (1975a), Γλαύκος Θρασάκης, Μπερλίνερ ανσάμπλ [*Glafkos Thrassakis, Berliner Ensemble*], Athens: Pleias.

Vassilikos, Vassilis (1975b), Γλαύκος Θρασάκης, η επιστροφή [*Glafkos Thrassakis, the Return*], Athens: Pleias.

Vassilikos, Vassilis (1978), *Un poète est morte*, trans. Gisele Jeanperin, Paris: Juilliard.

Vassilikos, Vassilis (1988), Γλαύκος Θρασάκης [*Glafkos Thrassakis*], Athens: Gnosi.

Vassilikos, Vassilis (1996), Γλαύκος Θρασάκης [*Glafkos Thrassakis*], Athens: Livanis.

Vassilikos, Vassilis (2002), *The Few Things I Know About Glafkos Thrassakis*, trans. Karen Emmerich, New York: Seven Stories.

Vassilikos, Vassilis (2014), *Lo poco que sé de Glafcos Zrasakis* [*The Few Things I Know about Glafkos Thrassakis*], trans. Angel Peréz González, Gijón, Spain: Hoja de Lata.

Venuti, Lawrence (1995), *The Translator's Invisibility: A History of Translation*, London: Routledge.

Venuti, Lawrence (1996), "Translation and the Pedagogy of Literature," *College English* 58 (3): 327–44.

Venuti, Lawrence (2013), *Translation Changes Everything: Theory and Practice*, London and New York: Routledge.

Venuti, Lawrence (2016), "Hijacking Translation: How Comp Lit Continues to Suppress Translated Texts," *boundary 2* 43 (2): 179–204.

Vlagopoulos, Panos (2016), "'The Patrimony of Our Race': Louis-Albert Bourgault-Ducoudray and the Emergence of the Discourse on Greek National Music," *Journal of Modern Greek Studies* 34 (1): 49–77.

von Soden, Wolfram (1958–81), *Akkadisches Handwörterbuch: unter Benutzung des lexikalischen Nachlasses von Bruno Meissner (1868-1947)* [*Akkadian Dictionary: Based on the Lexical Legacy of Bruno Meissner (1868-1947)*], Wiesbaden: Harrassowitz.

Voutier, Olivier (1826), *Lettres sur la Grèce, notes et chants populaires*. Paris: Firmin Didot Père et Fils.

Walkowitz, Rebecca L. (2015), *Born Translated: The Contemporary Novel in an Age of World Literature*, New York: Columbia University Press.

Walser, Robert (2010), *Microscripts*, trans. Susan Bernofsky, New York: New Directions.

Walser, Robert (2011), *Mikrogramme* [*Microscripts*], from the transcriptions of Bernhard Echte and Werner Morlang, ed. Lucas Marco Gisi, Reto Sorg, Peter Stocker, and Robert Walser-Stiftung Bern, Suhrkamp.

Warren, Austin and René Wellek (1977), *Theory of Literature*, New York: Harcourt Brace.

Werner, Marta L. (1995), *Emily Dickinson's Open Folios: Scenes of Reading, Surface of Writing*, Ann Arbor: University of Michigan Press.

Werner, Marta L. (1999), "The Poems of Emily Dickinson by R. W. Franklin: Emily Dickinson," *Text* 12: 255–63.

Werner, Marta L. (2007), "'A Woe of Ecstasy': On the Electronic Editing of Emily Dickinson's Late Fragments," *The Emily Dickinson Journal* 16 (2): 25–52.

Wirtén, Eva Hemmungs (2004), "Inventing F. David: Author(ing) Translation," *No Trespassing: Authorship, Intellectual Property Rights and the Boundaries of Globalization*, 38–56, Toronto: University of Toronto Press.

Woods, Michelle (2012), *Censoring Translation: Censorship, Theatre, and the Politics of Translation*, London and New York: Continuum.

Woods, Michelle, "Translating Topol: Kafka, the Holocaust, and Humor."
[Unpublished paper.]

Worthington, Martin (2012), *Principles of Akkadian Textual Criticism*, Berlin:
De Gruyter.

Young, Robert J. C. (2014), "Philosophy in Translation," in Sandra Bermann
and Catherine Porter (eds), *A Companion to Translation Studies*, 41–53,
West Sussex: John Wiley & Sons.

Zambelios, Spyridon (1852/1986), Άσματα δημοτικά της Ελλάδος, Εκδοθέντα
μετά μελέτης ιστορικής περι μεσαιωνικού ελληνισμού υπό Σπυρίδωνος
Ζαμπλεδίου, Λευκαδίου [*Folk Songs of Greece, Published with a Historical
Study Concerning Medieval Hellenism*], Athens: Karavia.

Index